KB244550

TEPS

서울대
텝스 관리위원회

최신기출
1200

문제집

SEASON

2

서울대 텝스 관리위원회 최신기출 1200 SEASON 2 문제집

문제제공 서울대학교 TEPS관리위원회
펴낸이 안용백
펴낸곳 (주)넥서스

초판 1쇄 발행 2012년 2월 10일
초판 32쇄 발행 2016년 10월 5일

출판신고 1992년 4월 3일 제311-2002-2호
10880 경기도 파주시 지목로 5
Tel (02)330-5500 Fax (02)330-5555
ISBN 978-89-5797-993-8 18740

www.nexusbook.com

TEPS

서울대 텝스 관리위원회 최신기출 1200

How to TEPS

서울대학교 TEPS관리위원회 기출문제 제공

문제집

SEASON 2

넥서스

⁝ PREFACE

2006년 넥서스에서 최초로 TEPS 기출문제집 〈유형별로 분석한 NEXUS 기출 800〉을 출간한 후 〈서울대 텝스 관리위원회 최신기출 1000〉 〈서울대 텝스 관리위원회 제공 최신기출 시크릿〉 〈서울대 텝스 관리위원 회 최신기출 1200〉에 이르기까지 대표적인 TEPS 기출문제집으로 자리매김할 수 있도록 많은 사랑과 관심 을 보여준 TEPS 수험생들과 학교 및 학원에서 강의를 담당하시는 선생님들께 다시 한번 감사의 마음을 전 한다. 다른 영어 능력 검정시험과 달리 많은 기출문제가 공식적으로 오픈된 TEPS 시험은 그만큼 과학적인 측정 도구와 신뢰할 수 있는 콘텐츠, 뛰어난 변별력 등 테스트로서의 투명성을 이미 인정받았다. 1999년 1월 첫 TEPS 시험 시행 이후 이러한 공인된 시험에 대한 신뢰도를 바탕으로 이제는 입시·입사·승진 등 여러 분 야에서 이 TEPS 시험 성적이 두루 활용되고 있는 것이 현실이다.

TEPS를 어떻게 공부해야 하느냐는 질문을 종종 받는다. TEPS 시험이 아직 한국인들에게는 만만한 시험이 아니라는 것을 너무 잘 알고 있기 때문에 제대로 된 교재와 학습법으로 TEPS 체질로 영어 공부 환경을 세팅 하라고밖에 조언해 줄 수 없다. 우리가 건강한 체력을 위해 몸에 좋은 음식, 심지어는 유기농을 섭취하려고 하 듯, 건강한 TEPS 체질을 갖고 싶다면 엉뚱한 TEPS 유사 문제들이 아닌 시험에 출제된 기출문제들을 많이 경 험해 볼 것을 권면한다. 시중에 이미 출간된 소위 베스트셀러라는 수험서에 수록된 TEPS 문제들을 분석해 보니, TEPS 시험이 아닌 다른 영어 시험 유형 문제를 수록해 혼동을 주는 경우가 많았다. TEPS 시험에 어떤 문제가 실제로 출제되었는지만 제대로 파악해도 시험 유형을 반 이상 경험한 거라고 볼 수 있다.

이번에 출간하는 〈서울대 텝스 관리위원회 최신기출 1200 SEASON 2〉는 〈서울대 텝스 관리위원회 최신기 출 1200〉에 이어 더욱 새로운 기출문제 6회분으로 구성, 학습자 편의를 위해 문제집과 해설집을 별도로 각 각 제작했다. 가장 최신 기출문제들만 선별해서 수록했고, 실제 TEPS 시험장에서 만났던 문제 그대로의 디자 인, 청해 방송에서 듣던 MP3 음원을 모두 고스란히 그대로 가져왔다. 또한 군더더기 없이 핵심만 짚어 주는 문제 해설을 위해 끝없이 원고를 수정 보완해서 질 좋은 TEPS 기출문제를 더 잘 이해할 수 있도록 해설집을 따로 만들었다. 방대한 TEPS 문제들을 편하게 각자의 도서관이나 강의실, 집, 카페에서 경험하고 TEPS 고사 장으로 향한다면 별로 긴장하지 않고 좋은 결과를 기대할 수 있을 것이다.

TEPS 기출문제집 출간을 위해 넥서스 TEPS연구소의 성가시게 많은 질문과 요구사항에도 적극적으로 도움 을 주신 서울대학교 TEPS관리위원회 관계자분들께 이 자리를 통해 다시 한번 감사의 마음을 전한다. TEPS 시험이 수험생 모두의 꿈을 실현하는 데 잘 활용되기를 응원한다.

넥서스 TEPS연구소 연구원 일동

:: CONTENTS

서문   5

특징   8

TEPS에 대하여   10

TEPS 만점 전략   12

서울대 최신기출 • 1

Listening Comprehension   39

Grammar   43

Vocabulary   51

Reading Comprehension   59

서울대 최신기출 • 2

Listening Comprehension   77

Grammar   81

Vocabulary   89

Reading Comprehension   97

서울대 최신기출 • 3

Listening Comprehension   115

Grammar   119

Vocabulary   127

Reading Comprehension   135

서울대 최신기출 • 4

Listening Comprehension   153
Grammar   157
Vocabulary   165
Reading Comprehension   173

서울대 최신기출 • 5

Listening Comprehension   191
Grammar   195
Vocabulary   203
Reading Comprehension   211

서울대 최신기출 • 6

Listening Comprehension   229
Grammar   233
Vocabulary   241
Reading Comprehension   249

Listening Comprehension **Scripts**   266
Answer Keys   326

i-**TEPS Review**   332
TEPS 등급표   334

: FEATURE

1 / TEPS 최신기출 1,200문항

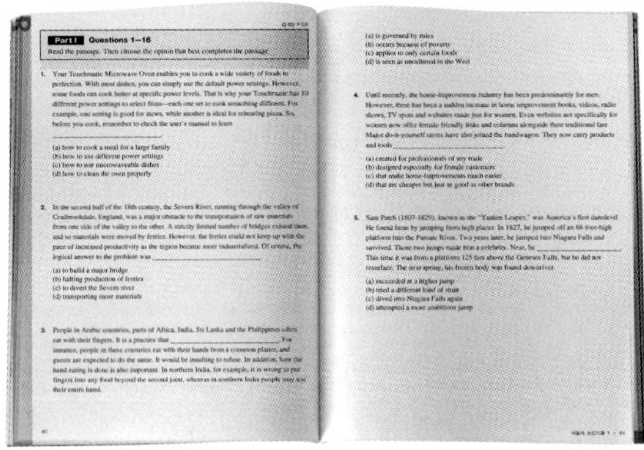

서울대학교 TEPS관리위원회가 공개한 현존 가장 최신 기출
문제 1,200문항을 실제 TEPS 시험지와 동일한 디자인 환경
으로 제공

2 / 수험생들에 꼭 필요한 TEPS 만점 전략

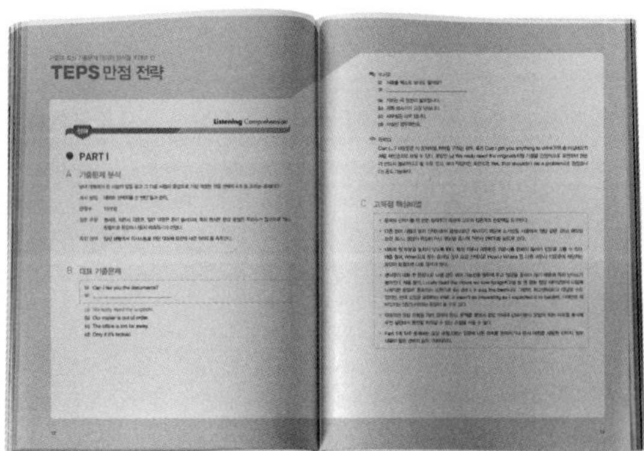

청해–문법–어휘–독해 4영역 13파트에 대한 TEPS 출제 경
향 및 고득점 대비 전략을 통합적으로 분석한 출제 비밀 노트
공개

3 / 군더더기 없는 완전 해설

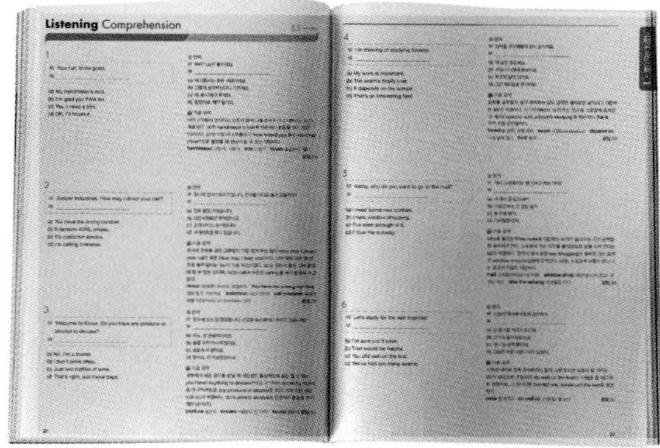

넥서스 TEPS연구소의 오랜 노하우가 녹아 있는 콤팩트한
알짜배기 해설로 오답에 대한 속시원한 해결책 제시

4 / 문제집과 해설집 별도 제작

학습자 편의를 위해 방대한 분량을 문제집과 해설집으로 별도
제작, 휴대하기 편할 뿐 아니라 학습 목적에 맞게 구매 가능

5 / 실제 고사장에서 듣던 청해 음성

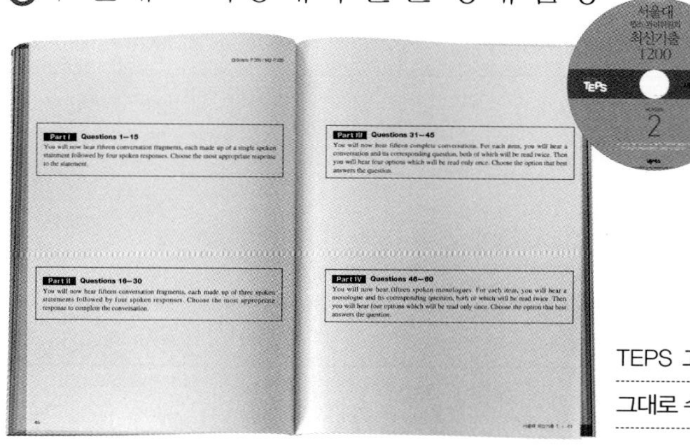

TEPS 고사장에서 청해 시험 시간에 사용했던 MP3 음원을
그대로 수록, 생생한 청해 시험 체험

1 / TEPS란?

❶ Test of English Proficiency developed by Seoul National University의 약자로 서울대학교 언어교육원에서 개발하고, TEPS관리위원회에서 주관하는 국가공인 영어시험

❷ 1999년 1월 처음 시행 이후 연 12~16회 실시

❸ 정부기관 및 기업의 직원 채용, 인사고과, 해외 파견 근무자 선발과 더불어 대학과 특목고 입학 및 졸업 자격 요건, 국가고시 및 자격 시험의 영어 대체 시험으로 활용

❹ 100여 명의 국내외 유수 대학의 최고 수준 영어 전문가들이 출제하고, 언어 테스팅 분야의 세계적인 권위자인 Bachman 교수(미국 UCLA)와 Oller 교수(미국 뉴멕시코대)로부터 타당성을 검증받음

❺ 말하기 – 쓰기 시험인 TEPS Speaking & Writing도 별도 실시 중이며, 2009년 10월부터 이를 통합한 *i*-TEPS 실시

2 / TEPS 시험 구성

영역	Part별 내용	문항수	시간/배점
청해 Listening Comprehension	Part I : 문장 하나를 듣고 이어질 대화 고르기 Part II : 3문장의 대화를 듣고 이어질 대화 고르기 Part III : 6~8 문장의 대화를 듣고 질문에 해당하는 답 고르기 Part IV : 담화문의 내용을 듣고 질문에 해당하는 답 고르기	15 15 15 15	55분 400점
문법 Grammar	Part I : 대화문의 빈칸에 적절한 표현 고르기 Part II : 문장의 빈칸에 적절한 표현 고르기 Part III : 대화에서 어법상 틀리거나 어색한 부분 고르기 Part IV : 단문에서 문법상 틀리거나 어색한 부분 고르기	20 20 5 5	25분 100점
어휘 Vocabulary	Part I : 대화문의 빈칸에 적절한 단어 고르기 Part II : 단문의 빈칸에 적절한 단어 고르기	25 25	15분 100점
독해 Reading Comprehension	Part I : 지문을 읽고 빈칸에 들어갈 내용 고르기 Part II : 지문을 읽고 질문에 가장 적절한 내용 고르기 Part III : 지문을 읽고 문맥상 어색한 내용 고르기	16 21 3	45분 400점
총계	13개 Parts	200	140분 990점

☆ **IRT** (Item Response Theory)에 의하여 최고점이 990점, 최저점이 10점으로 조정됨.

3 / TEPS 시험 응시 정보

현장 접수
❶ www.teps.or.kr에서 인근 접수처 및 준비물(응시료, 사진) 확인
❷ 접수처 방문: 해당 접수기간 평일 오후 12시 ~ 오후 5시

인터넷 접수
❶ 서울대학교 TEPS관리위원회 홈페이지 접속 www.teps.or.kr
❷ 준비물: 스캔한 사진 파일, 응시료 결제를 위한 신용 카드 및 은행 계좌

4 / TEPS 시험 당일 정보

❶ 고사장 입실 완료: 9시 30분(일요일) / 3시(토요일)
❷ 준비물: 신분증, 컴퓨터용 사인펜, 수정테이프, 수험표, 시계
❸ 유효한 신분증
　성인: 주민등록증, 운전면허증, 여권, 공무원증, 현역간부 신분증, 군무원증, 주민등록증 발급 신청 확인서, 외국인 등록증
　초·중고생: 학생증, 여권, 청소년증, 주민등록증, 주민등록증 발급 신청 확인서, TEPS 신분확인 증명서
❹ 시험 시간: 2시간 20분 (중간에 쉬는 시간 없음, 각 영역별 제한시간 엄수)
❺ 성적 확인: 약 2주 후 인터넷에서 조회 가능

TEPS 만점 전략

청해

● PART I

A 기출문제 분석

남녀 대화에서 한 사람의 말을 듣고 그 다음 사람의 응답으로 가장 적절한 것을 선택지 4개 중 고르는 문제이다.

제시 방법   대화와 선택지를 한 번만 들려 준다.

문항수   15문항

질문 유형   평서문, 의문사 의문문, 일반 의문문 등이 출제되며, 특히 평서문 응답 유형은 무리수가 많으므로 어느 방향으로 응답이 나올지 예측하기가 어렵다.

측정 영역   일상 생활에서 의사소통을 위한 대화체 표현에 대한 이해도를 측정한다.

B 대표 기출문제

M	Can I fax you the documents?
W	________________________

✔ (a) We really need the originals.

   (b) Our copier is out of order.

   (c) The office is too far away.

   (d) Only if it's factual.

💬 우리말

M 서류를 팩스로 보내도 될까요?

W _______________________________

(a) 저희는 꼭 원본이 필요합니다.

(b) 저희 복사기가 고장 났습니다.

(c) 사무실은 너무 멉니다.

(d) 사실인 경우에만요.

📡 공략법

Can I...? 의문문은 이 문제처럼 허락을 구하는 경우, 혹은 Can I get you anything to drink?(뭐 좀 마실래요?) 처럼 제안문으로 쓰일 수 있다. 정답인 (a) We really need the originals처럼 거절을 간접적으로 표현하여 원본이 반드시 필요하다고 할 수도 있고, 보다 직접적인 표현으로 Yes, that shouldn't be a problem(네, 괜찮습니다) 등도 가능하다.

C 고득점 핵심비법

- 문제와 선택지를 한 번만 들려주기 때문에 고도의 집중력과 순발력을 요구한다.

- 다른 영어 시험과 달리 선택지들이 음성으로만 제시되기 때문에 소거법을 사용해서 정답 같은 것(o), 애매모호한 것(△), 정답이 확실히 아닌 것(x)을 표시해 가면서 선택지를 듣도록 한다.

- 대화의 첫 부분을 놓치지 않도록 한다. 특히 의문사 의문문은 의문사를 정확히 들어야 정답을 고를 수 있다. 예를 들어, When으로 묻는 문제일 경우 오답 선택지로 How나 Where 등 다른 의문사 의문문에 해당하는 응답이 함정으로 나올 경우가 많다.

- 평서문이 대화 첫 문장으로 나올 경우 여러 가능성을 염두에 두고 정답을 골라야 하기 때문에 특히 난이도가 높아진다. 예를 들어, I really liked the movie we saw tonight(오늘 밤 본 영화 정말 재미있었어) 다음에 나옴직한 응답은 동의하는 표현으로 So did I. It was the best(나도 그랬어. 최고였어)라고 대답할 수도 있지만, 반대 입장을 표현하는 Well, it wasn't so interesting as I expected it to be(글쎄, 기대만큼 재미있지는 않았는데)라는 응답이 올 수도 있다.

- 대표적인 오답 유형을 미리 정리해 둔다. 문제를 풀면서 정답 이외의 선택지들이 오답이 되는 이유를 분석해 두면 실전에서 함정을 피해갈 수 있는 스킬을 키울 수 있다.

- Part 1에 자주 출제되는 오답 유형으로는 질문에 나온 어휘를 반복하거나 유사 어휘를 사용한 선택지, 일부 내용이 틀린 선택지 등이 대표적이다.

● PART II

A 기출문제 분석

남녀 대화에서 세 번째 대화까지 듣고 그 다음 이어질 응답으로 가장 자연스러운 것을 4개의 선택지 중에서 고르는 문제이다.

제시 방법 대화와 선택지를 한 번만 들려 준다.

문항수 15문항

질문 유형 평서문, 의문사 의문문, 일반 의문문 등이 출제되며, 이 중 특히 평서문인 경우 어느 방향으로 응답이 나올지 예측하기 어렵다.

측정 영역 일상 대화 속 표현에 대한 이해도 측정이라는 점에서 Part 1과 동일한데, 이와 더불어 전반적인 대화 흐름의 이해도를 측정하기도 한다.

B 대표 기출문제

> M We've been invited to Amy's for dinner.
> W What for?
> M I'm not sure, but we shouldn't go empty-handed.
> W _______________________________

(a) Why don't we invite her?

(b) She's going to cook for us.

(c) I'd love to go with you.

✔ (d) Let's bring a bottle of wine.

💬 우리말

M 에이미네 저녁식사 초대를 받았어.

W 무슨 일인데?

M 무슨 일인지는 모르겠지만 빈손으론 가면 안 될 것 같아.

W _______________________________

(a) 그녀를 초대하는 게 어때?

(b) 그녀가 우릴 위해 요리할 거야.

(c) 나도 같이 가고 싶어.

(d) 와인 한 병 사가자.

📶 공략법

We shouldn't…/ We must…/ We have to… 등은 상대방을 강하게 설득하는 문장이다. 파티에 갈 때 빈손으로 가면 안 된다는 말에, (d) Let's bring a bottle of wine과 같이 적극적인 동의 방법을 답으로 선택해야 한다. 이렇듯 서구 문화에서는 집으로 초대받은 경우 와인이나 케이크 혹은 꽃 등 간단한 선물을 준비해 가는 것이 예의라는 것도 기억해 두자.

C 고득점 핵심비법

- 한 번만 들려주는 세 줄의 대화를 정확하게 잘 듣도록 한다. 첫 문장을 잘 들어야 그 다음에 이어지는 두 줄의 대화를 잘 이해할 수 있기 때문에 Part 2 역시 고도의 집중력을 요한다.

- 만일 첫 줄을 놓쳤다면 당황하지 말고 그 다음 이어지는 두 줄의 대화를 잘 듣도록 한다. 가장 이상적인 청취는 세 줄을 다 알아듣는 것이지만, 혹시 그렇지 못하더라도 선택지가 나오기 직전의 말을 잘 들으면 자연스럽게 이어지는 응답을 고르는 데 도움이 된다.

- 소서법을 활용해시 정답을 고르는 것도 들려 주기만 하는 선택지에 대처할 수 있는 한 방법이다.

- 남녀 각각 어떤 말을 했는지 구분해서 들어야 오답을 피해갈 수 있다.

- 풀어본 문제의 오답을 매번 분석해서 실전에서 신속하고 정확하게 오답을 피하도록 한다.

- Part 2의 대표적인 오답 유형으로는 대화의 앞부분을 일부 놓치고 착각해서 선택할 만한 선택지, 대화에 언급된 어휘로 만든 선택지, 대화에 등장한 어휘의 또 다른 의미를 가지고 만든 선택지, 질문한 사람이 이어서 할 만한 말로 만든 선택지 등이 있다.

● PART III

A 기출문제 분석

남녀가 세 번씩 주고받는 대화를 듣고 4개의 선택지 중 질문에 가장 적절한 답을 고르는 문제이다.

제시 방법　대화 → 질문 → 대화 → 질문 → 선택지 순으로 들려 준다.

문항수　15문항

질문 유형　대의 파악(7문항) → 세부 내용 파악(5문항) → 추론(3문항) 순으로 나온다.

측정 영역　일상 대화에 등장하는 다양한 표현에 대한 이해도를 바탕으로 전체 대의 파악, 세부 내용 파악, 추론 능력을 측정한다.

B 대표 기출문제

> M Any special plans for your three-week vacation?
> W I think I'll visit my family and relax somewhere.
> M Where do you plan on relaxing?
> W Oh, I don't know, maybe go somewhere warm.
> M What about Thailand?
> W Actually, that sounds good. I'll put it on my list.

Q What is the main topic of the conversation?

(a) The best way to spend a vacation.

✔ (b) The woman's vacation plans.

(c) Popular holiday destinations.

(d) Setting aside time to visit family.

💬 우리말

M 3주 휴가 동안 특별한 계획이 있나요?

W 집에 들렀다가 어디 가서 좀 쉴 생각이에요.

M 어디서 쉬려고 하는데요?

W 글쎄요. 모르겠어요. 아마 따뜻한 곳으로 가겠죠.

M 태국은 어때요?

W 좋은 생각이네요. 그곳도 고려해 봐야겠어요.

Q 대화의 중심 소재는?

(a) 휴가를 보낼 가장 좋은 방법.

(b) 여자의 휴가 계획.

(c) 인기 있는 휴양지.

(d) 가족을 방문하기 위한 시간을 남겨 놓기.

🛜 공략법

휴가 계획은 상당히 빈출도가 높은 토픽이다. 어디로 휴가를 갈 것인지, 혹은 휴가가 어땠는지에 대해 물어보는 두 가지 내용 중 하나로 예상할 수 있다. 여자는 따뜻한 곳에서 쉬려고 하고 남자는 태국을 권하고 있으므로, 이를 간단하고 함축적으로 표현한 (b) The woman's vacation plans가 정답이다. (d)는 visiting family를 응용한 오답이다.

C 고득점 핵심비법

- 처음 대화를 들을 때 전체 대화 내용을 파악한 뒤, 질문에 따라 집중할 부분에 더 집중하는 두 번째 듣기를 한다. 대화의 흐름을 파악해야 대의 파악 문제뿐 아니라 세부 내용 파악이나 추론 문제도 더 쉽게 풀 수 있다.

- 질문에 따라서 메모를 해야 하는 경우도 있다. 특히 세부 내용 파악 문제의 경우 숫자, 연도, 물건의 종류 등을 명확하게 기억하는 것이 유리하고, 남녀 각각 어떤 말을 했는지 구분해서 알아 두는 것이 오답을 피하는 데 많은 도움이 된다. 추론 능력은 대의 또는 세부 내용을 바탕으로 하기 때문에 세부 내용도 간과할 수 없다.

- 선택지를 한 번밖에 들려주지 않기 때문에 대화 내용을 다 이해하고도 선택지를 놓쳐서 정답을 고르지 못하는 경우가 있다. 이를 방지하기 위해 소거법을 적용해서 선택지를 차례대로 표시하면서 최종 정답을 고르도록 한다.

- 질문 종류별로 오답 확률이 높은 유형을 알아 두는 것도 도움이 된다.

  – 대의 파악 오답 유형: 대화 중 일부 세부 사항만 포함한 선택지, 너무 일반적인 내용의 선택지, 대화 중 특정 키워드를 조합한 전혀 엉뚱한 내용의 선택지 등이다.

  – 세부 내용 파악 오답 유형: 대화에서 언급된 어휘를 반복한 선택지, 대화와 전혀 무관한 선택지, 일부 내용만 사실인 선택지, 남녀의 역할이 뒤바뀐 선택지, 시제가 대화 내용과 일치하지 않는 선택지 등이 있다.

  – 추론 오답 유형: 상식적으로는 맞는 진술이지만 대화 내용과는 무관한 선택지, 대화에서 언급된 어휘로 만들었지만 대화 내용과 무관한 선택지, 추론 가능한 내용과 정반대인 선택지 등이 있다.

- 대의 파악이나 세부 내용 파악 유형에 대비해 패러프레이징(paraphrasing) 연습을 하는 것이 좋다. 대화에서 언급된 어휘가 그대로 사용된 경우는 오답일 확률이 높은 반면, 언급된 어휘를 비슷한 말로 바꾸어 만든 선택지는 정답일 확률이 높으므로 paraphrasing 연습이 많은 도움이 된다.

● PART IV

A　기출문제 분석

담화문을 듣고 4개의 선택지 중 질문에 가장 적절한 정답을 고르는 문제이다.

제시 방법　담화문 → 질문 → 담화문 → 질문 → 선택지 순으로 들려 준다.

문항수　15문항

질문 유형　대의 파악(7문항) → 세부 내용 파악(5문항) → 추론(3문항) 순으로 나온다.

측정 영역　영어 연설, 강의, 라디오 방송 등에 나오는 다양한 표현에 대한 이해도 측정을 바탕으로 전체 대의 파악, 세부 내용 파악, 추론 능력을 측정한다.

B　대표 기출문제

> Earlier this week, animal control officials killed a bear responsible for wounding a camper. The 21-year-old camper was sleeping when the 280-pound male black bear ripped through the side of his tent. The camper sustained bite wound and scratches but was able to scare the bear off. Earlier this month, two other bears were killed in the same area after attacking several Boy Scout members at a camp.

Q　What happened to the camper who was attacked by the bear?
(a)　He died from wounds.
(b)　He got lost in the woods.
✔ (c)　He was bitten and scratched.
(d)　He was rescued by Boy Scouts.

💬 우리말

이번 주 초에 동물 관리국 직원들은 야영하던 사람을 다치게 한 이유로 곰 한 마리를 사살했다. 280파운드의 검은 수컷 곰이 텐트 한 쪽을 찢었을 때 야영을 하던 21세의 피해자는 자고 있었다. 그는 물리고 긁혔지만 곰을 놀라게 해서 쫓아낼 수 있었다. 이달 초에는 막사에 있던 보이스카우트 회원 여러 명을 공격한 다른 두 마리의 곰이 같은 곳에서 사살됐다.

Q　곰에게 공격당한 야영객에게 무슨 일이 일어났는가?
(a)　상처 때문에 죽었다.
(b)　숲 속에서 길을 잃었다.
(c)　물리고 긁혔다.
(d)　보이스카우트에 의해 구조되었다.

📶 **공략법**

이 문제는 질문 What happened to...?(~에게 무슨 일이 일어났는가?)에 초점을 맞춰 두 번째 들을 때 답을 골라 낼 수 있으며, The camper sustained bite wound and scratches를 바꿔 쓴 (c) He was bitten and scratched를 정답으로 선택해야 한다. 이 문제처럼 특정 사실을 묻는 문제도 출제된다.

C 고득점 핵심비법

- 먼저 담화문의 전체 흐름을 파악한 뒤, 두 번째 듣기에서 질문과 연계된 부분에 집중하여 정확하게 듣는다.

- 질문 유형에 따라 맞춤식 메모를 한다. 특히 세부 사항 파악 유형 문제에 대비해서는 숫자, 연도, 물품 종류 등을 세세하게 메모해야 하고, 추론 능력은 대의 또는 세부 내용을 바탕으로 하기 때문에 세부 내용도 간과할 수 없다는 것을 기억한다.

- 질문 종류별로 오답일 확률이 높은 경우를 알아 두는 것이 도움이 된다.
  - 대의 파악 오답 유형: 담화문 내용의 일부에 해당하는 세부 사항으로 만든 선택지, 주제와 관련은 있으나 너무 범위가 넓은 일반적인 내용의 선택지, 언급된 어휘로 구성된 점 외에는 내용과 전혀 관련이 없는 선택지 등이 오답일 확률이 높다.

  - 세부 내용 파악 오답 유형: 담화문에 언급된 어휘로 만들어진 선택지나 내용과 전혀 무관한 선택지, 일부만 사실인 선택지 등이 오답으로 제시될 가능성이 크다.

  - 추론 오답 유형: 상식적으로는 맞지만 내용과는 무관한 선택지, 담화문에서 언급된 어휘로 만들었지만 내용과는 무관한 선택지, 추론 가능한 내용과 정반대의 선택지 등이 종종 사용되는 오답 유형이다.

- 대의 파악이나 세부 내용 파악 유형의 문제를 위해서는 paraphrasing 연습을 하는 것이 좋다. 언급된 어휘를 그대로 사용하면 오답일 확률이 높은 반면, 정답의 경우 언급된 어휘를 paraphrasing해서 만드는 경우가 많다.

● PART I

A 기출문제 분석

두 줄의 대화문을 읽고 빈칸에 문법적으로 적절한 표현을 4개의 선택지 중에서 고르는 문제이다.

제시 방법 두 줄의 대화문이 주어진다.

문항수 20문항

측정 영역 실시간과 비슷한 시간 제약 속에서 문법적으로 정확한 영어를 대화 속에서 구사할 수 있는지 측정한다.

빈출 토픽 일상 생활 대화 중에 흔히 접할 수 있는 주제가 많이 사용되므로 청해나 어휘 영역의 대화 부분과 비슷한 내용이 나온다.

B 대표 기출문제

> A   When is the paper due?
> B   It _________________ by Friday.

✔ (a) has to be done

  (b) is done

  (c) will do

  (d) has to do

💬 **우리말**

A   리포트 기한이 언제까지죠?

B   금요일까지입니다.

📶 **공략법**

주어가 It이므로 수동태가 돼야 한다. 하지만 (b)를 사용해 It's done이라고 하면 '그것은 끝났다'라는 뜻이 되어 by Friday와 어울리지 않는다. 따라서, 수동태이며 by Friday와의 연결도 자연스러운 (a) has to be done이 정답이다.

- 정확한 영어를 적재적소에 사용하는 능력이 중요하므로 눈으로만 익히는 문법 지식을 배제한다. 대화체를 소리 내어 읽는 연습을 해서 문법이 내재화되어 상황에 맞게 즉각적으로 사용할 수 있는 수준까지 끌어올리도록 한다.

- 문법 네 가지 Part 중 비교적 평이한 난이도이기 때문에 시간 안배 차원에서 신속하게 풀고 다음 Part로 넘어가도록 한다. 단, 첫 줄은 빈칸에 올 적절한 답을 찾는 데 단서가 되므로 생략하고 넘어가면 함정에 빠지는 경우가 종종 있다. 신속하게 문제를 읽어나가되 읽지 않고 건너뛰는 일은 없어야 한다.

- 문법 문제의 빈칸은 주로 두 번째 줄에 오지만 일부 문제는 첫 번째 줄에 빈칸이 오기도 한다. 이런 유형에서는 두 번째 줄을 제대로 읽어야 출제자의 함정에 걸려들지 않는다. 즉, 빈칸 위치에 상관없이 문제에 나오는 대화는 모두 다 읽고 정확한 내용을 파악해야 오답 함정을 피해 정답을 찾을 수 있다.

- 문법 문제라고 해서 대화의 문법적인 요소만 신경 쓰면 안 된다. 상황에 적절한 어법을 고른다는 자세로 문제를 풀도록 한다. 예를 들어 대화 내용에 현재 시제가 여러 개 나온다고 무조건 현재 시제를 답으로 고르면 오히려 오답일 경우가 많다.

- 일상 대화 구문의 어법을 묻는 Part이므로 대화체의 정확한 표현을 익히는 것이 도움이 된다. 즉, 문법책의 모든 문법 요소를 처음부터 공부하는 것보다는 일상 대화 구분 표현 위주로 외울 수 있는 수준까지 익혀 두면 짧은 시간 내에 정확하게 구사할 수 있는 표현들이 많아질 것이다. 이렇게 되면 문법 Part 1도 쉽게 정복할 수 있다.

● PART II

A 기출문제 분석

한 개의 문장을 읽고 빈칸에 문법적으로 가장 적절한 표현을 4개의 선택지 중에서 고른다.

제시 방법　한 개의 문어체 문장이 주어진다.

문항수　20문항

측정 영역　문어체 영어의 정확한 어법 구사력을 측정한다.

빈출 토픽　학술문과 실용문 등 일상에서 접하는 문어체 문장에 언급되는 주제가 주로 사용된다.

B 대표 기출문제

> ______________________ David would be late was given to his boss.

　✔ (a) The message that
　(b) A message is that
　(c) From the message
　(d) The message which

💬 우리말

데이빗이 늦을 거라는 메시지가 그의 상사에게 전달되었다.

📶 공략법

빈칸에는 동사 was given의 주어가 필요하므로 (b)와 (c)는 제외된다. David would be late는 완전한 문장이므로 관계대명사 which가 앞에 쓰일 수 없고, 동격절을 이끄는 that이 적절하므로 정답은 (a)가 된다.

C 고득점 핵심비법

- 구어체 문장보다 문어체 문장은 의미 파악이 힘들 수 있으므로 평상시 문어체 문장의 직독직해 연습을 충분히 한다. 특히 관계사들로 연결된 문장, 절 안에 또 다른 절이 있는 문장 등 복잡한 문장을 평상시에 많이 접해 보도록 하자. 난해한 문장을 만났을 때 바로 의미를 파악할 수 있어야 문법 Part 2 문제를 신속하게 해결할 수 있다.

- 주어와 동사가 여러 개 나오는 긴 문장은 주절의 주어와 동사를 파악한 후, 다른 문법 사항들을 따져 보도록 한다. 특히 가장 빈출되면서도 기본이 되는 주어–동사 수 일치 문제는 주절의 주어와 동사를 파악해야만 풀 수 있는 문제이다.

- 영어를 외국어로 사용하는 한국인을 위한 TEPS 시험에서는 한국인이 특히 취약한 관사와 문장 구조 등에 대해 묻는 문제가 다수 출제된다. 이를 대비하기 위해서는 문장 내 쓰임새를 익혀 두는 것이 낱낱의 문법 지식을 알고 있는 것보다 신속하고 정확하게 문제를 푸는 데 많은 도움을 줄 것이다. 영어 활용 능력 수준 측정을 위해 TEPS가 고안된 점을 염두에 두고, 평소에 정확한 영어 구사 능력 함양에 집중하도록 한다.

- 문법 Part 1과 마찬가지로 정확한 어법을 익히려면 청해 Part 4 긴 담화문 속에 나오는 문장이나 어휘 Part 2 문장을 익혀 두는 것도 좋다. 각 분야별 어휘와 구문에 익숙해질수록 읽고 이해하는 속도가 자연히 빨라지게 되고, 아울러 문장 안에서 정확한 쓰임새도 익힐 수 있기 때문이다.

● PART III

A 기출문제 분석

네 줄의 대화문을 읽고 문법적으로 이상한 부분이 있는 문장을 고르는 유형의 문제이다.

제시 방법   네 줄의 대화문이 주어진다.

문항수   5문항

측정 영역   길어진 대화에서 비문법적 요소를 가려내는 능력을 측정한다.

빈출 토픽   일상 생활에서 접하는 대화에 나오는 주제가 주로 사용된다.

B 대표 기출문제

> (a) A   You said you had something to discuss with me.
> (b) B   Yeah, I have been debating whether to go back to work or not.
> (c) A   Are you actually thinking about becoming a full-time mom?
> ✔ (d) B   That's which I want to discuss with you.

💬 **우리말**
(a) A   나와 의논할 게 있다고 했지.
(b) B   응, 다시 일을 시작할지 고심 중이야.
(c) A   정말 전업 주부가 될 생각이야?
(d) B   그게 바로 의논하고 싶은 점이야.

📡 **공략법**

관계대명사 용법을 물어보는 문제이다. (d)에서 discuss의 목적어가 없고, which는 관계대명사인데 선행사가 없으므로 선행사를 포함하는 관계대명사 what으로 고쳐야 한다.

C 고득점 핵심비법

- 주어진 선택지가 따로 없어서 어떤 문법에 관한 문제인지 전혀 알 수 없고 주어진 대화 내용을 읽으면서 틀린 부분을 골라야 하기 때문에 보다 적극적인 태도로 문제에 임해야 한다. 즉, 각 대화에서 어느 문법 요소가 틀렸는지 모르는 상태에서 틀린 부분을 찾아야 하기 때문에 대화 내용을 파악함과 동시에 모든 품사와 구문 요소가 정확한지도 일일이 확인하는 습관을 평소에 들여야 당황하지 않고 실전에서 실력 발휘를 할 수 있다.

- 주어진 시간 내에 틀린 문법 사항을 골라야 하기 때문에 즉각적으로 비문법적인 부분을 찾아내는 훈련이 평상시에 필요하다. 이렇게 하기 위해서는 다른 문법 Part의 문제 대비와 마찬가지로 일상 대화 및 학술문과 실용문을 많이 접해서 다양한 문장에 익숙해져야 한다.

- 모든 문법 학습 요소들이 다 출제되는 것이 아니라 단골로 출제되는 문법 사항이 있음을 알자. 문장 구조, 시제, 수 일치, 관사 등에 해당하는 문법 요소들을 집중해서 훈련하는 것도 단기간에 Part 3을 정복할 수 있는 길이다. 하지만, Part 3 역시 제한된 문법 사항에만 국한해 다른 문법 요소를 무시했다가 낭패를 볼 수 있다는 것을 유의하자.

- Part 4에 비해 짧은 대화체라 약간 수월하게 보일 수 있겠지만 선택지가 주어진 Part 1과 2보다는 고난이도인 경우가 많다. 특히 재빨리 읽으면서 틀린 문법 사항도 찾아내야 하므로 평상시 대화문의 정확도를 분석하는 것도 실전에서 틀린 부분을 파악하는 데 도움이 될 것이다. 즉, 정답을 찾는 데에만 급급하지 말고 한 문제를 풀더라도 문법적으로 옳고 그른 부분들에 대한 분석을 자세히 하다 보면 실전에서 당황하지 않고 틀린 부분을 찾아낼 수 있다는 것이다.

PART IV

A 기출문제 분석

4개의 문어체 문장을 읽고 문법적으로 어색한 부분이 있는 문장을 고르는 유형의 문제이다.

제시 방법 4개의 문어체 문장이 하나의 지문으로 주어진다.

문항수 5문항

측정 영역 문어체 문장으로 구성된 지문에서 비문법적인 요소를 가려내는 능력을 측정한다.

빈출 토픽 신문, 잡지, 교재 등 일상 생활에서 문어체로 접하게 되는 주제가 사용된다.

B 대표 기출문제

> (a) Major League Baseball will begin mandatory testing for steroids. (b) From next March, each player will be tested and samples thoroughly analyzed. ✔ (c) The penalty for a first positive test will submit to treatment. (d) After their fifth positive test, players will receive a one-year suspension.

💬 우리말

(a) 메이저리그 야구에서 의무적으로 스테로이드 검사를 시작할 것이다. (b) 내년 3월부터, 모든 선수들이 검사를 받을 것이며, 혈액 샘플들은 철저히 분석될 것이다. (c) 첫 양성 반응에 대한 처벌은 치료를 받는 것이다. (d) 양성 반응을 다섯 차례 보인 선수들은 1년 동안 출전 정지된다.

📡 공략법

(c)에서 서수(first) 앞에는 정관사 the가 오는 것이 원칙이다. 물론 이 원칙이 깨지는 경우도 있지만, the first positive test가 올바른 형태이다.

C 고득점 핵심비법

- Part 3 대화체에 비해 Part 4는 지문 길이도 더 길고 문어체라서 내용 파악이 훨씬 더 어렵고 시간도 가장 많이 걸린다. 그렇기 때문에 비문법적인 요소를 찾기가 특히 더 어려울 수 있으므로 신속하게 문어체 문장들을 읽고 직독직해를 통해 내용을 즉시 파악할 수 있는 능력을 평상시에 훈련하도록 한다.

- 지문 내용은 물론 문제에서 요구하는 문법 사항 예측이 어렵기 때문에 더욱 적극적인 문제 풀이 전략이 필요하다. 4개의 문장을 읽으면서 내용 파악을 하는 동시에 모든 가능성을 열어 두고 비문법적으로 보이는 부분을 찾아 나가야 하는데 이때 가능성이 있는 부분을 일단 밑줄 그어 놓은 뒤 신속하게 다시 그 부분들을 재확인하는 것도 정확도를 높이는 한 방법이 될 수 있다.

- 주어진 시간 내에 틀린 문법 사항을 골라야 하기 때문에 즉각적으로 비문법적인 부분을 찾아내는 훈련이 필요하다. 이를 위해서는 정확한 표현을 즉각적으로 사용할 수 있을 정도로 알고 있어야 한다. 즉, Part 3 대비를 위해서 대화체를 많이 익혀 둠으로써 신속하게 비문법적인 대화 부분을 알아차리는 훈련을 하듯이, Part 4 대비책으로 학술문과 실용문을 접하면서 거의 암기할 정도로 정독하는 것도 문법 내재화를 도울 것이며, 이런 훈련 과정을 거치고 나면 자연스럽게 틀린 부분이 눈에 잘 띌 것이다.

- Part 2에 나오는 문장 네 개가 한꺼번에 출제된다고 생각하면 좀 부담이 덜어질 것이다. Part 2 문장들에서 문법적 오류를 찾는다고 생각하면 이제 마음 편해질 것이다.

  - 시제 문제: 각 문장마다 여러 시제가 혼합되어 있는 경우가 대부분이기 때문에 시제의 형태만 참고해서 틀린 시제를 찾는 것은 거의 불가능하다고 봐야 한다. 내용 파악이 선행되어야만 시제가 잘못 쓰인 곳을 찾을 수 있다.

  - 관사 문제: a와 the의 쓰임 여부는 4개 문장에서 어떤 명사가 이미 앞서 언급된 것이고 아닌지를 이해한 후에 결정되므로 내용 파악이 우선되어야 한다.

어휘

● PART I

A 기출문제 분석

두 줄의 대화문을 읽고 빈칸에 가장 잘 어울리는 어휘를 고르는 문제이다.

제시 방법   두 줄의 대화문이 주어진다.

문항수   25문항

측정 영역   대화에서 사용하는 구어체 표현을 적소에 활용할 수 있는지 측정한다.

빈출 토픽   일상 생활과 관련 있는 주제가 많이 출제된다.

B 대표 기출문제

> A   How did Beth hurt her leg so bad?
> B   I heard she _________________ coming down the mountain yesterday.

(a) faltered
(b) limped
(c) lingered
✔ (d) tripped

💬 우리말
A   베스는 어쩌다 그렇게 다리를 심하게 다쳤니?
B   어제 산을 내려오다가 걸려 넘어졌대.

(a) 흔들리다
(b) 절뚝거리다
(c) 버티다
(d) 발을 헛디디다

📶 공략법
다리를 다친(hurt her leg) 이유로는 산을 내려오다(coming down the mountain) '넘어졌을' 가능성이 가장 크다. '넘어지다'는 표현에는 (d)에 사용된 trip 외에 fall, tumble down 등이 있다.

고득점 핵심비법

- 짧은 시간 내에 문맥에 어울리는 어휘를 골라야 하기 때문에 많은 어휘를 알고 있는 것뿐만 아니라 문맥 (context)에 적절한 어휘를 사용할 수 있는 능력을 키우는 것도 중요하다. 따라서 어휘를 처음 접할 때엔 참고 자료를 동원해서 문장 내에서 쓰이는 다양한 예문을 동시에 익혀 두어야 한다. 시간 내에 모든 어휘 문제를 잘 풀기 위해서는 특히 문맥 속에서 각 어휘의 쓰임을 거의 외우다시피 알고 있어야 시간 낭비 없이 즉각적으로 빈칸에 올 정답을 고를 수 있을 것이다.

- 해당 어휘의 우리말을 단순하게 암기하는 것은 별 도움이 안 된다. 우리말로는 그럴듯해도 쓰임이 어색한 어휘의 뉘앙스 차이를 구분할 줄 알아야 하므로 문장 전체로 어휘를 이해하는 것이 장기적으로 유리하다.

- 청해의 대화 파트뿐만 아니라 문법 Part 1과 3에 언급된 대화들도 어휘 실력 향상을 위해 활용될 수 있음을 기억하고 어휘 영역 이외의 빈출 표현도 문맥 속에서 익혀 두도록 한다.

- 대화를 신속히 읽고 즉각적으로 빈칸을 채워 넣어야 하기 때문에 실제 대화를 하면서 적절한 어휘를 사용할 수 있을 정도의 실력이 되도록 많은 표현을 통째로 익혀 두어야 한다.

- 일상적인 대화 속에서 자주 등장하는 어휘뿐만 아니라 이어동사, 이디엄 등도 출제되므로 숙지해 두도록 한다.

- 형태상·의미상 혼동되는 어휘, 의미 덩어리로 사용되는 연어 등이 정확한 활용법도 아울러 알아 둔다.

● PART II

A 기출문제 분석

한 개의 문어체 문장을 읽고 빈칸에 가장 잘 어울리는 어휘를 고르는 문제이다.

제시 방법　한 개의 문어체 문장이 주어진다.

문항수　25문항

측정 영역　일상 생활에서 접할 수 있는 문어체 표현을 즉각적으로 사용할 수 있는지 측정한다.

빈출 토픽　학술문뿐만 아니라 실용문에 이르기까지 매우 다양한 주제를 다룬다.

B 대표 기출문제

> The management has decided to ________________ a complex strategy to resolve the crisis.

(a) breach
(b) withdraw
(c) alternate
✔ (d) implement

💬 우리말

경영진은 위기를 해결하기 위해 복합적인 전략을 이행하기로 결정했다.

(a) 위반하다
(b) 철수하다
(c) 번갈아 나오게 만들다
(d) 시행하다

📶 공략법

'전략을 수행하다'에 해당하는 동사를 골라야 한다. 위기 해결을 위해선(to resolve the crisis) 다양한 전략을 세우거나(establish)나 수행(implement)해야 한다. 선택지 중 이와 가장 어울리는 동사는 (d) implement이다.

C 고득점 핵심비법

- 학술문과 실용문의 주제별 빈출 어휘를 익혀 둔다. 빈출 어휘는 정답 선택지뿐만 아니라 오답 선택지에 나오는 어휘도 포함한다. 주제별로 자주 출제되는 어휘는 한정되어 있기 때문에 기출 어휘가 다시 출제될 확률이 높다.

- Part1과 마찬가지로 각 어휘의 쓰임새를 알아야 하기 때문에 전체 문장을 익히도록 한다. 그래야만 문법적으로도 정확한 어휘 활용 능력을 키울 수 있기 때문이다.

- 미묘한 뉘앙스 차이가 있는 쉬운 어휘의 용례 예문을 적극적으로 활용해야 한다. 의미가 비슷해 보이는 어휘들끼리 묶어서 따로 정리하면 도움이 될 것이다.

- 신문 기사, 잡지, 광고, 학술지, 비평 등의 실용문과 전문적인 학술문에서 다양하게 출제되므로 평상시 이런 종류의 글을 많이 접하는 것이 도움이 된다. 15분이라는 짧은 시간 내에 50문항이나 되는 문제를 무리 없이 풀기 위한 대비법 중 하나가 주제별로 다양한 문장을 평소에 자주 읽는 것이다. 이렇게 함으로써 필수 어휘를 자주 접할 수 있을 뿐만 아니라 문장 이해 속도도 향상될 수 있다.

- 대화체 문제와 마찬가지로 주제별 어휘뿐만 아니라 연어 및 형태상 · 의미상 혼동되는 어휘를 잘 알아 두도록 한다.

독해

● PART I

A 기출문제 분석

100단어 내외의 단일 지문을 읽고 빈칸에 들어갈 적절한 선택지를 고르는 문제이다. 14문항은 구나 절을 고르는 문제이고, 나머지 2문항은 문장과 문장 사이를 이어주는 연결어를 찾는 문제이다.

제시 방법　지문의 처음 문장이나 마지막 문장, 드물게 중간 문장에 빈칸이 있는 한 개의 글이 주어진다.

문항수　16문항

측정 영역　글의 전반적인 이해 능력 및 논리적인 흐름 파악 능력을 평가한다.

빈출 토픽　학술문과 실용문에서 골고루 출제된다.

B 대표 기출문제

> The idea that people live according to how others will perceive them has been established as the rule, not the exception. The real question now lies in the reasons for this way of life. It was hypothesized by C. S. Lewis that this desire to belong and to fit in is a natural human characteristic. He believed that people have _______________.

(a) a tendency to regard themselves as normal

(b) no idea how to deal with human nature

(c) a need to distinguish themselves as unique

✔ (d) an instinctive drive to belong to a group

💬 우리말

다른 사람이 자신을 어떻게 인식하느냐에 따라 인간의 행동이 결정된다는 개념은 예외가 아닌 법칙으로 굳어졌다. 이런 상황에서의 현실적인 물음은 왜 그렇게 사느냐이다. C. S. 루이스는 어딘가에 소속되고 맞춰지고 싶은 욕망은 인간의 본능적인 특성이라고 가정했다. 그는 사람들은 특정 그룹에 소속되고자 하는 본능적 욕구를 갖고 있다고 믿었다.

(a) 자신을 평범하다고 여기는 성향을

(b) 인간의 본성을 어떻게 다룰지에 대해 아무런 생각도 없는

(c) 자신을 특별한 존재로 여기고자 하는 욕구를

(d) 특정 그룹에 소속되고자 하는 본능적 욕구를

첫 문장에서 people live according to how others will perceive them이라는 내용과 세 번째 문장의 desire to belong and to fit in이라는 표현에서, 사람들에게는 집단에 소속되고자 하는 욕구가 있다는 (d)를 추론할 수 있다.

C 고득점 핵심비법

- 모든 지문을 자세히 읽겠다는 생각을 접는다. 1분에 한 문제씩 풀어야 하기 때문에 정독을 하기에는 절대적으로 시간이 부족하므로 주요 어휘 위주로 대의 파악 및 흐름 파악에 주력해야 시간 내에 문제를 다 풀 수 있다.

- 주제별 어휘를 평소 많이 알아 둔다. 청해, 문법, 어휘 등 TEPS의 다른 영역과 마찬가지로 방대한 어휘 지식을 갖추고 있어야 독해 속도도 빨라지고 정확한 이해가 가능하다.

- 빈칸의 위치에 따라 독해의 목적이 달라져야 한다. 빈칸이 첫 문장에 있는 경우 대의 파악만 해도 되지만 마지막 문장에 올 때에는 대의 파악뿐만 아니라 논리적 흐름도 염두에 두면서 독해를 해야 한다.

- 오답 함정 선택지 유형을 연습해 둔다.

  – 지문에 나오는 어휘로 만들었지만 문맥과 전혀 상관없는 선택지

  – 너무 일반적인 내용으로 만든 선택지

  – 상식적으로는 괜찮아 보이지만 내용과는 무관한 선택지

  – 지문 내용의 일부처럼 보이기는 하지만 논리적인 흐름 면에서는 어울리지 않는 선택지

● PART II

A 기출문제 분석

100단어 내외의 단일 지문을 읽고 주어진 질문에 적절한 답을 4개의 선택지에서 고르는 유형이다.

제시 방법　한 개의 지문에 한 개의 질문이 주어진다.

문항수　21문항

측정 영역　단일 지문에 대한 전체 및 세부 내용 이해 및 추론 능력을 측정한다.
대의 파악(6문항) → 세부 내용 파악(10문항) → 추론(5문항) 순으로 나온다.

빈출 토픽　학술문과 실용문에서 모두 골고루 출제된다.

B 대표 기출문제

> After years of negotiations, an agreement on ownership of five islands off of Queensland, Australia, has been finalized. The state government has finally agreed that the islands should become private property. For the past two years, it had argued that the islands belonged to the government rather than the natives of the islands. The agreement ends years of anguish. Native Don Banu, who has been following the debate for many years, said, "It's a great relief for all of us. Now we can start to move forward." The government is currently consulting islanders and expects to hand over the deeds of ownership in December.

Q What can be inferred about the decision made by the government?
(a) It was about who can own the island businesses.
✔ (b) It favored the local inhabitants of the islands.
(c) It could result in widespread disagreements.
(d) It was made sooner than expected.

💬 우리말

수년간의 협상 끝에, 호주 퀸즐랜드 근해의 다섯 개 섬에 대한 소유권 협정이 체결되었다. 주 정부는 결국 섬을 개인 소유로 하는 데 동의했다. 정부는 지난 2년 동안 섬이 원주민 소유가 아닌 정부 소유라고 주장해 왔다. 이번 협정으로 인해 수년 간 지속된 고통도 끝이 났다. 많은 세월 동안 논쟁을 지켜본 원주민 돈 바누는 "이번 일은 우리 모두에게 커다란 안심이 됩니다. 이제 우리는 새로운 일을 시작할 수 있게 되었습니다"라고 말했다. 정부는 현재 섬 주민들과 논의 중이며, 12월 소유권 이양을 할 작정이다.

Q 정부가 내린 결정에 대해 추론할 수 있는 것은?
(a) 누가 섬 사업을 소유할 수 있는가에 관한 것이었다.
(b) 섬 지역 주민들을 지지했다.
(c) 광범위한 반대를 야기할 수 있었다.
(d) 예상보다 일찍 이루어졌다.

📡 공략법

두 번째 문장에서 섬이 개인 소유(private property)가 되었다는 것은 결국 섬이 원주민의 소유임을 의미하며, 세 번째 문장의 natives가 local inhabitants of the islands와 같은 의미임을 파악할 수 있으면 쉽게 정답이 (b)임을 찾을 수 있다.

C 고득점 핵심비법

- 직독직해하는 습관을 들인다. 우리말로 번역하려 하지 말고 신속하게 영어 지문을 읽으면서 내용을 이해하는 습관을 들여야 한다.

- 지문을 다 읽겠다는 생각을 버려라. 대의 파악 문제의 경우 주요 내용어 중심으로 읽고, 세부 내용 파악 문제는 질문에 따라 선택지의 진위 여부를 한 개씩 확인해 가며 읽거나 육하원칙 문제는 질문 내용을 제대로 파악하고 해당 부분을 신속히 찾아서 그 부분을 자세히 읽는다. 추론 문제는 대의 파악 및 세부 내용 파악이 선행되어야 하기 때문에 좀 더 시간을 할애해야 할 것이다.

- 오답 함정을 각 문제 유형마다 미리 알아 두고 잘 피하도록 한다.
  - 대의 파악 오답 유형 : 세부 사실을 대의로 혼동하게 하는 오답이 자주 출제된다.

  - 세부 내용 파악 오답 유형 : 일부 내용만 사실인 경우, 지문에서 언급된 어휘로 만들었지만 내용과는 상관없는 선택지를 주의하자.

  - 추론 오답 유형 : 그럴듯해 보이지만 지문 내용과는 상관없는 오답, 정답과 정반대 진술이 선택지로 제시되기도 한다.

PART III

A 기출문제 분석

5개의 문장으로 구성된 100단어 내외의 단일 지문을 읽고 글의 흐름상 어색한 문장을 찾는 유형의 문제이다.

제시 방법　　주제문에 이어 4개의 문장이 제시된다.

문항수　　3문항

측정 영역　　지문의 응집력 파악 능력을 측정한다.

빈출 지문 토픽　학술문과 실용문 모두 골고루 출제된다.

B 대표 기출문제

In 1871, American Indians were placed on federal land reservations. ✔ (a) Today, American Indian tribes must be understood as nations within the nation of the United States. (b) The Indians had no control of their communities and no power to affect federal polices over them. (c) They were under the jurisdiction of the Bureau of Indian affairs, which decided what they would eat, where they would live, and ultimately how they would live. (d) Thus, they were stripped of their political rights and even their cultural heritage.

💬 **우리말**

1871년 미국의 인디언들은 연방정부가 정한 거주지로 옮겨졌다. (a) 오늘날 인디언 부족은 미국이라는 나라 안에 존재하는 별개의 나라로 이해되어야 한다. (b) 인디언들은 공동체에 대한 지배권도, 그들에 대한 연방정부의 정책에 영향을 미칠 힘도 없었다. (c) 무엇을 먹을지와 어디서 살지, 그리고 궁극적으로 어떻게 살 것인지를 결정하는 것도 인디언 사무국의 관할이었다. (d) 이런 식으로 그들은 정치적 권리와 심지어 문화적 유산마저 빼앗겼다.

📡 **공략법**

첫 문장(주제문)과 (b), (c), (d)는 1871년 이래 인디언들이 미국에서 겪어온 박해와 수탈에 대해 언급하고 있다. 그러나 (a)는 인디언 부족을 미국 안에 존재하는 별개의 국가로 인정해야 한다는 내용으로, 미국과 인디언 부족을 동등한 위치에서 언급하고 있으므로 개연성이 없다.

C 고득점 핵심비법

- 처음 제시되는 주제문에서 벗어난 문장을 찾는 것이므로 4개의 선택지 문장을 읽을 때에 항상 주제문과의 연관성을 염두에 두고 읽도록 한다. 문법 Part 4의 경우 각 문장 간의 연관성까지 염두에 두고 내용을 파악할 필요는 없으나 독해 Part 3에서는 주제문과의 연관성이 문제 풀이의 핵심이다.

- 주제문과 연관성은 있으나 문장의 위치가 잘못되어 흐름을 깨는 유형도 있으니 흐름상 잘 어울리는지도 살피도록 한다.

- 글의 어조가 갑자기 바뀌는 경우도 어색한 문장에 해당하므로 어조의 변화도 주의하도록 한다.

- 주어진 주제문에 대한 문장이 3개 나온 뒤 새로운 주제문이 4번째 문장으로 나오게 되면 어색한 문장이 된다는 것도 기억한다.

서울대 최신기출 1

Listening Comprehension

Grammar

Vocabulary

Reading Comprehension

LISTENING COMPREHENSION

DIRECTIONS

1. In the Listening Comprehension section, all content will be presented orally rather than in written form.

2. This section contains 4 parts. In parts I and II, each passage will be read only once. In parts III and IV, each passage and its corresponding question will be read twice. But in all sections, the options will be read only once. After listening to the passage and question, listen to the options and choose the best answer.

○ Scripts P 266 / 정답 P 326

Part I　**Questions 1—15**

You will now hear fifteen conversation fragments, each made up of a single spoken statement followed by four spoken responses. Choose the most appropriate response to the statement.

Part II　**Questions 16—30**

You will now hear fifteen conversation fragments, each made up of three spoken statements followed by four spoken responses. Choose the most appropriate response to complete the conversation.

Part III   Questions 31—45

You will now hear fifteen complete conversations. For each item, you will hear a conversation and its corresponding question, both of which will be read twice. Then you will hear four options which will be read only once. Choose the option that best answers the question.

Part IV   Questions 46—60

You will now hear fifteen spoken monologues. For each item, you will hear a monologue and its corresponding question, both of which will be read twice. Then you will hear four options which will be read only once. Choose the option that best answers the question.

GRAMMAR

◐ 정답 P 326

Part I **Questions 1—20**

Choose the best answer for the blank.

1. A: Tina, do you prefer watching movies or playing sports?

B: Well, watching movies __________ me more.

(a) interest
(b) interests
(c) is interested
(d) are interested

2. A: How did you do on the exam?

B: I think I did __________ well.

(a) far
(b) such
(c) quite
(d) much

3. A: People living in large cities are usually stressed.

B: That's a generalization __________.

(a) I not agree
(b) that I don't agree
(c) I don't agree with
(d) I don't agree with that

4. A: I feel like a failure for dropping out of school.

B: That __________ have been a mistake, but try to learn from it.

(a) may
(b) shall
(c) would
(d) should

5. A: If only I were thinner and richer!

B: You really ought to learn to accept __________.

(a) of yourself
(b) yourself as are you
(c) yourself as you are
(d) yourself of who you are

6. A: Where do I submit my résumé?

B: At the Personnel Department, __________ is just down the hall.

(a) that
(b) what
(c) where
(d) which

7. A: What did you find most difficult about living abroad?

B: __________ communicate with the people around me was depressing.

(a) Not able to
(b) Be able not to
(c) Not able being to
(d) Not being able to

8. A: It's too bad Mike lost his license.

B: Well, he was driving __________ the influence of alcohol.

(a) on
(b) with
(c) under
(d) through

9. A: Jim, you didn't take out the garbage this morning, did you?

   B: No, but I'll remember ___________ tonight, for sure.

   (a) taking it out
   (b) taking out it
   (c) to take out it
   (d) to take it out

10. A: Did you buy any bread?

    B: I ___________, but I forgot.

    (a) should
    (b) should have
    (c) should have to
    (d) should have to do

11. A: Is your organization focused on pollution issues?

    B: Yes. The environment, not profits, ___________ us the most.

    (a) concern
    (b) concerns
    (c) was concerning
    (d) were concerning

12. A: I'm going to quit smoking.

    B: ___________ that millions of times before.

    (a) You say
    (b) You've said
    (c) You had said
    (d) You're saying

13. A: Do you think Jesse lied to us?

    B: No. He's an honest man. He ___________ not have done that.

    (a) may
    (b) must
    (c) could
    (d) should

14. A: Did you manage to tour all the exhibitions?

    B: No, there was ___________.

    (a) in the museum so much to see
    (b) much to see so in the museum
    (c) to see in the museum so much
    (d) so much to see in the museum

15. A: Did you hear about the seminar?

    B: Yes, but I ___________ of the speaker yet.

    (a) hadn't informed
    (b) haven't informed
    (c) hadn't been informed
    (d) haven't been informed

16. A: World peace seems impossible.

    B: I know. The obstacles to peace ___________ so huge.

    (a) is
    (b) are
    (c) is to be
    (d) are to be

17. A: What impressed you most about the movie?

    B: ___________ several roles was very impressive.

    (a) The same actor played
    (b) That the same actor played
    (c) The same actor playing that
    (d) That the same actor playing

18. A: What do you picture yourself doing
five years from now?

B: ___________ a famous comedian.

(a) I probably became
(b) I've probably become
(c) I'm probably becoming
(d) I'll probably have become

19. A: I heard drinking wine is healthy.

B: Yes, but too much has ___________.

(a) the opposite effect exact
(b) the exact opposite effect
(c) the effect the exact opposite
(d) the effect exact the opposite

20. A: There are so many homeless people.

B: I know. The newspaper says poverty
is ___________.

(a) at a growing rate alarming
(b) alarming at a growing rate
(c) at an alarming rate growing
(d) growing at an alarming rate

Part II Questions 21—40
Choose the best answer for the blank.

---

21. Arabic script can be used to write
languages other than Arabic just
___________ the Roman alphabet is used
for many different languages.

(a) as
(b) so
(c) that
(d) because

22. The terms "broad" and "hard" are used
___________ a wide range of cheeses.

(a) to describing
(b) to describe
(c) described
(d) describe

23. The European beaver is ___________
rodents known to man.

(a) one of the largest
(b) one largest of the
(c) the large one of
(d) the one of large

24. The 2014 World Cup ___________
played in Brazil.

(a) is
(b) was
(c) will be
(d) has been

25. __________ of Joe's friends seem to understand why he is so interested in car engines.

(a) Few
(b) Little
(c) Lesser
(d) Fewest

26. Over the past decade, Japan __________ from being a major exporter of textiles to a major importer.

(a) changes
(b) is changing
(c) will change
(d) has changed

27. __________ is a great pastime and also helps to keep you fit.

(a) Canoeing
(b) To canoe
(c) Canoed
(d) Canoe

28. __________ it not been for the scholarship, the boy would not have been able to graduate.

(a) Has
(b) Had
(c) Was
(d) Were

29. It is wise to plan for your future now, even by just __________ small steps.

(a) taking
(b) to take
(c) to be taking
(d) having taken

30. Mr. Hope's son was not doing well at school, so he discussed __________ with his teacher.

(a) problem
(b) a problem
(c) the problem
(d) any problem

31. South Korea's government was established in 1948 through a general election __________ in accordance with a United Nations resolution.

(a) held
(b) to hold
(c) holding
(d) was held

32. Picasso's *Guernica* was a response to the German bombing of a Spanish town of that name, __________ sixteen hundred civilians died.

(a) to where
(b) in which
(c) of when
(d) for that

33. __________ he had digressed, the professor returned to his planned lesson.

(a) He realized
(b) To realize
(c) Realizing
(d) Realized

34. Computer repairmen should explain the jargon __________.

(a) customers not understand
(b) customers do not understand
(c) not customers understanding
(d) not understanding customers

35. The Boy Scout troop made camp in conditions __________ one scout described as "truly forlorn."

(a) whose
(b) where
(c) what
(d) that

36. It is the responsibility of each adult, parent, or guardian to supervise __________ children under your care while at SeaWorld Park.

(a) a few
(b) some
(c) such
(d) any

37. Part of the reason why police officers are sometimes impatient is that __________.

(a) at times stressful their jobs are
(b) stressful are at times their jobs
(c) their jobs are stressful at times
(d) at times are their jobs stressful

38. Salsa music might __________ as a fad in the early 1990s, but now it is a part of mainstream culture.

(a) start out
(b) be started out
(c) have started out
(d) have been started out

39. __________ to dry conditions for months, the forest was looked upon by authorities as a fire hazard.

(a) Subjecting
(b) To be subjecting
(c) Had been subjected
(d) Having been subjected

40. We can only guess what is __________ the surface of an individual's personality.

(a) upon
(b) along
(c) above
(d) beneath

Part III **Questions 41—45**

Identify the option that contains an awkward expression or an error in grammar.

41. (a) A: I'm going to England this summer.

(b) B: What a coincidence. So I am!

(c) A: Really? When are you going?

(d) B: Most likely in early July.

42. (a) A: You're in great shape for someone over 50.

(b) B: Well, I go to the gym every other days.

(c) A: How much time do you spend working out?

(d) B: Usually around an hour and a half.

43. (a) A: Tom, could you carry my purse?

(b) B: No way. What if I happen to run into my friends on the street?

(c) A: Come on. It's just a bag. Besides, I'm very tired.

(d) B: You wouldn't have had to ask me to do that if you didn't bring it.

44. (a) A: How is your experience of an American classroom different from a Korean?

(b) B: Well, I just listened in Korea, but here I actually participate in classroom activities.

(c) A: Do you think that has helped you learn more?

(d) B: Sure. I definitely learn more when I'm expected to participate actively.

45. (a) A: Oh, I wish I were more like you.

(b) B: Why? You seem to be living a great life!

(c) A: Well, although you have many friends, I don't know how to mingle.

(d) B: Oh, that's not so hard once you get the hang of it. I'll show you how.

Identify the option that contains an awkward expression or an error in grammar.

46. (a) Elbow pain has a variety of causes. (b) Inflammation of the tendons, or tendonitis, is one of them. (c) People who play racquet sports are prone to tendonitis. (d) However, any repetitive use of elbow can lead to pain.

47. (a) Some of us knew from childhood what we were being as adults. (b) Others, of course, had to search longer to discover their life's path. (c) A lack of childhood dreams, however, does not mean a life without success. (d) There are many successful people who grew up without any clear goals.

48. (a) Although deaf people can be taught to speak, they can never understand speech as well as a hearing person. (b) Seventy-five percent of spoken English words cannot be understood accurate through lip reading alone. (c) Therefore, the ability of many deaf individuals to comprehend spoken language is remarkable. (d) What they do is interpret lip movements along with facial expressions to determine what is being said.

49. (a) A big part of stress is feeling out of control. (b) So learn to handle stress by not overloading your day. (c) Take control by setting aside for yourself some time. (d) This will give you a chance to rest and reflect on events.

50. (a) One problem for livestock farmers who want to begin organic farming is that it reduces their ability to sell products at a premium price. (b) This loss of the ability to sell at the maximum price has to be compensated for somehow before organic farming can become financially viable. (c) Having overcome these financial issues, animal health stands as the next major problem farmers need to tackle. (d) What farmers face here is that many of the organic means of controlling disease in livestock are not satisfactory.

This is the end of the Grammar section. Do NOT move on to the next section until instructed to do so. You are NOT allowed to turn to any other section of the test.

VOCABULARY

DIRECTIONS

This part of the exam tests your vocabulary skills. You will have 15 minutes to complete the 50 questions. Be sure to follow the directions given by the proctor.

Part I Questions 1—25

Choose the best answer for the blank.

---

1. A: Why are you leaving so early?

B: I have a train to ___________.

(a) catch
(b) obtain
(c) attend
(d) occupy

2. A: I didn't like what you said to me yesterday.

B: If I hurt you in any ___________, I'm really sorry.

(a) line
(b) rule
(c) way
(d) style

3. A: Hello. May I speak to Caroline, please?

B: I'll go and ___________ if she's in.

(a) notice
(b) check
(c) seek
(d) find

4. A: Hi, Jones. Fancy meeting you here.

B: Oh, hi, Dan. I didn't expect to ___________ you here at Sara's party!

(a) get
(b) tell
(c) see
(d) bring

5. A: Can I eat these wild berries I found in the forest?

B: No, you can't. They may be ___________.

(a) poisonous
(b) needless
(c) vicious
(d) useless

6. A: My kids are always fighting. How about yours?

B: Actually, mine ___________ with each other quite well.

(a) fall out
(b) come up
(c) get along
(d) space out

7. A: This pie tastes really good.

B: Yeah, I think I'll have another ___________.

(a) thing
(b) piece
(c) shape
(d) chunk

8. A: Excuse me, does the Kennedy Center bus stop here?

B: No, that stop is ___________ further down.

(a) located
(b) prepared
(c) extended
(d) distanced

9. A: Your desk doesn't look very strong.

B: I know. But actually, it's quite __________.

(a) broad
(b) rough
(c) sturdy
(d) simple

10. A: Want to come for a walk in the park?

B: Sure. I'd love to go out for a __________.

(a) move
(b) stroll
(c) pace
(d) gaze

11. A: Tom changed his exercise routine.

B: Yeah, he started a new __________ to strengthen his back.

(a) regimen
(b) pattern
(c) schism
(d) jaunt

12. A: When does our flight arrive?

B: Here, I printed out a copy of our whole __________ for you.

(a) method
(b) itinerary
(c) procedure
(d) destination

13. A: It's hard to keep students disciplined.

B: I know. My students have been really __________ lately.

(a) handy
(b) unruly
(c) forceful
(d) restrained

14. A: Does your new job pay better?

B: No, but it has __________, like two months' paid vacation.

(a) tips
(b) value
(c) worth
(d) benefits

15. A: I hope Mike fits in at his new school.

B: I'm sure he won't have any difficulty in __________ to the new environment.

(a) progressing
(b) proceeding
(c) adjusting
(d) applying

16. A: How much is all of your jewelry worth?

B: I'm not sure. I haven't gotten it __________ yet.

(a) financed
(b) esteemed
(c) appraised
(d) measured

17. A: Let's shut the door. It's drafty in here.

B: But it feels __________ to me.

(a) stuffy
(b) illusive
(c) gloomy
(d) freezing

18. A: Do you like dancing to Mambo
    music?

    B: Not really. The __________ is too
    fast.

(a) notation
(b) accent
(c) tempo
(d) pitch

19. A: I'm glad you're on the company's
    social committee.

    B: Thanks, I appreciate your

       __________.

(a) relief
(b) profit
(c) aspect
(d) support

20. A: Was your Dad mad you quit school?

    B: He sure was. He __________ when
    I told him.

(a) hit the roof
(b) took the plunge
(c) was tickled pink
(d) kicked up his heels

21. A: Checkout time is noon, but I don't
    think we'll make it.

    B: Hopefully, the hotel will give us a
    short __________ period.

(a) plus
(b) grace
(c) excess
(d) mercy

22. A: Hasn't it been terribly hot lately?

    B: Yes, the heat has been __________.

(a) unbearable
(b) temporary
(c) intensive
(d) critical

23. A: I'm so mad at Jane. She wore my
    new sweater to school today.

    B: Well, you can __________ by
    wearing one of her new outfits first!

(a) set her up
(b) point her out
(c) get back at her
(d) look down on her

24. A: Judge Brown's ruling is
    controversial.

    B: Yes. It'll __________ a lot of
    debate.

(a) flaunt
(b) spawn
(c) procure
(d) brandish

25. A: Hey, I just got an email saying I've
    won a huge cash prize!

    B: I'm sure it's not true. Don't be so
    __________!

(a) cryptic
(b) gullible
(c) obstinate
(d) incessant

Part II **Questions 26—50**

Choose the best answer for the blank.

26. If you are a victim of discrimination, ___________ a complaint.

    (a) file
    (b) order
    (c) enable
    (d) suggest

27. All cigarette packets must carry a warning that ___________ smoking is bad for one's health.

    (a) says
    (b) deals
    (c) writes
    (d) records

28. In his autobiography, the statesman often ___________ to his upbringing as a time of great happiness.

    (a) pertains
    (b) submits
    (c) appeals
    (d) refers

29. So ___________ is Harvard University that many of the world's brightest young people aspire to study there.

    (a) relevant
    (b) decisive
    (c) allowable
    (d) prestigious

30. Lion prides ___________ of up to 18 adult females and their offspring accompanied by one or two adult males.

    (a) consist
    (b) control
    (c) discard
    (d) dispose

31. To keep your dog looking healthy and clean, ___________ him or her regularly.

    (a) shine
    (b) polish
    (c) groom
    (d) restore

32. The Great Chicago Fire of 1871 began with a small fire in a barn, but no conclusion has ever been ___________ as to what started the fire.

    (a) initiated
    (b) stepped
    (c) reached
    (d) pressed

33. To increase production, employees will be required to work a(n) ___________ hour a day.

    (a) extra
    (b) raised
    (c) reared
    (d) explicit

34. Cologne, Germany is a large city with over one million __________.

(a) tenants
(b) residuals
(c) inhabitants
(d) settlements

35. It is unlikely that we will see peace in Afghanistan in the __________ future.

(a) ominous
(b) prevailing
(c) foreseeable
(d) anticipatory

36. The French artist Christophe Petyt could plausibly __________ claim to being the world's greatest painter of fake art.

(a) fix
(b) lay
(c) rein
(d) grasp

37. On a warm spring day, the woman heard birds __________ outside her window.

(a) twittering
(b) twinkling
(c) grumbling
(d) glimmering

38. Music from years ago can fill people with __________ because it reminds them of their youth.

(a) inertia
(b) fantasia
(c) amnesia
(d) nostalgia

39. The religious devotee decided to make a __________ to several important holy sites.

(a) rendezvous
(b) pilgrimage
(c) fallacy
(d) quest

40. A lack of consistent communication concerning policy is often __________ as the greatest cause for concern among office staff.

(a) cited
(b) touted
(c) steered
(d) pursued

41. After extensive training over many years, the girl became a(n) __________ pianist.

(a) unconditional
(b) accomplished
(c) unequivocal
(d) authorized

42. Our Internet service is guaranteed to work when it is needed, providing the most __________ connection of all service providers in the city.

(a) traceable
(b) believable
(c) applicable
(d) dependable

43. The ambulance crew was unable to __________ the heart attack victim, who passed away before arriving at the hospital.

(a) desist
(b) dispel
(c) revive
(d) restate

44. While the US fought to throw off British rule, other former colonies gained their ___________ peacefully.

(a) autonomy
(b) uniformity
(c) unification
(d) articulation

45. The country granted ___________ to the illegal immigrants and allowed them to stay.

(a) censure
(b) amnesty
(c) pretense
(d) reproach

46. The roller coaster ride at the new park is too short, making the thrill ___________.

(a) transient
(b) minimum
(c) inconsistent
(d) spontaneous

47. The chairman was asked to ___________ the meeting for three days to allow shareholders time to submit new voting instructions.

(a) muster
(b) adjourn
(c) presage
(d) convoke

48. The politician's ___________ behavior was considered morally reprehensible, so he was not reelected.

(a) austere
(b) reticent
(c) licentious
(d) translucent

49. The Mexican War was one of the most ___________ events in American history, as it was essentially a shameless land grab.

(a) scurrilous
(b) derogatory
(c) redoubtable
(d) ignominious

50. The old woman attributed her good health to an optimistic outlook and a ___________ diet.

(a) rigorous
(b) hygienic
(c) precarious
(d) contentious

This is the end of the Vocabulary section. Do NOT move on to the Reading Comprehension section until instructed to do so. You are NOT allowed to turn to any other section of the test.

READING COMPREHENSION

Part I Questions 1—16

Read the passage. Then choose the option that best completes the passage.

1. Orangutans _______________________________. For most of them, the leafy canopy of the tropical forest provides everything they need in life, and they rarely descend from it. Another reason they live in trees is for safety. In the upper levels of the forest, they have no natural enemies. At night, when predators prowl below, orangutans sleep in nests far above the ground.

   (a) find safety in large groups
   (b) face greater competition for food
   (c) are superbly adapted for life in trees
   (d) are much more active in the day time

2. To outsiders, the Hindu taboo against eating cows might seem strange amid widespread poverty and periodic famine. The custom makes more sense, however, once it is understood how important cows are to survival. The death of any cow would be a great loss. Cows eat waste like rice straw and husks; they provide bull calves that grow up and plow the soil; their dung is used as fuel; and many provide milk. Therefore, to Hindus, it does not make sense to _______________________________.

   (a) kill a cow for food
   (b) eat meat regularly
   (c) continue their taboo
   (d) ignore a hungry cow

3. Carlos Moore, an African-Cuban militant, regards the Cuban government's moves to absorb blacks into the mainstream white community as a denial of black culture. He sees it as humiliating, as blacks constitute a large portion of the Cuban population. But others argue that the government's changes have brought about educational opportunities that can help blacks attain higher standards of living. They do not feel blacks should

   _______________________________.

   (a) give their support to black leaders
   (b) integrate with the rest of Cuban society
   (c) reject black culture in favor of white culture
   (d) keep to themselves in a separate community

4. _______________________________ on our website is easy. All you do is click on the Profile link located at the top left of the screen. Then look for the Contacts tab and click on that to edit your personal contact details. Once your personal details have been entered, it's a good idea to create a résumé. Click on the Resume tab and enter your résumé information or, alternatively, upload a completed résumé. Now you're ready to advertise your work skills, conduct searches and, of course, apply for jobs!

(a) Joining a social network
(b) Building a personal job profile
(c) Conducting effective job searches
(d) Advertising your services or products

5. In the 18th century BC, the Hittites established an empire in an area to the northwest of Babylonia, in what is now Turkey and Syria. They made a great contribution to civilization by starting the transition from the Bronze Age to the Iron Age. In the 13th century, they began to refine iron ore and use it to produce tools and weapons. As such, they can be described as the forerunners to the Iron Age. Indeed, many artifacts in museums around the world show how _______________________________.

(a) Hittites later migrated from Turkey
(b) Hittites dominated the ancient world
(c) iron was a major part of Hittite culture
(d) bronze tools were invented by the Hittites

6. Reporters and politicians often talk about the "Middle East," but in fact, this is _______________________________. It has become a useful way of referring to the lands of southwest Asia and northeast Africa. However, because it is not clear, some people might not think it includes African countries, while others might not think it includes countries in central Asia. In the past, traditional names—like Asia Minor, Mesopotamia, the Near East, the Holy Land, or the Levant—were used to refer to areas in the region.

(a) politically controversial
(b) a geographical error
(c) an imprecise term
(d) culturally biased

7. Empires seem to be a thing of the past in this day and age of more than 190 nations
    worldwide. Yet many countries are still recognized as the progeny of the great
    empires of the past. The countries founded or influenced by the British Empire
    are a good example, such as Australia, Canada, and the US. Other countries
    unfortunately bear the scars left by imperial rule. For instance, regional conflicts
    from Central Africa to the Middle East are often traceable to the imperial sins of
    war, slavery, exploitation, and cultural domination. In short, we live in a world that
    _______________________________________.

    (a) is a product of when the British Empire spanned the globe
    (b) has different forms of empires to those that once existed
    (c) suffers border conflicts because of religious intolerance
    (d) bears the recognizable imprints of empires now gone

8. A Harvard Medical School study has found that those who are obese during
    adolescence are more likely to die by middle age than their slimmer peers. The
    finding seems to be explained by the tendency of obese teens to remain so as adults,
    with their obesity in adulthood increasing their risk of developing serious medical
    conditions that can lead to death. The study clearly supports the idea of programs
    _______________________________________.

    (a) focused on improving the self-esteem of teens
    (b) geared toward adolescents with a troubled past
    (c) targeted at obese adults with a medical condition
    (d) aimed at preventing obesity in school-aged children

9.

> Dear Mr. Fields,
>
> This email is in regard to our meeting two weeks ago on the trial run of the website you designed for our company, Trendy Fashion Outlet. As I related to you at the meeting, customer response to the trial run was poor. I also pointed out numerous glitches in the site and asked that these be remedied within a week. That week has now passed, but the glitches remain. Thus, I have no choice but to
>
> ____ .
>
> Sincerely,
> J. Todd
> Manager, Trendy Fashion Outlet

(a) put my trust entirely in your artistic vision
(b) reevaluate the negative customer response
(c) hand over the project to another designer
(d) create a website incorporating your ideas

10. The National Union of Laborers (NUL) is an organization committed to improving the working conditions of America's employees. We are America's largest trade union, representing over half a million members across the country. The NUL champions the cause of employees in diverse industries, such as education, health care, airlines, and social services. We also strive to protect rights, negotiate better salaries, and gain better working conditions for our members. Staff at our 65 offices across the country ____ so you do not have to.

(a) have created a sophisticated workforce
(b) are now arguing the case internationally
(c) continue to fight for these essential rights
(d) negotiate with NUL officials for better pay

11. Efforts in the UK to become more environmentally friendly are ___________________.
According to statistics, people have become greener, and indeed recycling has increased
from 7% to 31% over the past 10 years. But a steady rise in total domestic energy
consumption has thwarted gains from a greener lifestyle. Analysts suggest that changing
family structures is a contributing factor, especially an increase in the number of people
living alone, as this results in more energy use.

(a) being closely tracked by government agencies
(b) causing significant reductions in energy use
(c) getting more families involved in recycling
(d) being undermined by other social changes

12. With the release on Wednesday of the English translation of *The Kind Soldier,* publishers
___________________. The 846-page novel by Jonathan Pallet is a
fictional memoir of a Nazi officer who is as brutal as he is remorseless. The novel
attracted controversy when first published in France in 2006, with one critic comparing
it to Tolstoy's *War and Peace* while another insisting that it was "absolutely disgusting."
One early review of the English version derides its "cheap sensationalism" and calls it
"willfully repellent," yet another in a different publication hails it as a masterpiece.

(a) defied critics who had protested its publication
(b) expected sales to be well above those in France
(c) had anticipated a polarized critical response
(d) were elated with reviews of the novel

13. It has recently come to light that ___________________. This revelation
is thanks to a spate of popular toy recalls drawing attention to the Consumer Product
Safety Commission and its failings. The Commission is responsible for 15,000 different
products and yet it only has one toy tester. The tester is unable to test all products, which
is why import companies are now solely responsible for product safety, the results of
which have been clearly demonstrated.

(a) imported toys are outselling local toy products
(b) customs authorities are still letting contraband through
(c) manufacturers are prioritizing profits over the safety of workers
(d) government agencies have not been properly testing imported toys

14. In the mid-1950s, a visual art movement known as Pop Art emerged in the UK and US. It challenged the fine arts establishment by representing the products of mass production and popular culture as if they were worthy subjects for art. The subjects of pop art frequently came from mainstream sources such as cinema, advertising, and comic strips. Pop artists depicted well-known people, images, and icons as artistic objects in a medium radically different from their original context, often with humorous or ironic intent. Thus, in effect, the movement ____.

(a) added a seriousness to the 1950s art world that was lacking
(b) reinforced popular culture's inferiority to fine art works
(c) eroded the gulf between so-called high and low art
(d) criticized the highbrow perspectives of Pop artists

15. Early Christian thinkers opposed astrology because it undermined the idea of free will and was linked to fortune-telling. The theologian St. Augustine (354–430) even declared that astrology was the devil's work. Despite such objections, astrology was practiced throughout the Middle Ages. Its popularity even increased during the Renaissance, in part due to rekindled interest in science. ________________________________, many of that era's great scientists practiced astrology as a way of earning money.

(a) In fact
(b) Even so
(c) Meanwhile
(d) Nevertheless

16. Are you an online seller who wants to increase revenue and spend less time on tasks? Then Market Pro's complete listing, pricing and order management system is for you. It will save you days in listing and pricing tasks, allowing you to focus on your business and not your process. ________________________________, Market Pro's auto-repricing is giving Charles Inman of BestAuctions.com a 30–40% boost in daily orders. It easily handles Charles' 10,000-plus book inventory and helps to quickly and conveniently fill orders with its postage printing program. Market Pro is definitely the way to go to keep your business running smoothly.

(a) What's more
(b) In consequence
(c) On the contrary
(d) As an illustration

Read the passage and the question. Then choose the option that best answers the question.

17. No parent would let a six-year-old wander into a big city alone. Parents know the dangers of the world, and it is their responsibility to teach children how to avoid them. Rules are set and enforced. Protecting children in cyberspace isn't any different. The only problem is that it may be more difficult for parents to know exactly what the dangers are. Our advice? Take the time to figure them out. Then make a point of setting rules and enforcing them, just like in the real world. It's really that simple.

Q: What is the main idea of the passage?
(a) Kids should be protected in cyberspace as in the real world.
(b) Cyberspace has clear-cut dangers in need of addressing.
(c) Kids' computer education should be closely supervised.
(d) Cyberspace has its own enforced rules and regulations.

18. Introducing Bartko's Carbot, the car you can assemble yourself and easily program for remote control or robotic action! After assembling your Carbot, control it remotely or download robotic missions via the Bartko's Carbot website and upload them into your Carbot's onboard computer. Your Carbot is now ready for either remote or automatic "robot" mode. You can download various missions, such as those for navigating obstacle courses or fighting with other Carbots. Get your very own Carbot today!

Q: What is the advertisement mainly about?
(a) A new toy car that is controlled verbally
(b) A new toy car with a variety of features
(c) A newly released robotic program
(d) A website-controlled new robot

19. Samuel Richardson's novel *Pamela*—written in the form of a series of letters—was published in 1740. It tells the story of a young female servant who, while struggling to protect her virtue against a lascivious master, records her experiences in a series of letters. Richardson's readers enjoyed the letter format for the sense of immediacy it created and because it allowed for intimate insights into Pamela's mind and character.

Q: What is the passage mainly about?
(a) Richardson's *Pamela* and its format
(b) The habits of the 18th century readers
(c) The surprising success of Richardson's *Pamela*
(d) Richardson's literary fame in the 18th century

20.

Dear Mr. Brann,

This letter is in regard to our recent telephone conversation about Grayson, Inc.'s credit and banking requirements. As you know, we are a growing business with increasing capital requirements. We have enclosed for your information our recent financial statements along with our business plan and budget for the forthcoming fiscal year. Based upon our forecasts, we anticipate requiring $750,000 in credit. Please provide us with a financing proposal which you believe would satisfy our requirements. We look forward to your response.

Sincerely,
Candice Trent

Q: What is the letter mainly about?
(a) The state of a company's credit history
(b) Mr. Brann's economic speculations for next year
(c) Mr. Brann's strict credit application requirements
(d) A request for a proposal on obtaining a line of credit

21. Manto Tshabalala-Msimang's removal as Health Minister of South Africa in 2008 brought relief and joy to AIDS treatment campaigners. For years campaigners had fought against Tshabalala-Msimang for spreading confusion about AIDS and promoting nutritional supplements instead of conventional medicine for HIV. They maintain that tens of thousands of South Africans lost their lives because of what they see as her ridiculous policies on HIV/AIDS.

Q: What is the news report mainly about?
(a) HIV/AIDS treatment campaigners' promotion of alternative medicine
(b) Criticism of Tshabalala-Msimang's policies regarding HIV/AIDS
(c) HIV/AIDS treatment campaigners' disease prevention tactics
(d) Tshabalala-Msimang's cutting-edge approach to HIV/AIDS

22. The proliferation of drug-resistant strains of potentially deadly bacteria such as E. coli is a serious medical problem. Antibiotic-resistant bacteria were first identified in the 1940s, but the consequences were not appreciated at that time. Today, excessive use of antibiotics, compounded by the paucity of new agents, has meant the problem of antibiotic resistance is fast escalating into a global health emergency. There is a consensus that overuse of these drugs in human beings has contributed to the increasing rates of resistance; and the use of antibiotics in animal food has also recently come under scrutiny.

Q: What is the main idea of the passage?
(a) Deadly E. coli has developed a resistance to new antibiotics.
(b) Misuse of antibiotics is creating a crisis of bacterial resistance.
(c) Both humans and animals are susceptible to resistant bacteria.
(d) New antibiotic-resistant strains of bacteria have been discovered.

23. The movement of a flock of Dunlin birds is a marvel of coordinated precision flying. With no apparent leader, they take off in large numbers, turning in the air as a flock and then landing with such expert coordination that collisions are extremely rare. The secret to their skill is that all birds watch the birds around them and duplicate their actions. They also watch for the mass movement of birds farther away in the flock and follow what they do. This is how a maneuver spreads through a whole flock in a smooth wave in a fraction of a second.

Q: Which of the following is correct about Dunlin birds according to the passage?
(a) They follow a leader when flying.
(b) They tend not to fly in great numbers.
(c) They signal their movements with sound.
(d) They mimic the actions of their fellow birds.

24. I am a 30-year-old American seeking Korean friends for international exchange and friendship. I live in Los Angeles and travel to Korea quite often. I can help you with your English if you show me around Seoul and help me with my very limited Korean while I am there. I like travel, red wine, Korean food, movies, exercising and reading. I will be in Korea on business for most of August and again next year. E-mail me at john_duck@ babal.com and let's meet up!

Q: Which of the following is correct according to the advertisement?
(a) The writer lives in Korea.
(b) The writer speaks little Korean.
(c) The writer is going to Korea on vacation.
(d) The writer will be in Korea during November.

25. The Errol Public School Parent-Teacher Association (PTA), in collaboration with other public school PTAs, has officially begun its campaign to convince the mayor to enforce more stringent safety regulations on school buses. In particular, it is calling for all buses to have 24-inch seat backs, 4 inches higher than the current regulation. It also recommends 3-point safety belts on smaller buses, since they are more prone to rolling over than larger buses.

Q: Which of the following is correct according to the passage?
(a) The Errol School PTA is campaigning alone.
(b) The mayor is enforcing stricter school bus safety.
(c) The proposed seats would be 24-inches higher than now.
(d) The 3-point safety belts were requested for smaller buses.

26. Benjamin Franklin, a legendary figure in American history, was a multi-talented man. Besides being one of the signatories of the Declaration of Independence, he founded the first fire insurance company in America, published an influential and popular magazine called *Poor Richard's Almanac*, and was sent to Paris as America's first ambassador to France. Franklin invented many useful items, including the lightning rod and bifocal glasses. He also coined some famous sayings, such as "Early to bed and early to rise makes a man healthy, wealthy, and wise."

Q: Which of the following is correct about Benjamin Franklin according to the passage?
(a) He was considered talented in one main area.
(b) He drafted the Declaration of Independence.
(c) He was a former US ambassador to France.
(d) He popularized sayings of famous people.

27. Whether or not Tiger Woods is the best golfer ever is open to debate. However, one thing is for sure: his impact on the sport has been considerable. He rejuvenated the game in the US so that it was no longer seen as a game for rich, out-of-shape men with too much time on their hands. The hugely popular Mr. Woods—the only man to have held four major championships simultaneously—extended golf's appeal beyond the affluent. Now people from all walks of life are taking it up.

Q: Which of the following is correct about Tiger Woods according to the passage?
(a) Everyone agrees Woods is the best golfer in history.
(b) Woods' impact on golf in America has been minor.
(c) Golf's appeal has broadened because of Woods.
(d) Woods mainly inspires poor kids to play golf.

28. John Fitzgerald, a retired professor of political science from Aspen University, is 80 years old. He is slightly hunched, and his voice is somewhat hoarse. Yet listening to him deliver the annual History Society lecture on Monday, I found myself hoping that he would return to speak every year. Fitzgerald manages to be both bold and modest at the same time—dazzling us with daring speculations, while apologizing for speaking longer than the hour allotted for his presentation.

Q: Which of the following is correct about John Fitzgerald according to the passage?
(a) He retired from his post as a history professor.
(b) He delivered a lecture to the Science Society.
(c) He made speculations in the lecture he gave.
(d) He finished his lecture earlier than expected.

29. It is often not acknowledged, but every one of America's early 13 colonies partook in the slave trade. However, slavery was not the same in all of them. Colonies had differing percentages of slaves. Few African slaves lived in the northern colonies, while 90 percent of all slaves lived in the southern colonies. Conditions for slaves differed as well. Generally, as the numbers of slaves were fewer in the North than in the South, the physical demands and punishments for disobedience were less severe. Conditions were much worse for slaves in the South.

Q: Which of the following is correct according to the passage?
(a) Some colonies in early America did not have slaves.
(b) American colonies had different slave populations.
(c) Slave conditions were similar in all the colonies.
(d) Southern colonies treated slaves more gently.

30. In 2001, America was shocked to discover that envelopes containing deadly anthrax powder had been sent to East Coast newsrooms and congressional offices in Washington, DC. Over several months, five people died from different mailings. The FBI initially thought the attacks were the work of foreign bioterrorists, but later the agency's focus turned to scientists at home. Seven years later, the FBI finally identified microbiologist Dr. Bruce Ivins as the man responsible for sending the anthrax. However, Ivins committed suicide before he could be charged.

Q: Which of the following is correct according to the article?
(a) Dr. Bruce Ivins committed one anthrax attack in total.
(b) Five people died after receiving anthrax in the mail.
(c) Foreign bioterrorists launched the anthrax attacks.
(d) Investigators finally charged the anthrax culprit.

31.

> Dear Thomas,
>
> I regret to inform you that your temporary employment at Addison Systems will be terminated at the end of next month. It was the decision of our managerial downsizing committee to remove all temporary positions. Rest assured that this decision does not reflect the company's attitude toward your performance over the past 18 months. Rather it is, regrettably, a result of the economic downturn in the fiber optics industry over the past year. A letter from the Human Resources Department with information on severance arrangements will follow in due course. Please do not hesitate to contact me should you require a recommendation letter.
>
> Sincerely,
> Fred Shandling
> Unit Manager

Q: Which of the following is correct according to the letter?
(a) A decision on Thomas's employment will be made next month.
(b) A managerial committee has decided to hire more employees.
(c) Thomas's termination is unrelated to the quality of his work.
(d) A downturn has affected the industry for 18 months.

32. Anthropological research suggests that prehistoric warfare between tribes was bound by ritual and limited in intensity. First, special battle sites or arenas were chosen as the venue for resolving the dispute. Before the actual battle began, each side would typically put on a display of martial prowess for intimidation purposes. Then the two hostile parties would battle it out in a series of one-on-one engagements using weapons such as stone axes, knives, and flint-tipped spears and arrows. Deaths, however, were few, as the point of the battle was to solve a problem, not kill.

Q: Which of the following is correct according to the passage?
(a) Prehistoric battles were fought collectively between groups.
(b) Warfare in prehistoric times was typically ritualized.
(c) Ancient warriors fought with their bare hands.
(d) Prehistoric warfare resulted in many deaths.

33. Want to get your product well-known fast? MTV can advertise your product 24 hours a day, seven days a week, 365 days a year. We call it our 360-degree coverage campaign. This full-circle approach to brand promotion means you are part of an integrated multi-media strategy that exposes your product to the 15 to 34-year-old age group at every angle: on-air, online, on-ground, and through MTV's many other merchandising opportunities. And let's face it. If your product is on MTV, it's going to look pretty cool.

Q: What can be inferred from the advertisement?
(a) MTV is increasing its advertising budget.
(b) MTV does not do business with people over 40.
(c) Advertising with MTV could result in big sales.
(d) Advertising with MTV will be fairly inexpensive.

34. Writer Vladimir Nabokov left behind an unpublished manuscript at the time of his death, as well as a will explicitly requesting that the manuscript, known as *The Original of Laura*, be destroyed. However, it was not destroyed but was put into the vault of a Swiss bank. Nabokov's son Dmitri, now 73, has been urged to release it by Nabokov's admirers, but he has tarried because of his father's request. His dilemma has highlighted the question of who "owns" a work of art, especially when its creator is deceased.

Q: What can be inferred from the passage?
(a) The manuscript will eventually be destroyed.
(b) Nabokov's will does not mention the manuscript.
(c) The authorship of the manuscript was once in doubt.
(d) Nabokov's fans hope the manuscript will be published.

35. Global Golf Learning is a world-renowned Internet-based seller of quality golf instructional aids. Our website is full of learning tools containing the distilled wisdom of dozens of retired professional golfers. What's great is that becoming a member of our site not only allows you to purchase these tools, but also to communicate via email with the professionals themselves. Want to improve your golf game? Join now and in no time you will be playing like a pro!

Q: What can be inferred about Global Golf Learning from the advertisement?
(a) Its membership fees depend on skill level.
(b) It has just started selling golf training aids.
(c) It is a website primarily for experienced golfers.
(d) It works closely with retired professional golfers.

36. Business managers in the US are increasingly recognizing that shorter work hours give employees an incentive to be more productive. This attitude shift over the last decade is based on evidence of productivity improvements resulting from reduced workweeks. One example is Metro Plastics Technology in Indiana. After switching to 30 hours' work for 40 hours' pay in July, 2008, the company saw product returns drop by 72 percent— an indication of quality improvements. Moreover, costs were reduced and workers became more efficient, energetic and enthusiastic.

Q: What can be inferred from the passage?
(a) Increased leisure time can increase employee motivation.
(b) Worthy business improvements initially incur extra costs.
(c) Metro Plastics Technology is reconsidering its change in working hours.
(d) Many workers are willing to accept pay cuts in return for shorter hours.

37. Since its publication in 1651, Thomas Hobbes' *Leviathan* has intrigued readers with its political philosophy. While its ultimate conclusion that an absolute sovereign best guarantees justice and order may not be attractive to modern readers, Hobbes' reasoning on morals and politics throughout the book does compel readers to question their widely shared assumptions about freedom and the scope of political authority. What Hobbes proposed was a distinctive and powerful basis for a political order that conforms to reason and secures the conditions under which human beings can pursue happiness.

Q: What can be inferred about Hobbes' *Leviathan*?
(a) It rejects the idea of placing political authority in the hands of the wealthy.
(b) It implies that political principles cannot be rationally deduced.
(c) It entirely divorces political philosophy from morality.
(d) It does not advocate a system of democracy.

Part III **Questions 38—40**

Read the passage. Then identify the option that does NOT belong.

38. Water is essential for human health. (a) Water helps with the balance of fluids necessary for optimum cell and organ functioning. (b) The percentage of a person's body that consists of water varies with weight and build. (c) It is essential in the transportation of nutrients, as well as in the elimination of body wastes. (d) Water works to lubricate joints and organs, maintain blood volume, and regulate body temperature.

39. During the Tang Dynasty (618-907), China was the wealthiest and most populous empire in the world. (a) Trade thrived via the Silk Road on land and by sea with India, Japan and Korea. (b) The country's overall population tripled between 630 and 755, and its capital, Changan, became a renowned metropolis. (c) Tea drinking culture in China did much to promote tea drinking and its medicinal properties elsewhere. (d) And the city was a cultural magnet at a time when China was particularly open to outside influences.

40. Elizabeth, New Jersey, is the last place you'd expect to find a collection of antique cars. (a) Nevertheless, my father founded a vintage car museum in the city, appropriately named the Davis Collection. (b) At the museum's opening, 200 friends, colleagues, auto mechanics and family members gathered to marvel at what my father had done. (c) While my father adores driving anything made before 1960, his current vehicle of choice is a 1955 Hagerman Jaguar, a lightweight racing car. (d) It's basically one luxurious, polished parking lot for 43 cars that includes an extremely rare 1938 Talbot-Lago that he calls a rolling sculpture.

This is the end of the Reading Comprehension section. Please remain seated until the proctor has instructed otherwise. You are NOT allowed to turn to any other section of the test.

: 서울대 최신기출 2

Listening Comprehension

Grammar

Vocabulary

Reading Comprehension

LISTENING COMPREHENSION

DIRECTIONS

1. In the Listening Comprehension section, all content will be presented orally rather than in written form.

2. This section contains 4 parts. In parts I and II, each passage will be read only once. In parts III and IV, each passage and its corresponding question will be read twice. But in all sections, the options will be read only once. After listening to the passage and question, listen to the options and choose the best answer.

Part I **Questions 1—15**

You will now hear fifteen conversation fragments, each made up of a single spoken statement followed by four spoken responses. Choose the most appropriate response to the statement.

Part II **Questions 16—30**

You will now hear fifteen conversation fragments, each made up of three spoken statements followed by four spoken responses. Choose the most appropriate response to complete the conversation.

Part III **Questions 31—45**

You will now hear fifteen complete conversations. For each item, you will hear a conversation and its corresponding question, both of which will be read twice. Then you will hear four options which will be read only once. Choose the option that best answers the question.

Part IV **Questions 46—60**

You will now hear fifteen spoken monologues. For each item, you will hear a monologue and its corresponding question, both of which will be read twice. Then you will hear four options which will be read only once. Choose the option that best answers the question.

GRAMMAR

Part I Questions 1—20

Choose the best answer for the blank.

1. A: Have you seen my keys?

B: Yes. I saw ___________ on the table.

(a) one
(b) that
(c) each
(d) them

2. A: Let me introduce myself. My name is Bronwyn.

B: ___________ to meet you.

(a) I delight
(b) I'm delighted
(c) I'm delighting
(d) I was being delighted

3. A: I don't like winter at all.

B: Yeah, ___________.

(a) so do I
(b) so I do
(c) neither I do
(d) neither do I

4. A: I think Marie and Stephen ___________ each other perfectly.

B: Yeah, they really are a nice couple.

(a) suit
(b) suits
(c) is suiting
(d) are suiting

5. A: Were there ___________ messages while I was away?

B: Yes, there were a few. Here, I wrote them down.

(a) any
(b) those
(c) much
(d) whatever

6. A: Is it too late to go to Susan's party?

B: Yes, everybody ___________ home by the time we arrive.

(a) went
(b) will go
(c) has gone
(d) will have gone

7. A: Well, it's getting late. I'd better go.

B: OK, ___________ to you.

(a) nice it's been to talk
(b) talking it's been nice
(c) it's been nice talking
(d) to talk has been nice for me

8. A: How did you scratch your knee?

B: ___________ to catch the bus, I fell and hurt myself.

(a) Ran
(b) Running
(c) Had run
(d) To have run

9. A: Have you finished your homework
    yet?

    B: No, I ___________.

    (a) just finishing that up
    (b) have finished it with
    (c) have it finished with
    (d) am just finishing up

10. A: Are you going to the high school
    reunion?

    B: If I ___________ find a babysitter for
    my daughter, I will.

    (a) can
    (b) may
    (c) shall
    (d) might

11. A: Did you really quit your job because
    you didn't have much to do?

    B: That's right. I ___________, so I quit.

    (a) bored
    (b) am boring
    (c) was bored
    (d) am being bored

12. A: Is Hannah still at work?

    B: No, she ___________ for home
    already.

    (a) left
    (b) leaves
    (c) will leave
    (d) was leaving

13. A: Can I speak to Jenny, please?

    B: I'm sorry, but she's ___________.

    (a) at the unavailable moment
    (b) the unavailable at moment
    (c) available not at the moment
    (d) not available at the moment

14. A: You seem to know a lot of French
    vocabulary.

    B: Thanks, but I still have ___________
    with grammar.

    (a) trouble
    (b) a trouble
    (c) the trouble
    (d) every trouble

15. A: Is it true Jake finally asked Wendy to
    marry him?

    B: Yes, but ___________ after she
    threatened to leave him.

    (a) proposed only to her
    (b) only to her proposed
    (c) he only proposed to her
    (d) to her he only proposed

16. A: I was surprised to hear you went to a
    night club after your work dinner.

    B: I wasn't ___________, but my
    co-workers insisted.

    (a) going to do
    (b) going to it
    (c) going so
    (d) going to

17. A: ___________ you smell something
    burning?

    B: Oh no! I forgot to turn off the oven!

    (a) Do
    (b) Will
    (c) Shall
    (d) Must

18. A: I'm really worried about the test.

B: But it's just a small test. It's not __________ big deal.

(a) a
(b) so
(c) many
(d) either

19. A: How did you like my speech?

B: It was __________ the best you've given.

(a) such
(b) very
(c) by far
(d) as ever

20. A: We need to hire another secretary.

B: No, in my opinion, __________.

(a) there need to be one only
(b) only one there need to be
(c) there need be only one
(d) one only need there be

Part II **Questions 21–40**

Choose the best answer for the blank.

---

21. Students were asked if they wanted __________ at school after class hours.

(a) study
(b) studied
(c) to study
(d) studying

22. To attract talented students, many state universities __________.

(a) to them merit aid offer
(b) offer to them merit aid
(c) offer merit aid them
(d) offer them merit aid

23. The ideal time to make a big investment is __________ likely to be at the beginning of the next quarter rather than now.

(a) ever
(b) more
(c) much
(d) farther

24. Many artifacts __________ back to ancient Egypt can be found in Greek sites.

(a) dating
(b) to date
(c) being dated
(d) having dated

25. Fifty-eight percent of people __________ think that only the rich will benefit from the proposed tax cuts.

(a) survey
(b) surveys
(c) surveyed
(d) surveying

26. __________ plants need lots of water and sunlight to grow.

(a) Most
(b) A most
(c) Most of
(d) The most

27. As the 19th century __________, so did methods for reproducing images using various photographic techniques.

(a) progresses
(b) progressed
(c) has progressed
(d) will have progressed

28. Taxes on cigarettes should be kept high __________ people who want to quit smoking will be more motivated to do so.

(a) after
(b) unless
(c) even if
(d) so that

29. During the 1950s, the US economy __________ in a sustained and substantial fashion.

(a) grew
(b) has grown
(c) will be growing
(d) will have grown

30. __________ by the paramedics.

(a) The patient was taken well care of
(b) Care was well taken of the patient
(c) The patient was well taken care of
(d) Of care well was the patient taken

31. The teacher recommended the textbook __________ he himself had found helpful.

(a) what
(b) which
(c) whatever
(d) whichever

32. The flu virus is spread in tiny drops of moisture that we __________ into the air when we cough or sneeze.

(a) spray
(b) sprayed
(c) are sprayed
(d) were sprayed

33. Some people mistakenly think __________ adventurers, like Hollywood's Indiana Jones.

(a) archaeologists as romantic
(b) of archaeologists as romantic
(c) of archaeologists romantic as
(d) romantic archaeologists that are

34. The Food and Drug Administration requires that the use of tartrazine, an artificial coloring, __________ on food packaging.

(a) identify
(b) identified
(c) is identified
(d) be identified

35. Ancient Greek texts were the fountains __________ Western philosophy arose.

(a) that
(b) which
(c) in what
(d) from which

36. When __________ dental products, look for an official Seal of Acceptance.

(a) choose
(b) chosen
(c) choosing
(d) to choose

37. What __________ is that Rome was never a democracy as we understand it today.

(a) in mind needs to keep
(b) needs to be kept in mind
(c) is needed to keep in mind
(d) to be kept in mind is needed

38. Amazingly agile __________ their size, hippos are good climbers and are able to scale steep river banks.

(a) of
(b) by
(c) for
(d) over

39. __________ consume over half of their daily calories at night.

(a) Percentage large of obese people
(b) Of obese people large percentage
(c) Obese people of a large percentage
(d) A large percentage of obese people

40. __________ panda cubs only weigh about 170 grams at birth, they grow quickly and can weigh up to 20 times more than that in just eight weeks.

(a) Also
(b) Since
(c) While
(d) Before

Part III   Questions 41—45

Identify the option that contains an awkward expression or an error in grammar.

41. (a) A: Has the suspect finally confessed to commit the robbery?

(b) B: No. He keeps denying it.

(c) A: Well, I don't believe him. What do you think?

(d) B: I think he's definitely the one who stole all that money.

42. (a) A: This is one of the best seafood restaurants in town.

(b) B: Is there anything in particular you suggest that I am ordering?

(c) A: That depends on what you feel like eating. How about chili shrimp?

(d) B: Sounds good to me. I'll get that with some rice on the side.

43. (a) A: We can't cook eggs for dinner. We've run out.

(b) B: Can you go buy some at the grocery store?

(c) A: OK. Do you need anything else while I'm there?

(d) B: Yes, get a can of tunas and some mushrooms.

44. (a) A: I ordered a new DVD online, but it was damaged when it arrived!

(b) B: You should call customer service and ask for a refund.

(c) A: Complaining about faulty goods or bad service are never easy for me.

(d) B: But you have to get your money's worth. I'd call them right away.

45. (a) A: Mr. Chairman, no one has any more questions for today.

(b) B: Very well. Have all topics for today's meeting been covered?

(c) A: Yes, I think we've satisfactorily dealt with all the tabled issues.

(d) B: In that case, I'd like to move that this meeting is adjourned.

Part IV Questions 46—50

Identify the option that contains an awkward expression or an error in grammar.

46. (a) Ireland's economy is growing faster than expected, according to official data. (b) Its gross domestic product grew by 5.7% this year. (c) And in terms of gross national product, the economy grew by 6.5%. (d) This growth is expected to continue, and the central bank is expecting growth of 8.5% at next year.

47. (a) The Herricks school district has seen a huge increase in Asian enrollment over the past five years. (b) Nowhere this increase is more evident than at Stamford High School. (c) Last year the district reported an enrollment that was 45% Asian. (d) As schools such as Stamford have gained good reputations, more Asian students are entering them.

48. (a) Many mammals are able to deter attackers of their own species without causing bodily harm to them or to themselves. (b) They use techniques such as displays of physical strength and superiority to persuade others not to seek confrontation. (c) This form of non-violent conflict resolution in part evolve to assist in the long term survival of mammal species. (d) It makes mammals less likely to wound or kill others of their species, so they are less likely to suffer a decrease in numbers.

49. (a) One of the myths about the origin of tea tells how the Chinese Emperor Shen Nong discovered it while in his garden. (b) Preparing to drink a cup of hot water, a leaf broke free from a nearby plant and fell into the Emperor's cup. (c) The water turned brownish, but the Emperor decided to taste it and found it to his liking. (d) He then began searching for different varieties of leaves to try in hot water, and that is how tea was invented.

50. (a) Harold Pinter is an English playwright whose plays are noted for their use of silence to increase tension and add meaning. (b) Equally characteristic are Pinter's themes of nameless menace, memory, territorial control, violence, communication breakdown, and alienation. (c) Many of his major plays are set in a single room that occupants are threatened by forces or people with unclear intentions. (d) Pinter refuses to provide rational justifications for the action in his work, and instead focuses on existential issues in human interactions.

This is the end of the Grammar section. Do NOT move on to the next section until instructed to do so. You are NOT allowed to turn to any other section of the test.

VOCABULARY

Part I Questions 1—25

Choose the best answer for the blank.

1. A: Mark, this is my friend Peter.

B: Hi Peter. It's a ___________ to meet you.

(a) wonder
(b) comfort
(c) pleasure
(d) happiness

2. A: I've been studying for hours. I'm so tired.

B: You should take a ___________ .

(a) gap
(b) time
(c) leave
(d) break

3. A: Can Judy and I go in your car?

B: Sure, I can ___________ you.

(a) lift
(b) drive
(c) speed
(d) wheel

4. A: I can't thread this needle.

B: The ___________ is too small for that thread.

(a) eye
(b) line
(c) horn
(d) mouth

5. A: OK, Jonathan. You'll be playing on the team this week.

B: Thanks for giving me a(n) ___________ to play, coach.

(a) luck
(b) deal
(c) entry
(d) chance

6. A: Can you hear me OK? I'm calling from the subway.

B: Sorry, I can't hear you ___________ .

(a) clearly
(b) closely
(c) soundly
(d) strongly

7. A: I was upset by how rude the boss was.

B: Don't mind him. He ___________ everyone like that.

(a) takes
(b) treats
(c) mixes
(d) soothes

8. A: I think I can win this chess game.

B: Don't get your ___________ up too high.

(a) goals
(b) plans
(c) hopes
(d) results

9. A: I'm tall enough to touch the ceiling.

    B: Wow, I can only do that if I
       ___________.

    (a) jump
    (b) hurdle
    (c) spread
    (d) prolong

10. A: Shall I book you into the Meridian
       for the Tokyo conference?

    B: OK, as long as it doesn't
       ___________ the travel budget.

    (a) limit
    (b) exceed
    (c) restrict
    (d) succeed

11. A: Would you like some more cake?

    B: Yes, please. I'd love another
       ___________.

    (a) cut
    (b) pick
    (c) dish
    (d) slice

12. A: How come you ran out of time in the
       exam?

    B: I didn't ___________ it was only one
       hour long!

    (a) insure
    (b) realize
    (c) ponder
    (d) finalize

13. A: Should I make a left turn here?

    B: Yes, it's our best ___________.

    (a) option
    (b) version
    (c) division
    (d) reaction

14. A: Joan is thinking of dropping out of
       university.

    B: It'll be a ___________ if she does.

    (a) guilt
    (b) shame
    (c) neglect
    (d) mischief

15. A: You must be glad your exams are
       over.

    B: Yes, I'm so ___________ that they're
       finished.

    (a) concerned
    (b) fascinated
    (c) relieved
    (d) alerted

16. A: Can I have a chat with you later?

    B: Sure, just ___________ my office
       after lunch.

    (a) step on
    (b) drop off
    (c) come by
    (d) stand up

17. A: What's the biggest cause of air
       pollution in this city?

    B: Automobile ___________ are the
       main cause.

    (a) releases
    (b) issuances
    (c) emissions
    (d) dismissals

18. A: Can you come to my party, Jesse?

B: It ___________ on what day you have it.

(a) varies
(b) focuses
(c) matters
(d) depends

19. A: I'm busy, but I still want to join a club.

B: Don't ___________ more than you can manage.

(a) do over
(b) rack up
(c) take on
(d) work up

20. A: Do you think there's such a thing as the Loch Ness monster?

B: No, I don't believe it ___________.

(a) lives
(b) exists
(c) occurs
(d) survives

21. A: Why can't I take fresh fruit through customs?

B: Contaminated fruit can lead to a(n) ___________ of disease.

(a) gust
(b) misuse
(c) outbreak
(d) explosion

22. A: Did you hear about the latest political scandal?

B: Yes, and I think those involved should be ___________.

(a) delegated
(b) culminated
(c) diminished
(d) reprimanded

23. A: What made dad so angry at Anne?

B: He ___________ sneaking out on a weeknight.

(a) caught her red-handed
(b) breathed down her neck
(c) followed in her footsteps
(d) gave her the cold shoulder

24. A: Has Mary heard back from the universities she applied to?

B: No, she's waiting with ___________ anxiety.

(a) rooting
(b) heaping
(c) stacking
(d) mounting

25. A: I don't understand a word of this new contract. Do you?

B: No, it's completely ___________ to me, too.

(a) effusive
(b) prodigal
(c) inclement
(d) inscrutable

Part II   **Questions 26—50**

Choose the best answer for the blank.

26. The crocodile uses strong jaws and teeth to ___________ prey and drag it under water.

  (a) clap
  (b) hold
  (c) stick
  (d) bend

27. Customers with items that ___________ our returns guidelines will receive a full refund.

  (a) make
  (b) catch
  (c) fetch
  (d) meet

28. A flood occurs when a river rises so much that it cannot be ___________ within its normal channel.

  (a) restored
  (b) produced
  (c) contained
  (d) conformed

29. Coleman's Foundation for the Disabled is a charity that is ___________ to helping people with physical disabilities.

  (a) referred
  (b) matched
  (c) addressed
  (d) committed

30. Significant advances have been made in finding ___________ for malaria in recent years.

  (a) contact
  (b) solution
  (c) assisting
  (d) treatment

31. This frying pan that ___________ for $20 everywhere else will cost you only $15 at Brannan's.

  (a) sells
  (b) pays
  (c) buys
  (d) prices

32. Societies have both formal and informal rules that ___________ how people should behave.

  (a) generate
  (b) indulge
  (c) cherish
  (d) specify

33. The question of inflation is not on the ___________ for today's conference, but nevertheless it should be discussed.

  (a) agenda
  (b) preface
  (c) formula
  (d) collusion

34. Adrian was ___________ by the fan mail he received after his new movie became popular.

(a) flattered
(b) enhanced
(c) harnessed
(d) backhanded

35. Writing good fiction is an art that many aspire to but few ___________.

(a) partake
(b) achieve
(c) originate
(d) contemplate

36. Michelle sometimes goes to department stores just to ___________ the latest fashions.

(a) browse
(b) obscure
(c) spectate
(d) acquaint

37. Despite progress in ___________ stricter laws against it, corruption still persists among politicians.

(a) identifying
(b) eliminating
(c) establishing
(d) understanding

38. These two parties have failed to ___________ an agreement and cannot even decide when to meet again.

(a) reach
(b) usher
(c) access
(d) harbor

39. Just as doctors encourage an annual medical exam, your business should ___________ a checkup each year.

(a) handle
(b) sustain
(c) undergo
(d) medicate

40. Despite the novel's focus on political intrigue and corruption, it is very original and never ___________ into cliché.

(a) lapses
(b) trumps
(c) derides
(d) jumbles

41. Childless couples are targeted by online marketers since they often have more ___________ income than others.

(a) affable
(b) laudable
(c) disposable
(d) vulnerable

42. The potato, ___________ to South America, became a staple in Europe soon after its introduction there in 1700.

(a) innate
(b) inborn
(c) intrinsic
(d) indigenous

43. Alta-Travel urges all customers to obtain traveler's insurance to cover any ___________ that might occur.

(a) liabilities
(b) feasibilities
(c) criminalities
(d) responsibilities

44. Our staff is dedicated to __________
each customer staying at our resort an
incredible summer of fun.

(a) catering
(b) ensuring
(c) gratifying
(d) organizing

45. The education authority is implementing
programs to __________ the number of
students quitting high school.

(a) adorn
(b) edify
(c) perk
(d) curb

46. Cheap electricity has attracted lucrative
industries to Utah, generating a lot of
__________ for the state.

(a) retinue
(b) revenue
(c) frugality
(d) providence

47. The abandoned house was __________
after failing a city safety inspection.

(a) warranted
(b) vindicated
(c) discharged
(d) condemned

48. Jill's __________ character is
refreshing in contrast to the cynical
customers she serves at the downtown
bar.

(a) subdued
(b) exuberant
(c) incredulous
(d) excruciating

49. In 1933, the US government sought
to raise crop prices by paying farmers
a __________ to compensate for
voluntary cutbacks in production.

(a) subsidy
(b) malpractice
(c) discrepancy
(d) commiseration

50. The government's changes have
intensified rather than __________
public concern about the efficacy of
public schooling.

(a) allured
(b) alleged
(c) allayed
(d) allotted

This is the end of the Vocabulary section. Do NOT move on to the Reading Comprehension section until instructed to do so. You are NOT allowed to turn to any other section of the test.

READING COMPREHENSION

Part I   Questions 1—16

Read the passage. Then choose the option that best completes the passage.

1. With globalization, the world is entering an era of multicultural exchange like never before. This is having the effect of expanding and broadening the cultural experience people have and in turn diversifying their sense of identity. For example, a young British man may see Japanese animation, Indian food, American jazz and Italian language as major parts of his life and identity. He is less likely to consider his identity as traditionally British. In other words, people the world over are _______________________.

   (a) seeing the loss of cultural traditions
   (b) now far more internationally minded
   (c) happy to do business on a global scale
   (d) confused about their citizenship status

2. Massachusetts Bay transportation authorities have released details today of an incident in which a 34-year-old man was accidentally strangled when the hood of his sweatshirt became entangled in an escalator. The incident, which occurred two weeks ago at Porter Square subway station, was not made public until investigators had found the cause. Authorities say that no other people were involved and that the man had been drinking. The case is now closed since it was confirmed that _______________________.

   (a) subway staff were at fault
   (b) the killer has been arrested
   (c) the man had committed suicide
   (d) alcohol was to blame for the accident

3. To prepare a fish for frying, first scale or skin it. Then, run your knife along the median bone to cut off the flesh on each side of the fish. This will give you two fillets. Next, heat a frying pan, add olive oil, and rub the fillets with salt before dropping them into the pan. Fry them until golden brown, which takes around 3-4 minutes. Next, take them out of the pan and drain any excess oil. Put them on a plate and add some lemon juice. That's all there is to it! Now you can _______________________.

(a) eat your delicious pan-fried fillets
(b) clean the fish and put it in the pan
(c) serve your fillets cooked in lemon juice
(d) grill your fish to your own specifications

4. Today, Germany is one of the most liberalized and civilized countries on earth. Human rights and civil liberties are even more effectively protected than in traditional homelands of liberty such as Britain. Through the professionalism of its historians, the seriousness of its reformers, the idealism of its moralists, and the creative genius of its artists, Germany has come a long way from the aggressive and discriminatory nation it was during World War II. In fact, it ___________________________________.

(a) is a proud part of its historical past
(b) is likely to see economic improvement
(c) is something of a complete turnaround
(d) is a country where the arts are flourishing

5.

Dear BigJet Lost & Found Department:

I am writing because I lost a wallet while on one of your flights and I hope you might help me locate it. I know I had the wallet with me when I boarded flight 703 at London Heathrow on May 30. However, it must have fallen out of my pocket on board. I was in seat 45B. The wallet is beige leather, and it had several credit cards in my name. It was not until I was in a taxi in New York that ________________.
Thanks in advance for any help you may be able to provide.

Sincerely,
Terry Kanski

(a) I realized I was late for the flight
(b) I discovered my wallet was missing
(c) I found my wallet but no credit cards
(d) I saw that my money had been stolen

6. A number of theories exist for why February 14 _________________________________.
    One suggests that it all started in ancient Rome. Among the pagan fertility celebrations
    of Rome was the Feast of Lupercalia. The festival began around mid-February, and one
    of its customs was that young marriageable girls would write their names on notes and
    leave them in large urns. Young men of Rome then drew out a girl's name from the urn
    and would be paired with her for the rest of the year. Quite often, love would bloom and
    the paired couple would soon marry.

    (a) was founded in the ancient world
    (b) became synonymous with romance
    (c) is given the name of Valentine's Day
    (d) has pagan and Christian significance

7. One of the key concepts emphasized in the new edition of *English Today* is the use
    of contractions and reductions in everyday language. Learners of English as a second
    language are often reluctant to use contracted and reduced forms. This reluctance can
    form a barrier to oral proficiency, not to mention listening comprehension. That is why
    our book includes them as _________________________.

    (a) a gift with each copy of *English Today*
    (b) new methods for learning contractions
    (c) an essential component of each chapter
    (d) ways to improve your basic writing skills

8. As the owner of one of the premier hotels in Chicago, I have enjoyed being able to dine
    at my hotel's restaurant any time I please. One evening at the restaurant, I could not
    decide between the lobster and the salmon. I told the waiter to bring whichever the chef
    recommended. Later, he _________________________. When I asked why, he
    told me it was because the chef said he did not want me to miss out on anything. Now,
    that's what I call first-class treatment.

    (a) came back with my lobster dish
    (b) recommended a fine vintage wine
    (c) brought out both lobster and salmon
    (d) gave my wife the same quality service

9. Filmmaker Marcel Carne's *The Children of Paradise* was made during the Nazi occupation of Paris and released in 1945. Though filmed under much duress, Carne managed to produce what is considered by some to be the greatest French film ever made. It was also the pinnacle of his career. He had been the leading French director of the 1940s, yet his filmmaking soon fell out of fashion. Carne continued to work into the 1970s, but ___________________________________.

(a) he was never to repeat the success of *The Children of Paradise*
(b) he still felt *The Children of Paradise* would become popular
(c) he refused all requests by film critics to make a sequel
(d) he did not make his comeback until the 1980s

10. Manutech is a leader in providing industrial technological information and analyses. We are committed to delivering all the up-to-date information you need on technology companies. Our database has over 100,000 detailed profiles of public and private companies, government labs, and non-profit organizations. Our easy-to-search system is based on hierarchical categories cross-referenced with 24 main technology classifications. Rely on Manutech for the best in ___________________________________.

(a) industry-wide classification system software
(b) information on the latest tech product releases
(c) data on leading tech companies and enterprises
(d) technological expertise for your networking needs

11. The British writer George Orwell was committed politically to the left, a leaning that was reflected in most of his writings. He was a believer in radical social democracy, and this belief was related to the sympathy he had for the poor and the outcast. He saw the poor as suffering under a capitalist system that created gross disparities of income between the callous rich and the near destitute. As such, he was an enemy to

___________________________________.

(a) those who had made him poor and destitute
(b) the ruling classes and their inequitable privilege
(c) those who were accepting of the idea of equality
(d) the critics of capitalist reform in his own country

12. In the Internet age, copyright infringement frequently happens online. However, if you have a federally registered copyright, then you can take the following steps to prevent anyone from using your material online. First, you can ask the infringer to stop using your material. If that fails, you can notify the web provider and demand they take action. If the provider does not take action, they will become liable. Many providers prefer not to become embroiled in legal problems and will take action. Thus, it is a good idea to
__________________________.

(a) warn the infringer first before taking action
(b) sue for infringement to get proper compensation
(c) avoid infringement by doing research on copyright laws
(d) obtain federal registration to protect yourself from infringement

13. Everything you need to start your own business at home can be found in one of our Business from Home packs. You will get information on over 10,000 business opportunities that involve working from home. Our pack includes free advertising, design, finance and marketing tips, plus a unique password to access our exclusive Business from Home website! It is easy and anyone can do it. Think of
__________________________. Visit www. businessfromhome.com now for more details.

(a) what you can do after you have won
(b) how your house will look once it is finished
(c) the money you will save through our investments
(d) all the benefits of working for yourself in your own home

14. According to the research of social psychologist Roy Baumeister, it is a myth that "pure evil" is behind any sadistic brutality inflicted on innocent victims. Baumeister concludes that most violence springs from ambition, lust, fear, pride, a desire for power or wealth, and even a misplaced idealism. In contrast to the traditional view that violence stems from sociological aberrance, he sees it as being derived from instinctual human elements. Therefore, to understand evil, Baumeister says, we must change the
__________________________.

(a) notion that victims of crime are innocent people
(b) comfortable belief that it is separate from ourselves
(c) way we view people with bad childhood experiences
(d) focus of analysis from individuals to society as a whole

15. It is not always easy to choose a career while still a college student. However, in today's rapidly-changing job market, this is not a big problem. You can be sure that challenging and interesting jobs not even created yet will be available when you leave college. So you need not be overly concerned if you have not chosen a specific career path. ______________________________, you should continue your education and develop broad skills you will need no matter what, such as verbal and written communication skills and the ability to think laterally.

(a) Rather
(b) Indeed
(c) In addition
(d) For instance

16. Under the rule of Genghis Khan, Mongol law was based around the concept of group responsibility and collective guilt. An individual's legal status was intimately tied with family and the larger group to which he or she belonged. That meant that a crime by one could bring punishment to all. In the case of a family, family members took responsibility of ensuring other members behaved correctly. ______________________________, a squad of soldiers was liable collectively for each individual's actions. Naturally, with this kind of law, a sense of collective responsibility pervaded Mongol culture at all levels.

(a) Consequently
(b) Incidentally
(c) Conversely
(d) Similarly

Read the passage and the question. Then choose the option that best answers the question.

17. Pompeii was a prosperous city until August 24, 79 AD, when the nearby volcano, Mount Vesuvius, erupted. Hot ash, stones and cinders rained down on the city, and the air was filled with poisonous gas. The showers of hot, wet ash and cinders covered and sealed most of the city, killing about 2,000 people. Some of the victims were trapped in their homes and killed. Others breathed the poisonous fumes and died as they ran away. When it was all over, Pompeii was buried under more than 30 feet of pumice and ash.

Q: What is the main topic of the passage?
(a) How ashes rather than lava buried Pompeii
(b) Why Mount Vesuvius killed so many people
(c) The complete volcanic destruction of Pompeii
(d) The end of Pompeii's prosperity in ancient times

18. We hope you are happy with the special offers and updates you have been receiving from UBuy.com. However, if you no longer wish to receive offers or updates such as this, simply change your UBuy.com preference details by unchecking the "Receive Email" box in your account. By making this change, you will no longer receive special promotions or offers. To begin receiving these emails again, just recheck the "Receive Email" box.

Q: What is the main topic of the passage?
(a) How to obtain a UBuy.com membership
(b) How to receive special offers from UBuy.com
(c) How to cancel email messages from UBuy.com
(d) How to get information about UBuy.com via email

19. This year Jack Haims, age 6, began kindergarten with abilities that put him ahead of other kids. He could already count to 100, read children's rhyming books and do simple writing. He acquired these valuable skills through attending preschool. Jack's experience is part of a growing trend, as an increasing number of parents all over the nation are enrolling their children in preschool prior to attending kindergarten. These children then carry the advantages with them through kindergarten and into primary school.

Q: What is the main idea of the passage?
(a) Preschool children can often read and write.
(b) Children today mature quicker than they used to.
(c) More children are attending preschool to gain skills.
(d) Parents are pushing children into kindergarten too early.

20. An orangutan moves through the forest using all four of its limbs to grasp the branches of trees. Not only does it have powerful hands designed for holding and grasping branches, but it also uses its feet for the same purpose. The big toe on each foot can be rotated to touch the ends of the other toes, like the thumbs on human hands. In effect, this gives the orangutan the equivalent of four "hands" for climbing trees and gripping branches.

Q: What is the passage mainly about?
(a) The unique limbs of the orangutan
(b) The way orangutans appear human
(c) The physical features of an orangutan
(d) The movement of orangutans among trees

21. Through internal reforms and military conquests from 768 to 814, Charlemagne earned his place in history as the father of Europe. When he became sole ruler of the kingdom of the Franks in 771, he was determined to expand his realm and bring order to Europe, which was falling into political decay. In 772, he began the first of many military campaigns, and by 800 he ruled over all of Western Europe, establishing a central government. In doing this, Charlemagne restored much of the unity of the old Roman Empire and paved the way for the development of modern Europe.

Q: What is the main topic of the passage?
(a) Historical milestones during Charlemagne's reign over Europe
(b) Charlemagne's role in laying the foundations of modern Europe
(c) Reforms instituted by Charlemagne throughout Medieval Europe
(d) Military conquest as Charlemagne's means of bringing order to Europe

22. While 16 million Americans served in the military during World War II, 42,000 conscientious objectors refused to take arms. *The Good War and Those Who Refused to Fight* is a documentary that closely follows the stories of a few of them. While some people might view conscientious objection as unpatriotic, the objectors are sympathetically portrayed. The film also focuses more on the contributions that pacifists made to World War II, whether as noncombatants serving in the military or as home-front volunteers, than on pacifist views.

Q: What is mainly being discussed about the documentary in the passage?
(a) Its focus on people who were unfit to fight in World War II
(b) Its criticism of people who refuse to defend their nation in wartime
(c) How it shows that not everyone was in support of fighting World War II
(d) How it presents a positive view of World War II's conscientious objectors

23. Irving Berlin's famous musical *Annie Get Your Gun* was based on the well-known American performer Annie Oakley. She was renowned for her skills with a rifle and used to demonstrate remarkable feats of marksmanship as a major attraction in Buffalo Bill's touring "Wild West Show." In 1901 she was involved in a railroad accident that left her partially paralyzed, but that did not stop her. She kept on demonstrating her shooting skill to audiences for another 20 years.

Q: Which of the following is correct about Annie Oakley according to the passage?
(a) She continued shooting after an accident.
(b) She was originally from the United Kingdom.
(c) She was paralyzed in a 1901 Buffalo Bill show.
(d) She played a small part in Irving Berlin's musical.

24. San Francisco's South of Market neighborhood is known for its many delightful attractions for tourists. It is where you can find the San Francisco Museum of Modern Art, the beautiful Yerba Buena Gardens and the famous Mission Streets. But that's not all. The area has acquired a new reputation and the name of Multimedia Gulch. Thanks to Internet age, it is now home to more Web and digital media companies per square meter than anywhere in the world.

Q: Which of the following is correct about South of Market?
(a) It is next to the Multimedia Gulch.
(b) It is popular with San Francisco artists.
(c) It has few significant tourist attractions.
(d) It has become home to multimedia firms.

25. The Miko candle set made from 100% natural beeswax is a perfect recreation of a six-piece sushi roll. To create this unique set, our craftspeople made colored waxes that look like seaweed, rice, cucumber, avocado and crabmeat, then skillfully combined them by hand. Fool your friends! Throw a sushi party—then bring out and light the candles before you serve the real thing. A great gift for all your sushi-loving friends, this set even comes with a pair of candle chopsticks.

Q: Which of the following is correct according to the advertisement?
(a) The pair of candle chopsticks costs extra.
(b) The chopsticks and sushi candles are edible.
(c) The candles are made with artificial ingredients.
(d) The candle set contains six sushi-shaped candles.

26. The Italian writer and Auschwitz survivor Primo Levi died on April 11, 1987, when he threw himself down the stairwell of his apartment building in Turin. The death of this apparently serene and self-controlled man stunned his readers. However, Levi's friend Ferdinando Camon said in an interview that Levi's suicide should be "backdated to 1945," since Levi had been waiting since then to do it—waiting until his work was complete. He may be right. Levi began his series of memoirs in 1946, soon after his release from Auschwitz, and had just finished the last book in 1986.

Q: Which of the following is correct according to the passage?
(a) Levi had survived a suicide attempt in 1945.
(b) Levi's series of memoirs was left unfinished.
(c) Levi killed himself after completing his memoirs.
(d) Levi's death was an accident according to Camon.

27. In Bay City on Monday the tires of the district's 78 school buses were deflated by vandals, giving public school students an extra day off for spring break. It is another in a series of incidents of vandalism in the area in recent months. The vandals struck sometime over the weekend, according to district school transportation director John Michaels. There was no damage to the fencing around the bus yard, so the vandals probably climbed the fence to let the tires down. Mr. Michaels said the vandals did not puncture the tires but simply opened the valves and took the cores out.

Q: Which of the following is correct about the vandalism in Bay City?
(a) It happened in the middle of the spring semester.
(b) It is the first act of vandalism in Bay City this year.
(c) Vandals did not damage the bus yard's enclosing fence.
(d) Vandals punched holes in the tires of all the school buses.

28. A study of bird flu patients has found that they have high levels of chemicals known as cytokines and chemokines in their systems. These chemicals trigger an inflammatory response from the immune system, drawing in white blood cells to attack the invading flu virus. In people with strong immune systems, the reaction to these chemicals is stronger. If it is too strong, the lungs can fill with fluids and this can trigger a deadly pneumonia. Medical historians believe that this is the reason why so many young and healthy people died in the 1918 pandemic known as the Spanish flu. Younger people today are similarly at risk if struck by bird flu.

Q: Which of the following is correct about bird flu according to the passage?
(a) White blood cells attack chemokine chemicals.
(b) Cytokines and chemokines are two deadly virus strains.
(c) A strong immune response to the flu virus can be dangerous.
(d) Young people with strong immune systems rarely contract the flu.

29.

Dear Mr. Plinker,

Please complete the enclosed application and send it using the envelope provided to the Admissions Office at Brandeis University before the closing date. Also, ensure that three letters of recommendation and official transcripts from all post-secondary schools you have attended are submitted before that date. Please have your referees use the enclosed forms and send them directly to the Admissions Office. Transcripts should also be sent directly by your schools. If you have any questions, please contact me by email.

Sincerely,
Sylvia Dander, Admissions Office

Q: Which of the following is correct according to the letter?
(a) Applicants can submit reference letters anytime.
(b) The application will arrive in a separate envelope.
(c) Transcripts should be sent in the provided envelope.
(d) References must be sent straight to the Admissions Office.

30. During last night's meeting, Hazleton's City Council approved the Illegal Immigrant Residency Act by a vote of 4 to 1. The Act imposes severe penalties on landlords who rent space to illegal immigrants. Under the new law, anyone seeking to rent a dwelling in the city will now have to hold a residency license or submit to an investigation of citizenship status. Landlords found renting to people without proper credentials could be fined up to $1,000 a day.

Q: Which of the following is correct according to the passage?
(a) The Illegal Immigrant Residency Act has been overturned.
(b) Those renting to illegal immigrants will have to pay a fine.
(c) Two council members opposed the Act for different reasons.
(d) Immigrants must show proof of employment to rent a house.

31. Scientists are genetically modifying mice to make them schizophrenic in the hopes of gaining a better understanding of the illness. The DNA of the mice is modified to mimic a mutant gene first discovered in the genetic make-up of a human family with a high incidence of schizophrenia. Brains of modified mice have been found to have features similar to those of humans with schizophrenia, which suggests that mice could be important tools for the study of factors that underlie mental illnesses and the testing of drug treatments.

Q: Which of the following is correct according to the passage?
(a) Schizophrenia in humans is not genetically transmitted.
(b) The modified genes do not appear to affect mice's brains.
(c) Studies with mice have led to new treatments for schizophrenia.
(d) Experiments on mice may help reveal causes of mental illnesses.

32. Delegates from cell phone companies around the world gathered in London this week for a conference to discuss the future of their industry. At the top of the agenda was discussion on pay-per-click advertising. Phone network operators are looking to profit from pay-per-click advertising revenue in much the same way Internet giants like Google have. By connecting cell phone users to online advertisers through link advertising, cell phone companies can expect to see huge profits. There are currently more than 2 billion cell phone users worldwide, and a growing number of them are now going online via cell phones rather than PCs.

Q: Which of the following is correct according to the passage?
(a) Giant Internet companies are entering the cell phone business.
(b) Two billion cell phone users are going online using cell phones.
(c) Cell phone companies plan to profit through online advertising.
(d) Growth in the cell phone industry has reached its saturation point.

33.

Dear Mr. Matthews,

I received your letter about your damaged shipment and regret any inconvenience it may have caused. A certain amount of breakage of this sort sometimes occurs in cross-country shipping. I must remind you to keep the damaged dishes in the same condition you received them until one of our representatives can inspect them, which should be within two weeks. If all is as you have stated, you can expect reimbursement two weeks after our inspection.

Sincerely,
Dave Andrews
Top Shipping Company

Q: What can be inferred from the letter?
(a) Dave Andrews will inspect the damaged dishes himself.
(b) Dave Andrews is unlikely to allow a reimbursement.
(c) Mr. Matthews accidentally damaged his new dishes.
(d) Mr. Matthews wants a refund for the broken dishes.

34. Incandescent and fluorescent bulbs are the most common types of household lighting. Incandescent bulbs are the least expensive to produce and the easiest to use, but they have a short lifespan and are somewhat expensive to run. Also, generating the electricity to power them yields large amounts of CO_2 emissions. Fluorescent lights are three to four times more efficient, resulting in fewer CO_2 emissions, and are therefore better for the environment. Compact forms of fluorescent lighting are becoming more popular and are set to be mandatory in places like Australia, where incandescent lighting will soon be banned.

Q: What can be inferred from the passage?
(a) Fluorescent light bulbs are impractical for domestic use.
(b) Australia's ban on incandescent lighting is ecologically motivated.
(c) More research will be done on producing better incandescent bulbs.
(d) Incandescent lighting is unlikely to be banned in developed countries.

35. Caribou are hoofed ruminant mammals that can be found above the tree line in Arctic North America and Greenland. Because they live on lichen in the winter, they are very well adapted to the harsh Arctic tundra through which they migrate great distances each year. Caribou cows and bulls both grow distinctive antlers, and bull antlers can reach 4 feet in width. A caribou calf can run within 90 minutes of its birth, which some must do to keep up with the migrating herds.

Q: What can be inferred about caribou from the passage?
(a) They feed exclusively on lichen.
(b) They dwell mostly in North America.
(c) Their calves have to migrate large distances.
(d) Female caribous' antlers can reach up to 4 feet in width.

36. As governor, I felt that I should write this editorial to address misapprehensions surrounding the demands of teachers and their threatened strike. First, I am required to balance the budget, and with the economy as it is, I am unable to authorize a pay raise to the extent that teachers are demanding. Second, given the circumstances, I made them a fair and final offer, and it is my hope that they accept it. Rest assured that strike action will not benefit anyone.

Q: What can be inferred from the editorial?
(a) Teachers want more money than they are worth.
(b) Teachers will go on strike to raise education standards.
(c) The governor is unlikely to be moved by any strike action.
(d) The governor is trying to hide his budget mismanagement.

37. At the close of the 18th century, there was a curious cultural shift from veneration to mockery in the words employed to describe elderly people. It was not so much that new labels were invented to express contempt for the old, but that new connotations were applied to old labels. For example, "gaffer," which was once a title of respect, even of endearment, came to describe an old man in a slightly derogatory way. In a similar aspect, "fogy" which had meant a wounded military veteran before 1780, came to refer to a foolish old person fixed in their habits.

Q: What can be inferred from the passage?
(a) Nineteenth-century youth venerated older people.
(b) New words do not have to be invented for a new concept.
(c) Older people receive less respect in periods following wars.
(d) Language changed more rapidly in the 18th century than today.

Part III   **Questions 38 — 40**

Read the passage. Then identify the option that does NOT belong.

38. The Uffizi gallery in Florence, one of the world's greatest public museums, was originally designed as an office building. (a) It is a three-sided structure that surrounds a long narrow plaza that runs off the Palazzo Vecchio. (b) Florence was an important city for trade and commerce during the Renaissance. (c) The Uffizi, which was built in the mid-sixteenth century, features typical Renaissance architecture. (d) It is three stories high and has marble floors and 45 rooms and galleries.

39. Through excavations, archaeologists seek to understand what life was like in the past. (a) Drawings on pieces of pottery may show the kinds of clothing people wore. (b) A bone needle may indicate that they made clothing by skewing skins together. (c) Heavy stone objects and animal bones are cleaned and sorted in a cleared area. (d) Various kinds of rubbing stones could mean that they knew how to grind wheat or make tools.

40. Many people believe that falling into quicksand means inevitable death. (a) However, the truth is that quicksand is mainly liquid, and it is possible to float on its surface. (b) Quicksand has been highly fictionalized throughout history and was often included in 20th-century adventure novels. (c) Taking deep breaths also helps, as this will keep one calm and increase one's buoyancy. (d) By using slow, gentle movements, it is usually possible to propel oneself to the edge of the quicksand and escape.

This is the end of the Reading Comprehension section. Please remain seated until the proctor has instructed otherwise. You are NOT allowed to turn to any other section of the test.

서울대 최신기출 3

Listening Comprehension

Grammar

Vocabulary

Reading Comprehension

LISTENING COMPREHENSION

Part I **Questions 1—15**

You will now hear fifteen conversation fragments, each made up of a single spoken statement followed by four spoken responses. Choose the most appropriate response to the statement.

Part II **Questions 16—30**

You will now hear fifteen conversation fragments, each made up of three spoken statements followed by four spoken responses. Choose the most appropriate response to complete the conversation.

Part III Questions 31—45

You will now hear fifteen complete conversations. For each item, you will hear a conversation and its corresponding question, both of which will be read twice. Then you will hear four options which will be read only once. Choose the option that best answers the question.

Part IV Questions 46—60

You will now hear fifteen spoken monologues. For each item, you will hear a monologue and its corresponding question, both of which will be read twice. Then you will hear four options which will be read only once. Choose the option that best answers the question.

GRAMMAR

DIRECTIONS

This part of the exam tests your grammar skills. You will have 25 minutes to complete the 50 questions. Be sure to follow the directions given by the proctor.

Part I   Questions 1—20

Choose the best answer for the blank.

1. A: My exams are all over.

B: ____________ that's the case, let's eat out somewhere nice.

(a) If
(b) Until
(c) Though
(d) Whereas

2. A: Could you dryclean this jacket in two days?

B: Sure, and I'll even have it ____________ to your home.

(a) deliver
(b) delivers
(c) delivered
(d) delivering

3. A: Do you go straight home after work?

B: No, I sometimes stop by a store ____________ some groceries.

(a) to buy
(b) buying
(c) for buying
(d) to be buying

4. A: Can I get you something to drink?

B: Sure. If you ____________ mind.

(a) shouldn't
(b) wouldn't
(c) couldn't
(d) mustn't

5. A: I think Tony is the smartest person in our class.

B: Yeah, so ____________.

(a) do I
(b) I do
(c) is he
(d) he is it

6. A: We've had wonderful weather lately.

B: Yes, it couldn't be ____________.

(a) better
(b) good
(c) well
(d) best

7. A: Which flower pots shall we take home?

B: The ____________.

(a) left three first pots
(b) first pots three on the left
(c) pots on the left first three
(d) first three pots on the left

8. A: Hi, Jane. I'm still at the airport due to the flight delay.

B: Really? I was sure you ____________ gone by now.

(a) will be
(b) have been
(c) will have been
(d) would have been

9. A: Dave has never turned homework in late before.

   B: Well, he ___________ this time.

   (a) did
   (b) was
   (c) has had
   (d) did have

10. A: How much does this snack cost?

    B: It ___________.

    (a) is cost for four dollars
    (b) costs for four dollars
    (c) is four dollars cost
    (d) costs four dollars

11. A: What took you so long to get back to the hotel?

    B: ___________ lost on the way.

    (a) I get
    (b) I got
    (c) I'll get
    (d) I've gotten

12. A: Can I invite my friends over?

    B: I can't see why ___________.

    (a) you not do
    (b) don't you
    (c) don't
    (d) not

13. A: Did you see Jake's new sports car? It's incredible!

    B: I know. I wish my car ___________ as nice.

    (a) is
    (b) be
    (c) were
    (d) will be

14. A: ___________ to move out of my office while it's being repainted.

    B: I hope you've been moved to a nice office in the meantime.

    (a) I asked
    (b) I was asked
    (c) I'll be asked
    (d) I'll have asked

15. A: Could you tell me where the rest room is?

    B: Sure, it's ___________.

    (a) the hall down on your right
    (b) your right side down the hall
    (c) on right side and down the hall
    (d) down the hall and on your right

16. A: How was the movie?

    B: Fairly good. Not the best one ___________ this year, though.

    (a) I see
    (b) I've seen
    (c) I had seen
    (d) I'm seeing

17. A: Have you been waiting long?

    B: Yes, and I was ___________.

    (a) to be leaving when you walked in
    (b) leaving about when you walked in
    (c) when you walked in about to leave
    (d) about to leave when you walked in

18. A: Sarah can't make it to the dinner on Friday.

B: Well, __________ she can't come, we'll still have it.

(a) since
(b) unless
(c) even if
(d) for instance

19. A: I'd like to check out now, please.

B: Certainly. I hope __________ your stay.

(a) you enjoy
(b) you'll enjoy
(c) you enjoyed
(d) you had enjoyed

20. A: I've never heard __________.

B: You should. She's really quite good.

(a) Kate piano play
(b) Kate play the piano
(c) piano by Kate played
(d) play the piano by Kate

Part II   **Questions 21—40**

Choose the best answer for the blank.

---

21. Labor Day is always __________ first Monday of September in the US and Canada.

(a) a
(b) the
(c) one
(d) this

22. Research shows that married people live longer, __________, and suffer from fewer diseases than single people.

(a) happier
(b) are happier
(c) to be happier
(d) being happier

23. If you suffer from dry mouth, your dentist may suggest __________ sugarless gum.

(a) chew
(b) to chew
(c) chewing
(d) to chewing

24. Researchers claim that the current tax policy widens the gap between __________.

(a) rich and a poor
(b) a rich and a poor
(c) rich and the poor
(d) the rich and the poor

25. __________ a parking space at this time of day.

(a) To find is impossible
(b) It is to find impossible
(c) It is impossible to find
(d) To find it is impossible

26. Damaged products can be returned for an exchange up to 30 days __________ the date of purchase.

(a) to
(b) on
(c) until
(d) from

27. Above the store's entrance was a sign __________, "Watch Your Head."

(a) say
(b) said
(c) to say
(d) saying

28. Modern airliners fly at extremely high altitudes __________ air pressure is so low that pressurized cabins are necessary to breathe normally.

(a) that
(b) what
(c) which
(d) where

29. Since tonight's concert is the last time singer Elle Merrat will perform live, it is __________.

(a) not to be missed
(b) to be not missed
(c) to be missing not
(d) not to be missing

30. In the early 1800s, only men __________ vote in the US.

(a) must
(b) could
(c) might
(d) should

31. __________ to create more scholarships, university officials sent many letters to alumni for more support.

(a) Wanted
(b) To want
(c) Wanting
(d) Have wanted

32. Analysts said that the CEO's illegal deals __________ the reason why the company fell into bankruptcy.

(a) was
(b) were
(c) was being
(d) were being

33. Multicultural education is the primary way __________ school educators combat racism.

(a) in what
(b) by what
(c) for which
(d) through which

34. Africa has diverse terrain, __________ from lush grasslands to harsh sandy deserts.

(a) ranges
(b) ranged
(c) ranging
(d) to range

35. ___________ a workforce or workplace so diverse as Velox Enterprises.

(a) Never there has been
(b) There has never been
(c) There have never been
(d) Never there have been

36. Halley's Comet ___________ to be seen by the naked eye every 76 years.

(a) is coming enough close to Earth
(b) to Earth comes close enough
(c) comes close enough to Earth
(d) to Earth is coming closer

37. Personal space is the distance that feels comfortable between you and ___________.

(a) other person
(b) another people
(c) another person
(d) the other people

38. Even though critics call Jack Sedgeworth's writing unoriginal and full of clichés, his latest book ___________ over $2 million in sales.

(a) grosses
(b) is grossed
(c) has grossed
(d) has been grossed

39. Treasure hunters ___________ a valuable hoard from its waters said that they were victims of a misunderstanding.

(a) accused by Spain taking
(b) by Spain accused to take
(c) accused by Spain of taking
(d) were accused of taking by Spain

40. ___________ any problems with your new television or require assistance, please contact customer service.

(a) If you had
(b) You should have
(c) Should you have
(d) Were you having

41. (a) A: How can we get to the theater if your car is at the mechanic's?

(b) B: We can always go there by bus.

(c) A: Is there a bus that stops near the theater?

(d) B: Sure, I had taken the bus many times before.

42. (a) A: You're taking a long time to get dressed.

(b) B: Actually, I finished getting dressed 10 minutes ago.

(c) A: Then, let's go. We're late for the party as it is.

(d) B: Wait. I need to decide on a necklace to go nice with the dress.

43. (a) A: How many classes are you going to take this semester?

(b) B: Just one. That's probably all I can handle with my full-time job.

(c) A: That might be a wise thing to do. So, how are you thinking of taking?

(d) B: I'll probably sign up for one of the classes you recommended.

44. (a) A: This article states that memory loss is common between elderly people.

(b) B: Does it suggest any ways to prevent it?

(c) A: It advocates exercise and a healthy diet.

(d) B: It seems that a healthy lifestyle is the key to preventing many problems.

45. (a) A: Fred made a critical error in this line of computer code.

(b) B: I find it hard to believe he did that.

(c) A: What do you mean? What makes you think he didn't do it?

(d) B: Fred has never made so a careless mistake in his entire career.

Part IV Questions 46—50

Identify the option that contains an awkward expression or an error in grammar.

46. (a) A standard language is a certain type of language that is given legal status. (b) Correctness, precision, and purity is the qualities of such a language. (c) This language becomes the benchmark by which we gauge all other variants of the language. (d) It is promoted in schools and used in law courts and government institutions.

47. (a) The spinal cord is bundle of nerves running through the center of the backbone. (b) It is a superhighway that carries messages from the body to the brain and vice versa. (c) Sensory nerves send information to the brain through the spinal cord, which the brain must interpret to produce an appropriate response. (d) Motor nerves then whisk the brain's instructions back to the body.

48. (a) Regular interactions between the winds and ocean currents produce predictable weather phenomena. (b) Two well-known examples are the El Niño effect and the transfer of heat from the tropics to the poles. (c) However, global warming can alter these patterns by melting glaciers that will in turn change ocean currents, affected the climate worldwide. (d) These changes in ocean currents may produce climate variations that could endure for centuries.

49. (a) Astronauts require 1.6 kg of drinking water daily and require 27 kg more water for other needs. (b) Each person on a 1,000-day mission to Mars would require 28,600 kg of water. (c) It takes about $25,000 to be launching into just a low Earth orbit. (d) So it is unlikely that astronauts can take a large amount of water with them to Mars.

50. (a) A flock of sheep recently produced a bale of wool that sold for $500,000. (b) The wool, which is about one-fifth the thickness of a human hair, is amazingly soft. (c) Being valuable, it was locked in a guarded vault to keep it safe. (d) The sheep are provided with a climate-controlled building where it can live in comfort.

This is the end of the Grammar section. Do NOT move on to the next section until instructed to do so. You are NOT allowed to turn to any other section of the test.

VOCABULARY

Part I　Questions 1—25

Choose the best answer for the blank.

1. A: Hello, I'm calling about your job ad in the paper.

B: I'm sorry, but the position has already been ___________ .

(a) held
(b) filled
(c) made
(d) worked

2. A: What's the problem, Officer? I was only going 50 miles an hour.

B: But the speed ___________ here is 40.

(a) top
(b) line
(c) limit
(d) check

3. A: Can you come to a party tomorrow?

B: I'm sorry, but maybe another ___________ .

(a) time
(b) piece
(c) option
(d) moment

4. A: Does everyone have to fill out an arrival card?

B: No, only non-residents and tourists need to ___________ it.

(a) fulfill
(b) manage
(c) approve
(d) complete

5. A: I don't like this tie. It's too bright.

B: But, it ___________ your suit.

(a) mixes
(b) blends
(c) matches
(d) switches

6. A: I hope I do well on the exam today.

B: Don't worry. You should pass ___________ .

(a) truly
(b) easily
(c) kindly
(d) specially

7. A: Sam was very timid during the group discussion.

B: Yeah, he really ___________ from conversation.

(a) sat down
(b) jumped up
(c) shied away
(d) turned back

8. A: What's so good about that book?

B: It ___________ as a great reference on Greek history.

(a) states
(b) serves
(c) relates
(d) maintains

9. A: I forgot Professor Ronen's office number. You remember it, right?

    B: Sorry, but I can't __________ it, either.

    (a) recall
    (b) repeat
    (c) replace
    (d) recount

10. A: Are you lost? Can I help you?

    B: Thanks for the __________, but I'm OK.

    (a) idea
    (b) offer
    (c) mark
    (d) advice

11. A: Wendy! I almost didn't __________ you.

    B: Hi, Pam. Yeah, I've changed a lot since high school.

    (a) perceive
    (b) recognize
    (c) appreciate
    (d) acknowledge

12. A: Why didn't the maid clean our room?

    B: Because I __________ the "Do Not Disturb" sign on the doorknob.

    (a) hung
    (b) noted
    (c) painted
    (d) centered

13. A: Are these shoes the right size?

    B: Yes, they're a perfect __________.

    (a) fit
    (b) suit
    (c) form
    (d) degree

14. A: How did you find your way back to the station?

    B: I had a map to __________ me.

    (a) find
    (b) read
    (c) guide
    (d) escort

15. A: I'm really satisfied with this hotel.

    B: Yes, the rooms are clean, the food is good and the service is __________.

    (a) veracious
    (b) legitimate
    (c) enervated
    (d) impeccable

16. A: Let's share a room when we're on the conference trip.

    B: Good idea. We can __________ the bill and save money.

    (a) split
    (b) assign
    (c) merge
    (d) change

17. A: Thanks for helping me move my things out of my house.

    B: It's my __________. Think nothing of it.

    (a) relief
    (b) chance
    (c) pleasure
    (d) intention

18. A: Why don't we go first class on the train?

B: OK, but that'll double the __________.

(a) sum
(b) price
(c) value
(d) ticket

19. A: Do you know what those people are talking about?

B: No, I don't have the __________ idea.

(a) fairest
(b) faintest
(c) broadest
(d) brightest

20. A: That movie is so funny.

B: Yeah, every time I see it, I __________.

(a) watch out
(b) crack up
(c) bust up
(d) flip out

21. A: Sally is having problems with her math teacher.

B: I can __________ with her because I also had problems with him last semester.

(a) prioritize
(b) familiarize
(c) sympathize
(d) synchronize

22. A: My boss is making me work more for less pay.

B: That's awful. It sounds like you're being __________.

(a) optioned
(b) exploited
(c) engrained
(d) overhanded

23. A: Hi, I made a reservation for two under Terrence Klein.

B: This way, sir. I'll __________ you to your seat.

(a) direct
(b) precede
(c) forward
(d) transport

24. A: Sorry for the delay. We're processing your auto insurance claim as quickly as we can.

B: Well, I'm __________ patience.

(a) turning over to
(b) getting in with
(c) running out of
(d) losing out on

25. A: Why was Jack elected class president?

B: I think it's because he __________ confidence.

(a) extols
(b) exudes
(c) exhales
(d) exhumes

26. Last year, Michelle ___________ a scholarship to attend Boston University.

(a) greeted
(b) received
(c) admitted
(d) absorbed

27. This blender will allow you to crush ice and blend frozen fruit ___________ in a few seconds.

(a) willingly
(b) effortlessly
(c) particularly
(d) intentionally

28. Abraham Lincoln's Emancipation Proclamation ___________ praise from many people in Great Britain and France.

(a) drew
(b) chose
(c) drove
(d) chased

29. Hailstones ___________ the roofs and walls of the houses for half an hour.

(a) bent
(b) spent
(c) struck
(d) dropped

30. While others spent their lives building their own wealth, Mother Teresa ___________ her life to the poor.

(a) set
(b) paid
(c) devoted
(d) approved

31. It is important to become ___________ about a company before purchasing its stock.

(a) determined
(b) unmistakable
(c) unforgettable
(d) knowledgeable

32. Some say that a shared taste in clothes is a strong ___________ of similar opinions and even compatible personalities.

(a) deterrent
(b) treatment
(c) indication
(d) regulation

33. You can confirm the ___________ of your order by checking our homepage.

(a) status
(b) locale
(c) place
(d) step

34. If the government does not take action now, the public is going to pay for it __________ later.

(a) dearly
(b) highly
(c) widely
(d) extremely

35. Those who undergo counseling will __________ more if they attend all of the sessions and take an active part in them.

(a) affirm
(b) benefit
(c) upgrade
(d) integrate

36. The general sat in the middle and was __________ by other military officers at the meeting.

(a) edged
(b) flanked
(c) bordered
(d) sequestered

37. Clinical social workers specialize in the __________ of mental health services to individuals and families.

(a) attention
(b) provision
(c) instruction
(d) manipulation

38. After saying something inappropriate, Robert smiled to __________ his embarrassment from others.

(a) achieve
(b) remove
(c) conceal
(d) deceive

39. As it was getting late, Jen thanked the party's hosts and took her __________.

(a) leave
(b) claim
(c) descent
(d) absence

40. The botanical garden __________ a collection of diverse flora.

(a) enters
(b) houses
(c) creates
(d) upholds

41. The television program has a large __________, with millions of people tuning in each week.

(a) clientele
(b) assembly
(c) gathering
(d) viewership

42. Many countries are aware of the dangers of greenhouse gases and have __________ stricter emission standards.

(a) inflicted
(b) imposed
(c) disclosed
(d) dissuaded

43. Hundreds of police __________ on the rally site and used tear gas and clubs to subdue protestors.

(a) conceded
(b) convulsed
(c) converged
(d) confronted

44. Art is a long-term investment option and can be a __________ against inflation.

   (a) plug
   (b) hedge
   (c) throttle
   (d) loophole

45. Sudden weight loss or gain can be __________ to a number of causes, including depression.

   (a) affordable
   (b) regrettable
   (c) responsible
   (d) attributable

46. The two impoverished neighborhoods have __________ into a single thriving community.

   (a) avowed
   (b) allocated
   (c) coalesced
   (d) counseled

47. Many flatworms are parasitic and can __________ a variety of hosts, including humans.

   (a) infest
   (b) deduce
   (c) ensnare
   (d) sublimate

48. When early traders visited ports of foreign countries, they communicated with locals by __________ a simplified language known as a pidgin.

   (a) adopting
   (b) releasing
   (c) submitting
   (d) denouncing

49. When the renowned tenor finished singing, the delighted audience applauded without __________.

   (a) reverence
   (b) resolution
   (c) resignation
   (d) reservation

50. A general "spend now, pay later" attitude has __________ itself in many countries.

   (a) entrenched
   (b) undulated
   (c) scoured
   (d) incised

This is the end of the Vocabulary section. Do NOT move on to the Reading Comprehension section until instructed to do so. You are NOT allowed to turn to any other section of the test.

READING COMPREHENSION

DIRECTIONS

This part of the exam tests your ability to comprehend reading passages. You will have 45 minutes to complete the 40 questions. Be sure to follow the directions given by the proctor.

Part I Questions 1—16

Read the passage. Then choose the option that best completes the passage.

1. The Savara Restaurant is committed to providing its customers with the best Indian cuisine. Our chefs are passionate about Indian cooking and create dishes only from the freshest ingredients while using the finest traditional Indian recipes. We also strive to create an authentic atmosphere with genuine Indian artwork and decor. And you can experience it all for a great price. Visit us today for __________________________________.

   (a) the cheapest food in town
   (b) a fun day out with the kids
   (c) the best in home-style cooking
   (d) an authentic dining experience

2. The Botard Art Museum, situated in the seaside resort of Mikkrob, Estonia, is __________________________________. The newly elected mayor of Mikkrob has petitioned for its shutdown to make way for a new shopping mall. The Botard Art Museum's director, Alar Bruns, who has run the museum for nearly 15 years on a small budget and with little government support, today expressed concern that the mayor's move is politically motivated. Mr. Bruns added that the cultural life of Mikkrob "should not be sacrificed for big business interests."

   (a) threatened with closure
   (b) in need of a new director
   (c) designed to attract tourists
   (d) seeking additional funding

3. When women grow older and enter the early stages of menopause, doctors will likely recommend hormone replacement therapy to relieve symptoms and prevent bone loss. Bone loss prevention is particularly important, since up to 20% of a woman's expected lifetime bone loss could occur in the years immediately following menopause. Some women may even shrink an inch in the first year. So, if you are experiencing menopausal symptoms, consult your doctor about receiving hormone treatment. Without it, you _________________________________.

(a) cannot decrease your bone size
(b) could suffer dramatic bone loss
(c) might be able to prevent menopause
(d) will run a risk of catching the disease

4. Being an effective foreign language teacher is a challenging task since learners within a classroom may have different learning styles. Some learners may learn better when engaged in peer or group work while others may do better when involved in individual exercises. So, it is important that foreign language teachers provide _________________________________.

(a) activities based on real-life situations
(b) more challenging tasks for fast learners
(c) appropriate feedback on student progress
(d) a range of tasks to match varied learning styles

5. Science fiction writers once imagined future technology that would reduce an entire three-course meal to a few small pills. Sous-chef Lyman Buchwald, however, has brought technology to the kitchen in ways sci-fi writers never envisioned. Buchwald has modified an ink-jet printer to create dishes printed on edible paper. Food critics have cheered, complimenting Mr. Buchwald for his _________________________________.

(a) tasty dishes that come in pill form
(b) advancements in printer technology
(c) unique contributions to science fiction
(d) creative blending of food and technology

6. Despite his tremendous success as a pioneer of the automobile industry, Henry Ford tyrannized his workers. Autocratic and puritanical, he fired his bookkeeping staff regularly and any workers that his spies caught smoking. Gangster tactics were used to maintain discipline in plants, and unions were kept out of Ford factories until 1941. Ford basically ________________________________.

(a) succeeded because of the risks he took
(b) cared little for those who worked for him
(c) improved factory conditions for all workers
(d) respected his workers as they respected him

7. *The Strange Case of Dr. Jekyll and Mr. Hyde* by Robert Louis Stevenson has long been admired by readers and critics as representing a duality in human nature where moral feelings are in conflict with sinful impulses. However, this was not how the novella was originally written. Stevenson simply wrote the story after recalling a dream. But at the suggestion of his wife, he reshaped it into a tale that

________________________________.

(a) is most suitable for children
(b) shocked the public by criticizing society
(c) stirred up a debate among literary critics
(d) portrays humanity's conflicting emotions

8.

Dear Brad,

We've been having a terrific vacation in Mexico. Every day we find new things to do: hiking among ancient Mayan ruins, scuba-diving, deep-sea fishing or dancing. Tomorrow we're even going to go up in a hot-air balloon over the jungle! I'm sorry you couldn't get time off work to join us. I know that you really wanted to see Mexico. Maybe next time ________________________________. Well, take care.

Cheers,
Monique

(a) you can come on a holiday with us
(b) you'll find Mexico more interesting
(c) you won't have to go home so early
(d) you might visit the museums instead

9. One of the aims of conservation science is to protect and maintain a region's biodiversity, the number and variety of organisms in a particular region. And one of the greatest threats to biodiversity is _______________________________. These can be invasive and pose a threat to local species. For example, they might deplete limited food resources by changing the composition of local plant communities through selective feeding. Through such actions, alien species dramatically change whole ecosystems. The complete eradication of these invaders is often the only way a region's natural equilibrium and biodiversity can be preserved.

(a) the rise of pollution
(b) the elimination of weeds
(c) the extinction of rare creatures
(d) the introduction of alien species

10. At university, I would have defined my writing style as animated, audience-centered and energetic. Bombastic would have been more accurate, but at that time I would never have admitted to that. Now I admit that my style was often wordy—something a good essayist should avoid. I cringe when I read my old essays and stories, as I imagine my readers did. Fortunately, I have learned to write _______________________________.
Now I try to serve my readers, to give them what they want and try not to impress them with indulgent verbiage.

(a) with a less conventional approach
(b) according to what publishers want
(c) about my own thoughts and feelings
(d) with greater clarity and more economy

11. Unlike animal species on the mainland, many of the species on islands cannot migrate elsewhere when food resources decline. They have no choice but to survive on whatever food is available or starve. Consequently, evolution on islands has favored smaller animals because the amount of food they require is smaller. So animals that _______________________________ on an island.

(a) require less food have a better chance of surviving
(b) have been introduced can create severe problems
(c) are smaller tend to be the first ones eaten
(d) blend into their environment can survive

12. Most scholars agree that history began with the advent of writing some 6,000 years ago. This was when humans could begin recording history and when cultures and civilizations were emerging. By the same token, scholars classify the events that took place before writing as prehistoric. This use of the invention of writing to distinguish the prehistoric and the historic, the uncivilized and the civilized, is logically valid. One need only measure the long period of incredibly slow-paced changes of prehistoric times against the rapid and dramatic changes of the past 6,000 years to see why. A link clearly exists between ___________________________________.

(a) the human condition of prehistoric and historic times
(b) the rise of civilization and a diligence in recordkeeping
(c) the way people wrote then and the way they write now
(d) the invention of writing and the speed of cultural progress

13. One of the obligations of allied Yanomamo tribes of Central Brazil is that they must give support and shelter to their allies if need be. For instance, if a tribe is driven away from its village and plantation by an enemy, it will be given shelter in an ally's village. However, this is only until it can establish a new plantation elsewhere that will provide for an independent existence. This could take a year or even longer. Regardless of how long it takes, however, the tribe ___________________________________.

(a) will fight until it has defeated the enemy tribe
(b) will not return to its village unless it is protected
(c) will work for its friends without complaint or regret
(d) will not move until a new plantation can support them

14. Our research team has organized a scientific expedition to Italy because we believe that volcanic eruptions ___________________________________. While some in the scientific community doubt this idea, we hope to confirm it through research into Mt. Etna in Italy. Our team will spend two weeks atop Etna, risking our lives to prove what may be a key to predicting volcanic eruptions. If we find that the moon indeed influences volcanic eruptions, it will stand as one of the great discoveries in volcanology.

(a) are causing a serious erosion of the Italian coastline
(b) have significant long-term effects on the environment
(c) follow patterns based on the moon's gravitational pull
(d) provide clues about what is going on at the earth's core

15. Statistics linking the consumption of wine rather than beer to health benefits could be misleading due to differing dietary preferences among wine and beer drinkers. This was the contention by researchers at the Gourmand Institute after they had surveyed consumer purchases throughout Europe. What they found was that people who only drank wine tended to buy cheeses, fruits, vegetables, and low-fat meats. _________________________________, beer drinkers purchased less healthy foods, such as frozen dinners, sausages, chips, and soft drinks.

(a) In fact
(b) In sum
(c) In contrast
(d) In addition

16. In order to determine the number of calories that you need to either gain, lose or maintain weight, nutritionists must calculate your basal metabolic rate (BMR). They have numerous formulas for doing this, but the most accurate one takes your lean body mass (LBM) into account. _______________________________, for all but the overweight or extremely muscular, an accurate BMR estimate is still possible with certain calculations that do not incorporate your LBM. One such example is the extremely accurate Harris Benedict formula, which uses nothing more than weight, height, age, and sex.

(a) Yet
(b) Instead
(c) Namely
(d) Likewise

Part II   **Questions 17—37**

Read the passage and the question. Then choose the option that best answers the question.

17. In some countries, a dowry, in the form of money or property, is given by a bride to her husband as part of their marriage. The size of this dowry is usually worked out according to the groom's social status. Thus, it is almost impossible for lower class women to marry into upper class families. Even worse, in some cases where a woman's family is too poor to afford any kind of dowry, she might never marry.

Q   What is the main topic of the passage?
(a) Reasons for paying a dowry
(b) Dowries given by poor women
(c) Marriages of rich and poor people
(d) A marriage custom in some countries

18. Tooth decay results from the actions of bacteria on the teeth. Bacteria ferment sugars that are present on a tooth and create lactic acid. The lactic acid then breaks down calcium, followed by proteins in the tooth's enamel. That process results in holes and weak spots. As this decay spreads deeper into the tooth's middle layer, the tooth starts to become sensitive to touch and temperature. Finally, when decay reaches the tooth's center, where its nerve is located, it creates an inflammation that causes a toothache.

Q: What is the passage mainly about?
(a) The progression of tooth decay
(b) The bacteria that cause tooth decay
(c) The threat of sugars to dental health
(d) The importance of preventing cavities

19. If you ever want to truly experience the local cuisine of Issan, in northeastern Thailand, you cannot pass up sampling dishes of fried insects. Issan is predominantly an agricultural region and used to be one of the poorest in Thailand—so poor that its people had to rely on eating insects as a cheap way of obtaining protein. The region experienced an economic boom in the early 1990s, but despite the prosperity, people continue the tradition of eating insects and actually savor them as delicacies.

Q: What is the best title for the passage?
(a) Insect Cooking Techniques
(b) The Increase in Insect Consumption
(c) Tasty Dishes in Various Thai Regions
(d) Insect Cuisine in Issan: Past & Present

20. Recent government initiatives in Malaysia to regulate the employment of foreign workers have had little effect, the president of the Malaysian Trade Union Congress Mr. Rajalan said in Kuala Lumpur today. Errant employers are still rarely punished, while the process of recruiting foreigners legally remains expensive and bureaucratic. Businesses, therefore, continue to hire illegal immigrants, safe from any risk of punishment. Mr. Rajalan said that as a result of this, possibly as many as 1.2 million illegal immigrants now work in the country.

Q: What is the passage mainly about?
(a) Economic effects of Malaysia's foreign labor market
(b) Malaysia's efforts to recruit a legitimate foreign workforce
(c) Malaysia's inability to stop the employment of illegal foreign workers
(d) Difficulties the Malaysian government has in formulating immigration laws

21. DrugWatch, the government-run safety information and adverse event reporting program, alerts all pharmacists to safety labeling revisions for FluGone, a prescription medication for influenza. The prescribing information that accompanies FluGone contains an incorrect dosing chart for the standard dose for children. The dosing frequency should have been listed as once daily, instead of twice daily, under the "Recommended Dosage for Ten Days" column. DrugWatch advises pharmacists to discard the original chart and consult the supplied chart for dosing information.

Q: What is the main purpose of the announcement?
(a) To inform healthcare professionals of new clinical practices
(b) To advise pharmacists of a mistake in dosage information
(c) To notify hospitals of a medicine's possible side effects
(d) To prevent doctors from prescribing FluGone to adults

22. For the Irish poet Patrick Kavanagh, a local Irish parish was where you could find all the truths about human life. The subject of his poetry was thus often the mundane rural life of his parish. Although such communities are traditionally disparaged as parochial and their inhabitants regarded as having sectarian, insular and limited views, Kavanagh regarded this parochialism as exemplifying how things were all over the world. For him, the local parish was a window through which all the world was revealed.

Q: What is the main point made about Patrick Kavanagh in the passage?
(a) He wrote poems in the small parish he lived in.
(b) He spent all of his life promoting traditional Irish values.
(c) He saw parish life as representative of all human societies.
(d) He concentrated on the good side of parochialism in his poems.

23.

Dear Mr. Brown,

Your outstanding account balance of $405 is now four months overdue. To date, we have not received any payment at all. In addition, you have not responded to the previous letters we have sent. If we do not receive payment within the next month, we will have to take legal action. We look forward to your prompt response.

Janet Lynch
Mira Financial

Q: Which of the following is correct according to the letter?
(a) Mr. Brown has not responded to previous letters.
(b) Mr. Brown's last payment was not enough.
(c) Mr. Brown will receive $405 next month.
(d) Mr. Brown has four months to pay $405.

24. Metropolis Suites currently has eight fully furnished short-term lease apartments located in the heart of Paris. These provide a wonderful alternative to hotel accommodations for visitors who plan to spend an extended period in the city. Our apartments are available for periods ranging from one week to one year. To ensure availability, you are advised to reserve an apartment at least six months in advance. Check our online calendar for availability now.

Q: Which of the following is correct according to the advertisement?
(a) Apartments can be rented for as long as a year.
(b) Apartment locations are spread throughout Paris.
(c) Apartment lodgings can be booked for a weekend.
(d) Apartments must be booked six weeks in advance.

25. My sister-in-law and her husband really annoy me. When my husband and I made a plan to go out for Chinese with some other couples recently, they insisted on coming along. At the restaurant, they just ordered fried rice each and then asked if they could try each of our dishes. That way they ended up with a full plate of food each. When the bill arrived, they only paid for their fried rice orders. They asked if they should pay a part of everyone's check, but of course, they knew no one would take them up on such a silly offer. I won't be having Chinese with them again.

Q: Which of the following is correct about the writer's sister-in-law and her husband?
(a) They ended up paying for everyone's meal.
(b) They were invited to a Chinese restaurant.
(c) They tasted other people's dishes for free.
(d) They did not pay for what they ordered.

26. It is now clear that millions of women around the world have an increased risk of developing breast cancer because of a drug that their mothers were prescribed during pregnancy. A new study of 5,000 women has found that those women whose mothers took the anti-miscarriage drug called DES between 1941 and 1975 were more likely to develop breast cancer. Although the drug was known to cause an increased risk of breast cancer for expectant mothers who took it, this is the first study to show that the drug affected their offspring as well.

Q: What has caused a greater risk of breast cancer for some women?
(a) A genetic flaw passed on from their mothers
(b) A drug their mothers took while pregnant
(c) A fertility drug they took to get pregnant
(d) A drug they took without a prescription

27. You undoubtedly know how important it is to reduce exposure to the sun's ultraviolet radiation (UV). But did you know that ordinary clothes do not protect you from UV? That's why we are pleased to bring you our latest product, UVstop, a UV treatment for clothing. Simply pour UVstop into your wash to transform your clothes into UV protective clothing that can block 96% of the sun's harmful rays from reaching your skin. UVstop is recommended by the Skin Cancer Foundation.

Q: Which of the following is correct about UVstop?
(a) It provides clothing with UV protection.
(b) It is generally used as a laundry detergent.
(c) It enables clothes to block out UV completely.
(d) It is a brand of high-potency sunscreen lotion.

28. Digital World will issue a full refund for items returned within 90 days of purchase in mint condition. If an item was sent to you as a gift, we can send you an e-voucher for the amount of the item. Unfortunately, we cannot perform direct item exchanges. Instead, you may exchange items by first obtaining a refund and then by placing a new order for the item you want. On the other hand, if you received an item that was in a damaged or defective condition, then a direct exchange is possible. Visit our website at www. digitalworld.com for return options.

Q: Which of the following is correct according to the passage?
(a) Damaged merchandise cannot be exchanged.
(b) Items can be exchanged directly if they were gifts.
(c) Items may be exchanged by returning and reordering.
(d) Customers may choose between a voucher and a refund.

29. Cleisthenes, a nobleman of Athens, is often considered the father of democracy for reforming the constitution of Athens and setting it on a democratic footing. In 507 BC, he divided Athens' citizenry into ten tribes according to geographic location. Then, he directed each tribe to choose 50 men to serve for one year on a so-called Council of Five Hundred. This council did not decide but rather proposed laws to an assembly made up of primarily wealthy citizens that debated and authorized laws. While this arrangement was not a fully realized democracy, Cleisthenes' system did anticipate modern democracy.

Q: Which of the following is correct according to the passage?
(a) Athens' ten tribes lived in different geographic locations.
(b) The number of men selected from each tribe was different.
(c) The job of the Council of Five Hundred was to decide laws.
(d) Cleisthenes' system was based on the world's first democracy.

30. If you suffer from persistent heartburn that fails to respond to antacids or changes in diet, it is likely that you have acid reflux disease. Acid reflux is a chronic condition that, if left untreated, can cause permanent damage to the delicate tissues of the esophagus. However, the disease can be controlled. For many, a prescription drug called Fluxnon, taken once daily, provides relief from acid reflux. Consult your doctor to see if Fluxnon is right for you.

Q: Which of the following is correct according to the passage?
(a) Damage caused by acid reflux can be permanent.
(b) Heartburn is a known cause of acid reflux disease.
(c) Antacids treats acid reflux disease very effectively.
(d) Fluxnon must be taken twice a day to treat acid reflux.

31. The word "refrigerator" dates back to 17th-century England, and it was used to describe a variety of chambers and vessels used for cooling. But what we know today as a refrigerator has a more recent history. It was not until 1918 that a company called Frigidaire began producing the first electric refrigerators. They were ungainly and expensive—the cheapest sold for around $900, which was as much as the cost of a good car. Not surprisingly, sales were slow. As late as 1921, only 5,000 refrigerators had been made in America. By 1931, however, with better models and prices, production of refrigerators had soared to a million a year.

Q: Which of the following is correct according to the passage?
(a) The electric refrigerator was originated by Frigidaire.
(b) One million refrigerators were manufactured in 1921.
(c) Refrigerator sales reached 5,000 in 1921.
(d) The first refrigerators sold well.

32. The saffron crocus is a flower that is cultivated for its red pollen receptors, which are dried to produce the flavorful spice called saffron. Compared to other seasonings, saffron is expensive since a field area of 2,000 square meters is required to produce one kilogram of the spice. Also, domestication has rendered the flower sterile, which means that human intervention is necessary for its propagation. This is a labor-intensive process that also contributes to the high cost of the spice.

Q: Which of the following is correct about the saffron crocus according to the passage?
(a) Its flowers are colored bright yellow.
(b) Its petals are used to produce a spice.
(c) It requires human assistance to reproduce.
(d) Its spice can be produced without much difficulty.

33. For effective relief of cold symptoms, take one Adex capsule with a full glass of water every four hours. Do not exceed six tablets in 24 hours. This medication may be taken with food or milk if stomach upset occurs. Reduce dosage if nervousness or dizziness occurs. Do not crush, chew or break the capsules, as this may destroy the long-term action of the drug and increase side effects. For children six to twelve years, give half the adult dosage. For children under six years old, consult your physician.

Q: What can be inferred from the instructions?
(a) Dizziness occurs more often in children than in adults.
(b) Doubling the dosage will help relieve symptoms quicker.
(c) Symptoms generally disappear within 24 hours of taking Adex.
(d) Not all children under six years old may be allowed to take the medicine.

34. After decades of rejection by the fashion world and consumers due to the abuse of animals, fur is back in fashion. Regrettably, a new generation of fashion designers and models, who were not a part of the anti-fur protests of the 80s and early 90s, are now promoting fur fashions. Earlier this year in Milan, design houses presented models in full-length fox and mink furs. And this month the influential glamour magazine *Fascination* ran a 12-page promotion featuring fur clothing designed by several up-and-coming designers. Given this pro-fur revival, it appears that even moral convictions and respect for other living things go in and out of fashion as easily as clothes do.

Q: Which of the following statements would the writer most likely agree with?
(a) Fashion models of this generation are as classy as ever.
(b) Fashion designers of today are at last showing originality.
(c) The revival of fur is a sad indictment of the fashion industry.
(d) The fashion industry is revitalized thanks to the revival of fur.

35.

Dear Mr. Mackson,

I am very pleased to be able to write to you and tell you that we have accepted your article for publication in our magazine *Educational Monthly*. Everyone on our editorial staff agreed that the article presents a very strong argument for the exclusion of computers from most public school classes. Your insight, ingenuity and originality are to be praised. Please find enclosed a check for the amount of $500. We would very much appreciate receiving any other articles you would like to submit for publication.

Yours sincerely,
Spencer Bisk
Senior Editor, *Educational Monthly*

Q: What can be inferred from the letter?
(a) *Educational Monthly* offers practical computing advice to teachers.
(b) Mr. Mackson will become a new employee of *Educational Monthly*.
(c) *Educational Monthly* staff were impressed by Mr. Mackson's article.
(d) Mr. Mackson may receive a higher payment for his next submission.

36. One of the first things that amazed anthropologist Jean Liedloff in her study of the Yequana, an indigenous tribe of the rain forests in Venezuela, was that the tribe did not have a word for work. Tribe members did not distinguish work from other ways of spending time, either. When Liedloff observed how they performed everything as a leisure activity, she realized how much modern societies have segregated life into the opposing conditions of work and leisure. The Yequana, in her view, had an incredibly relaxed way of living, even though they kept themselves busy.

Q: What can be inferred about the Yequana based on Jean Liedloff's experiences?
(a) They were ignorant about life's realities compared to Westerners.
(b) They could not understand why Liedloff was studying them.
(c) They did not work hard except when observed by Liedloff.
(d) They accomplished work without regarding it as a burden.

37. Izaak Walton was an English writer known for *The Complete Angler*, a book about fishing published in 1653. It was such a popular book during Walton's lifetime that it went through five editions. Not only does it describe angling techniques, but it also gives a picture of the peace and simple pleasure of country life. Up until the last century, lovers of fishing praised the book and its author unreservedly. But Walton's fame has diminished somewhat in recent years because of the discovery of a book called *The Arte of Angling* published in 1577, which contains some identical material.

Q: What does the passage imply about Izaak Walton?
(a) His book was not as successful as *The Arte of Angling*.
(b) He made more errors in his book than was previously thought.
(c) He plagiarized material from an earlier book for his fishing book.
(d) His attitude toward fishing changed after reading *The Arte of Angling*.

Part III **Questions 38 — 40**

Read the passage. Then identify the option that does NOT belong.

38. As societies become more multicultural, international food culture is becoming more commonplace. (a) Sushi bars in New York City draw restaurant-goers from a wide variety of backgrounds. (b) The national dish in Britain is a generous portion of fish and chips eaten with salt and vinegar. (c) In Tokyo, Western fast food of almost any variety can be found with little effort. (d) And, in Vladivostok, it is not difficult to find kimchi or Korean-style red pepper paste at local markets.

39. The growing popularity of E. Stuart's latest novel, *The Faded Past*, comes at a time when a flurry of attention is being paid to Canadian writers. (a) Stuart is one of the finest living writers in the English language, with a startling imagination and a piercing intellect. (b) Stuart's first collection of poetry was expected to sell well in the Canadian community, but failed to make any significant impact. (c) His new prose work has had broad appeal with its mix of realism and post-colonial themes. (d) Critics are proclaiming the novel a must-read, especially for its relevance to contemporary Canadians.

40. The Juvenile Drug Rehabilitation program helps young people overcome their substance abuse through a strict therapeutic program. (a) For the most part, incentives inspire juveniles to succeed and stick with the program. (b) The program is not easy and requires a strong commitment not just from juveniles but from parents or guardians. (c) Juveniles must agree to fulfill all weekly requirements and accept sanctions for certain transgressions. (d) Sanctions apply, for example, if a juvenile misses a therapy session or has been caught using drugs.

This is the end of the Reading Comprehension section. Please remain seated until the proctor has instructed otherwise. You are NOT allowed to turn to any other section of the test.

Listening Comprehension

Grammar

Vocabulary

Reading Comprehension

LISTENING COMPREHENSION

DIRECTIONS

1. In the Listening Comprehension section, all content will be presented orally rather than in written form.

2. This section contains 4 parts. In parts I and II, each passage will be read only once. In parts III and IV, each passage and its corresponding question will be read twice. But in all sections, the options will be read only once. After listening to the passage and question, listen to the options and choose the best answer.

Part I **Questions 1—15**

You will now hear fifteen conversation fragments, each made up of a single spoken statement followed by four spoken responses. Choose the most appropriate response to the statement.

Part II **Questions 16—30**

You will now hear fifteen conversation fragments, each made up of three spoken statements followed by four spoken responses. Choose the most appropriate response to complete the conversation.

Part III **Questions 31—45**

You will now hear fifteen complete conversations. For each item, you will hear a conversation and its corresponding question, both of which will be read twice. Then you will hear four options which will be read only once. Choose the option that best answers the question.

Part IV **Questions 46—60**

You will now hear fifteen spoken monologues. For each item, you will hear a monologue and its corresponding question, both of which will be read twice. Then you will hear four options which will be read only once. Choose the option that best answers the question.

TEPS

GRAMMAR

Part I Questions 1—20

Choose the best answer for the blank.

1. A: Why does your father upset you?
B: He ___________ my sisters but never me.

(a) praise
(b) praises
(c) is praising
(d) are praising

2. A: What did you think of Georgina's cooking?
B: Amazing. I was ___________ impressed.

(a) so
(b) too
(c) such
(d) many

3. A: I didn't buy a present for Dad.
B: I didn't do ___________ gift shopping, either.

(a) any
(b) each
(c) some
(d) every

4. A: I need another pen. Mine isn't working.
B: Here, ___________ a spare one you can use.

(a) I get
(b) I've got
(c) I was getting
(d) I'll be getting

5. A: Why didn't you send Mom a Mother's Day card last week?
B: Because ___________.

(a) you forgot to remind me
(b) forgot to remind you did
(c) you forgot reminding to me
(d) reminding you forgot to me

6. A: Why were you late for the meeting?
B: I didn't know that the schedule ___________.

(a) will change
(b) had changed
(c) will have changed
(d) has been changing

7. A: So, are you enjoying your visit?
B: Oh, yes. I ___________ to be here.

(a) delight
(b) am delighted
(c) was delighting
(d) have been delighted

8. A: What are you going to give to the relief fund?
B: I will just donate ___________ I can spare.

(a) whom
(b) which
(c) what
(d) that

9. A: Hi, I'd like to buy a webcam.

    B: OK, we have several different
    ___________ to choose from here.

    (a) those
    (b) them
    (c) ones
    (d) ours

10. A: Is Janet the only Spanish speaker in
    your family?

    B: No, Mom can speak Spanish and
    ___________ Sarah.

    (a) so
    (b) so can
    (c) so speaks
    (d) so can speak

11. A: Should I take calculus this semester?

    B: ___________ your problems with
    math, I wouldn't recommend it.

    (a) I know
    (b) Knowing
    (c) Have known
    (d) To be known

12. A: I ___________ be able to go to the
    party.

    B: That's a shame. It'll be a lot of fun.

    (a) shouldn't
    (b) couldn't
    (c) won't
    (d) can't

13. A: How long have you been getting
    your hair cut here?

    B: I think I ___________ here for almost
    10 years.

    (a) was coming
    (b) would come
    (c) would be coming
    (d) have been coming

14. A: Aren't you over the flu yet?

    B: No, the older you get, ___________.

    (a) the longer to recover it takes
    (b) to recover it takes the longer
    (c) it takes the longer to recover
    (d) the longer it takes to recover

15. A: What happened at your surprise
    party?

    B: ___________ the door, when
    everyone screamed "Surprise!"

    (a) I had opened no sooner
    (b) No sooner had I opened
    (c) I had not opened sooner
    (d) Not sooner I had opened

16. A: Sam's so courageous to go
    skydiving.

    B: Frankly, he is ___________.

    (a) crazier than braver
    (b) more crazy than brave
    (c) more crazy rather than brave
    (d) crazier more than is he braver

17. A: Elise is going to the airport to see Joel off.

    B: I suggest we ___________ there to see him off, too.

    (a) be
    (b) were
    (c) will be
    (d) are being

18. A: I can't believe we lost the game.

    B: ___________ we tried our best.

    (a) What important that it is
    (b) That's what is important
    (c) What's important is that
    (d) That important it is that

19. A: Did you pay off your loan?

    B: No, I just paid off ___________ portion of it.

    (a) a
    (b) the
    (c) any
    (d) every

20. A: I'm excited about studying overseas.

    B: Well, ___________ here in Seoul.

    (a) rather would you stay
    (b) I rather you would stay
    (c) you would rather stayed
    (d) I would rather you stayed

Part II   **Questions 21—40**

Choose the best answer for the blank.

---

21. Michael had a paper ___________ by the next morning, so he did not go out with his friends.

    (a) write
    (b) writing
    (c) to write
    (d) to be writing

22. It was the judge's opinion that ___________ contestants were very talented.

    (a) all
    (b) much
    (c) either
    (d) neither

23. Today almost 1.5 billion consumers own mobile phones ___________ various shapes and sizes.

    (a) of
    (b) at
    (c) to
    (d) for

24. The secretary was ___________ she had ever been to a meeting.

    (a) later than
    (b) as late than
    (c) more than later
    (d) than the most late

25. Developing skill related fitness, which includes coordination, reaction time, speed and power, __________ part of any balanced exercise program.

(a) is
(b) are
(c) was
(d) were

26. Being the first to set foot on the Moon's surface is an achievement __________ Neil Armstrong will always be remembered.

(a) where
(b) in what
(c) whatever
(d) for which

27. The couple __________ married for 60 years next month.

(a) is being
(b) had been
(c) was being
(d) will have been

28. So many trained staff __________ that there are few experienced staff left.

(a) are laying off
(b) will be laid off
(c) have been laid off
(d) had been laying off

29. Temperatures may still continue to rise __________ greenhouse gas emissions are immediately stabilized.

(a) yet
(b) that
(c) if only
(d) even if

30. In the 1500s, witch-hunts resulted in the execution of many innocent victims, __________ were women.

(a) about three-quarters of whom
(b) whom about three-quarters of them
(c) about them three-quarters of whom
(d) whom about of those three-quarters

31. The photographer rushed up to the woman, __________ he knew would make a great model, and gave her his business card.

(a) whose
(b) which
(c) who
(d) that

32. __________ installing more computers in our schools will not be a panacea for problems in our education system.

(a) Suffice it to say that
(b) It suffices that to say
(c) That suffices it to say
(d) To say it suffices that

33. __________ the report is left-of-center is a reflection of media bias.

(a) Once
(b) That
(c) As
(d) If

34. __________ if they do not want to run the risk of developing serious health complications later.

(a) Must quit the smokers
(b) Quitting the smokers must
(c) Must is for smokers to quit
(d) Quitting is a must for smokers

35. An unhealthy diet possibly reduces average life expectancy ___________ 1.2 years.

(a) by
(b) for
(c) through
(d) between

36. ___________ out in the country, the elderly couple rarely sees their adult children.

(a) They are living
(b) As they do living
(c) Living as they do
(d) So as they do living

37. Never ___________ a cruise before, Liz was concerned that she might get seasick.

(a) having taken
(b) have taken
(c) taking
(d) taken

38. With a number of opponents ___________ the law, there is a reasonable chance it will be passed.

(a) in favor of both houses
(b) that favor in both houses
(c) in both houses in favor of
(d) of both houses that favor in

39. The police chief, along with the mayor, ___________ committed to ending the crime wave before it gets worse.

(a) is
(b) are
(c) was
(d) were

40. Visitors to the zoo are not allowed near the polar bear mothers and cubs ___________ them.

(a) not so as to disturb
(b) so as not disturb to
(c) not as so disturb to
(d) so as not to disturb

Identify the option that contains an awkward expression or an error in grammar.

41. (a) A: It looks like food prices will be going up again, along with the price of gas.

(b) B: That's because the government didn't react fast enough to the economic downturn.

(c) A Yeah, if something was done earlier, we wouldn't be in this situation now.

(d) B: Right. This government clearly doesn't have a clue about how to run the economy.

42. (a) A: Do you think Professor Harvey would make a good supervisor for my PhD?

(b) B: I don't know. You should just go and discuss the matter with her.

(c) A But I wanted to find out what other people thought about her first.

(d) B: Just go and find out for yourself, since you know what you're looked for.

43. (a) A: I think I've studied enough chemistry for today.

(b) B: Me, too. I think I'm going to head home now.

(c) A Would you mind to drop me off on your way?

(d) B: No, not at all. We don't live far from each other.

44. (a) A: I might stay home tonight. I don't feel like going out.

(b) B: It makes me angry, hear you say that after we'd made plans.

(c) A But we didn't make definite plans. Besides, it's cold outside.

(d) B: Well, if you're going to be like that, I'll just go out with someone else.

45. (a) A: I'm so glad Monday's a holiday next week. I need a break.

(b) B: Yeah, we would take advantage of the extra long weekend.

(c) A I'm all for that, but what do you suggest we do?

(d) B: Let's take a trip up to one of the ski resorts for a change.

Part IV **Questions 46—50**

Identify the option that contains an awkward expression or an error in grammar.

46. (a) Which of the appliances in your home would be the hardest to live without? (b) The refrigerator was the answer most people give to that question in a recent survey. (c) That is hardly a surprising result considering the widespread use of the refrigerator in developed countries. (d) More than 99.5% of family kitchens in the US, for example, have a refrigerator.

47. (a) First-time car buyers should shop around before settling on a method of payment. (b) If your credit rating is excellent, you could get a loan from a bank to help purchase a car. (c) But remember, interest rates offering by lenders can vary according to their policies. (d) Before taking out a loan, compare interest rates at several different banks to find the best.

48. (a) Plague has been responsible for large numbers of deaths during several different periods of European history. (b) The most deadly outbreak occurred in the 14th century, from 1347 to the end of 1350. (c) The disease was brought to Sicily by infected crew and rats on trading ships that had come from the Black Sea. (d) From Sicily, it spread northwest across Europe, killing one-third of Europe's populations in less than three years.

49. (a) Until about two centuries ago, fossils were mysterious objects that cultures explained in varying ways. (b) Some thought fossils were weapons left behind by the gods or the remains of animals that had not made it onto Noah's ark. (c) In the 1800s, scientists realized that many fossils were of ancient animals to science known not, which they called dinosaurs. (d) Only then did people understand what fossils were and begin to show an enthusiasm for fossil hunting.

50. (a) As people age, they naturally develop what is known as short-term memory loss. (b) This loss is caused by the inevitable shrinking of a part of the brain that plays a key role in processing new information. (c) However, when short-term memory problems are more pronounced, it is called mild cognitive impairment. (d) People diagnosed with this have up to the 50% chance of developing Alzheimer's within four years.

This is the end of the Grammar section. Do NOT move on to the next section until instructed to do so. You are NOT allowed to turn to any other section of the test.

Vocabulary

Part I Questions 1—25

Choose the best answer for the blank.

---

1. A: How is your new job going?

B: It's hard work, but the ___________ is good.

(a) rental
(b) price
(c) pay
(d) fee

2. A: I lost my wallet, and then I slipped and fell while looking for it.

B: Wow. It certainly is not your ___________ day.

(a) easy
(b) busy
(c) lucky
(d) funny

3. A: Hi Denise. What have you been up to lately?

B: Oh, just trying to ___________ healthy.

(a) stay
(b) hold
(c) grow
(d) contain

4. A: Ouch! You stepped on my foot!

B: Oh, sorry. I didn't ___________ to.

(a) put
(b) will
(c) mean
(d) expect

5. A: Can you help me with this puzzle?

B: Well, I'm ___________ at the moment, but I can in twenty minutes.

(a) dug in
(b) tied up
(c) set down
(d) pulled off

6. A: Do you need help with that box?

B: No, I can ___________ it.

(a) suffer
(b) afford
(c) handle
(d) tolerate

7. A: It feels warmer today than it did yesterday.

B: Yes, temperatures are ___________.

(a) rising
(b) lifting
(c) falling
(d) dropping

8. A: Hi. Is your manager in?

B: I'm sorry, he's not ___________ at the moment.

(a) possible
(b) available
(c) reasonable
(d) convenient

9. A: Let's meet during the holidays.

    B: OK. I'll let you know when I'm
       __________.

    (a) free
    (b) idle
    (c) open
    (d) vacant

10. A: Excuse me, do you know where the
       nearest bank is?

    B: There's one down a __________
       between 2nd and 3rd street.

    (a) block
    (b) corner
    (c) square
    (d) section

11. A: Tom isn't himself these days.

    B: I know. He's been really __________
       lately.

    (a) over
    (b) away
    (c) down
    (d) under

12. A: Now we have to go through customs.

    B: It won't take long. We have nothing
       to __________.

    (a) lose
    (b) offer
    (c) record
    (d) declare

13. A: Hello, C&M department store.

    B: Could you __________ me to the
       Electronics department, please?

    (a) join
    (b) link
    (c) shift
    (d) connect

14. A: There's no way I'll finish my report
       on time.

    B: Then you had better ask for a(n)
       __________.

    (a) allowance
    (b) extension
    (c) renewal
    (d) delay

15. A: Congratulations on your promotion!
       You must be very excited.

    B: Yes. I'm really __________.

    (a) agitated
    (b) overjoyed
    (c) concerned
    (d) stimulated

16. A: I'd like to rent a car.

    B: Sure, we have all kinds of __________.

    (a) crafts
    (b) carriers
    (c) mobiles
    (d) vehicles

17. A: How did you know I'd want to see this movie?

B: Because your taste in movies is so ___________.

(a) anxious
(b) calculative
(c) mechanical
(d) predictable

18. A: What's wrong? You don't look well.

B: I'm OK. Just feeling a bit _________.

(a) off the cuff
(b) on the fence
(c) over the top
(d) under the weather

19. A: I can't believe how badly I did on the math test.

B: Me, neither. My score was ___________.

(a) flat
(b) base
(c) flimsy
(d) pathetic

20. A: I'm so glad we have a dishwasher.

B: Yes. It's great to have such modern ___________.

(a) techniques
(b) consolations
(c) conveniences
(d) machinations

21. A: Look at that comet in the sky.

B: Wow! It's ___________.

(a) prevalent
(b) florescent
(c) exuberant
(d) spectacular

22. A: Mike has a beautiful stone cottage near a lake in the country.

B: That sounds ___________.

(a) lofty
(b) idyllic
(c) gracious
(d) amicable

23. A: Is it true that Jim broke his arm?

B: It is. His arm is in a ___________.

(a) bust
(b) loop
(c) sling
(d) ridge

24. A: For some reason, John thinks I'm divorced when I've never even been married.

B: Then, go and ___________.

(a) set the record straight
(b) beat around the bush
(c) kick up your heels
(d) burst at the seams

25. A: This author publishes at least one book a year.

B: Wow. She's really ___________.

(a) prolific
(b) luxuriant
(c) abundant
(d) reproductive

Part II Questions 26—50

Choose the best answer for the blank.

26. The young sales assistant went to a great deal of ___________ to help customers.

(a) trial
(b) service
(c) trouble
(d) pressure

27. In summer, some businesses at Westfield Plaza put up a ___________ that says, "No shirt, no shoes, no service."

(a) guide
(b) mark
(c) post
(d) sign

28. The quarterly reports are ___________ by the end of the week.

(a) owed
(b) paid
(c) due
(d) fair

29. People are ___________ functionally illiterate if they cannot read or write well enough to do things like hold a job, finish school or vote.

(a) kept
(b) made
(c) nominated
(d) considered

30. Next year, a nationwide conference is scheduled for groups whose ___________ interest is in wild-life preservation.

(a) trivial
(b) partial
(c) neutral
(d) common

31. Early Spanish explorers returned to Europe with ___________ plants they had found in the New World.

(a) desolate
(b) innate
(c) exotic
(d) feeble

32. For security, passenger baggage must be placed on the conveyor belt for x-ray ___________.

(a) shooting
(b) screening
(c) mirroring
(d) projecting

33. BJ Electronics is well-known for making strong and ___________ home appliances.

(a) excitable
(b) minimal
(c) reliable
(d) factual

34. By observing how stars form elsewhere in our galaxy, astronomers can ___________ the conditions that led to the formation of our solar system.

(a) deduce
(b) presume
(c) implicate
(d) conjugate

35. The station's policy requires ___________ to be censored from TV documentaries.

(a) eulogies
(b) profanities
(c) extremities
(d) pleasantries

36. Although my grandmother is deaf now, she was ___________ in her earlier years for her innovative piano compositions.

(a) integrated
(b) authorized
(c) acquainted
(d) recognized

37. It is a myth that reading books in poor light can ___________ your eyes.

(a) fracture
(b) damage
(c) decay
(d) abuse

38. It is better to make supportive rather than ___________ comments to your children so that they do not feel like failures.

(a) ethical
(b) critical
(c) feasible
(d) hazardous

39. There is no ___________ that the quality and depth of research done by Dr. Lee's team have been outstanding.

(a) competition
(b) comparison
(c) question
(d) division

40. The new CEO quickly ___________ the people he liked to key positions.

(a) settled
(b) appointed
(c) appropriated
(d) implemented

41. At Crown Pharmaceuticals, we do not ___________ the benefits of our products.

(a) diffuse
(b) retaliate
(c) alternate
(d) exaggerate

42. Web designers strive to keep ___________ with the changing Internet industry.

(a) obedient
(b) suitable
(c) current
(d) tardy

43. In the poet Gerard Manley Hopkins's private letters, it is possible to detect his ___________ ambition to rival Christina Rossetti as a poetic artist.

(a) indented
(b) scribbled
(c) informed
(d) concealed

44. ___________, or chronic anxiety over imaginary health problems, can be treated with therapy and medication.

(a) Inertia
(b) Euphoria
(c) Aphrodisia
(d) Hypochondria

45. A local company will have to pay a hefty fine after it was caught making ___________ claims about its operations.

(a) fraudulent
(b) intentional
(c) meticulous
(d) rudimentary

46. In the 1500s, the Italian city of Venice ___________ a salt monopoly without actually being involved in salt production.

(a) credited
(b) mentored
(c) established
(d) conscripted

47. Generosity is no longer a virtue if it is ___________, making it an attempt to enhance one's status.

(a) impetuous
(b) punctilious
(c) ostentatious
(d) philanthropic

48. The advertising industry spends billions, ___________ consumers with endless advertisements via television.

(a) cascading
(b) indulging
(c) submerging
(d) bombarding

49. Many opposition leaders were ___________ during the violent military coup.

(a) reiterated
(b) liquidated
(c) brandished
(d) deteriorated

50. Since the College has not increased its enrollment, the argument for building more parking space is ___________.

(a) wont
(b) moot
(c) stalwart
(d) partisan

This is the end of the Vocabulary section. Do NOT move on to the Reading Comprehension section until instructed to do so. You are NOT allowed to turn to any other section of the test.

READING COMPREHENSION

DIRECTIONS

This part of the exam tests your ability to comprehend reading passages. You will have 45 minutes to complete the 40 questions. Be sure to follow the directions given by the proctor.

Part I Questions 1—16

Read the passage. Then choose the option that best completes the passage.

1. A recent study revealed that people who consume a high volume of snacks often select them based solely on their availability. Office workers, for instance, are likely to visit stores or vending machines stocked with unhealthy, sugary sweets simply because they are close. So, if you possess this tendency, keep your desk drawer filled with nutritious and healthy foods. As long as you have ________________________________, you will not be so tempted to frequent the vending machines.

   (a) a place to store things
   (b) a lower chance of overeating
   (c) a snack to give to your friends
   (d) a healthy snack within reach

2. We are seeking an individual to fill the spot of General Manager for a busy, high-profile company in Central London. The successful applicant will be asked to oversee a catering staff of more than 25 and be responsible for all financial accounts representing the board. Applicants must be well presented and are encouraged to have ten years or more of work experience in a similar position. Only applicants meeting these qualifications will be considered ________________________________.

   (a) to work as a staff secretary
   (b) for a temporary part-time job
   (c) to manage our product warehouse
   (d) for this managerial position

3. Fathers have ________________________________, maintain some psychologists. They insist that a great deal of future romantic relationships that take place in a female's life will be affected—positively or negatively—by the way she perceives and interacts with her father. If he rejects and ignores her, she will spend her life trying to find his replacement in her heart. If he is warm and affectionate, she will seek a partner to match him. If he expresses how beautiful, worthy and feminine she is, she will be inclined to see herself that way. If he ridicules her appearance, she will probably have self-esteem problems in her adult years.

(a) a tremendous impact on their daughters' lives
(b) often neglected their daughters' feelings
(c) less of an influence on children than mothers
(d) too little free time to spend with their children

4. I received a lot of useful gifts when my baby was born. Unfortunately, some were not so useful, but I was to blame for that. An example of a not-so-useful gift was sent by the wife of one of my law partners: a pink-and-white striped dress with a white apron. She had thought Ashton Jessie was a girl's name. I didn't help matters when I neglected to put a blue ribbon on the birth announcement. It was therefore my own fault that

____________________________________.

(a) the dress was too small for her
(b) she had confused my son for a girl
(c) the name sounded like a product brand
(d) she didn't know I had given birth to twins

5. Businesses have grown and prospered in port cities for centuries because of shipping. Then, in the 19th century, they spread across nations thanks to the development of railways. In the 20th century, automobile and motorways further helped businesses along major roads to grow and prosper. With increased air travel, the same pattern of development emerged. Businesses _______________________________. As with centers of transportation in the past, airports are becoming hubs of major business developments.

(a) have found it hard to survive nowadays
(b) are growing and thriving around airports
(c) are helping to build more airports worldwide
(d) have found airport crowding to be a big problem

6. After composing an environmental report related to a proposed development, you need to do two things to have it approved. First, turn in a copy of your environmental report to the Environmental Protection Agency for review and approval. Second, make your report and draft proposal public in a newspaper. The public should also have access to copies of all relevant documents for review and should have sufficient time to issue responses of approval or rejection. The Ministry of Environment alone may approve the proposal, provided that ___________________________________.

(a) the correct fees and charges are paid on time
(b) the site is not condemned by government officials
(c) a cost analysis shows that it is within budget
(d) a consensus is reached by all parties concerned

7. The Vietnam War ended in defeat for America, but many people still argue that the war could have been won. Some Vietnam veterans will say the only reason they lost was because of restrictions imposed on their operations by politicians in their own country. Others say they lost because their country was not united with a collective resolve to see the war through to victory. These opinions reflect how America ___________________________________. Ultimately, the war was fought on two fronts: one abroad and one at home.

(a) had underestimated the Vietnamese
(b) was a country divided against itself
(c) justified sending troops to Vietnam
(d) needed support from its key allies

8.

Dear Mr. Mitchell,

We have gone through your film script entitled *Hotel Flamingo* and ___________________________________. Though the chief producer clearly sees the message you are trying to convey, he feels that there is something missing, and I agree with him. However, we are both convinced there is a quality movie here based on the strength of the characters. Therefore, we were wondering if you could visit the studio on Monday after 9 to discuss possible revisions. We would very much appreciate it if we could discuss the script with you in person.

Sincerely,
J.B. Griffin

(a) are sorry but we could never use it
(b) congratulate you on getting it produced
(c) have some reservations about it as is
(d) are worried about the subject matter

9.   A two-day seminar hosted by the Federal Trade Commission began today, in which consumer advocates, IT industry representatives and academics addressed privacy issues surrounding online target advertising. The seminar was in response to concerns expressed by consumer protection groups about the practice of tracking users' activities online and so-called "behavioral advertising." Advertisers often collect user information, such as searches done, sites visited and content viewed, without user consent. Consumer protection groups, however, are insisting that ___________________________________.

(a) target advertising is in the consumer's interests
(b) users must be made more aware of online fraud
(c) online shopping is much safer than it used to be
(d) gathering data covertly is an invasion of privacy

10. The way people make judgments about others on the basis of body movements and facial expressions was the subject of a study done by Anderson and Rose in 1999. They presented students with 30-second silent videos of lectures by college professors and then had them rate the professors on a variety of personal qualities. The student's ratings, Anderson and Rose found, were fairly consistent. What's more, these ratings closely matched end-of-semester evaluations by the professors' own students. This suggests that ___________________________________.

(a) communication depends heavily on verbal skills
(b) using video lessons is an effective teaching method
(c) judgments based on body language can be fairly accurate
(d) a professor's popularity depends solely on lecture content

11. Motor skills develop with maturation, but, at the same time, application of these skills is also essential to that development. This point was dramatically demonstrated by a study done on institutionalized orphans in Iran, who had spent the majority of their first few years lying flat on their backs in cribs. These babies were never placed in a sitting position or even propped up on pillows. Deprived of normal opportunities to acquire and develop motor skills, none of the children could walk and less than half could even sit without help. The obvious conclusion was that _______________________________.

(a) infant motor skills develop poorly without practice
(b) child development depends on having an adequate diet
(c) institutionalization can destroy the lives of children
(d) maturation had little effect on hand-to-eye coordination

12. The origin of the Chinese writing system, which supposedly can be traced back to 2500-1900 BC, is still a mystery. The world's oldest form of writing dates back to about 3200 BC in Sumer, some 4,000 miles west of early Chinese urban centers, and by 2200 BC, writing was being practiced 2,600 miles west of Chinese urban centers in the Indus Valley. However, no ancient writing systems are known to have existed in the regions between the Indus Valley and China. This indicates that the Chinese most likely had no knowledge of foreign writing systems, at least during these times. Most scholars thus assume that _______________________________.

(a) Chinese evolved independently of other writing systems
(b) Chinese writing was influenced by Indus Valley languages
(c) Chinese predates the writing system developed in Sumer
(d) Chinese writing inspired other outlying writing systems

13. Famed author Jorge Luis Borges wrote about eternal life, and other topics of immortality, perhaps more provocatively and interestingly than any other writer. In his short story *The Immortal*, he creates a people whose acquisition of immortality has ruined their joy of being alive. As implications of their immortality, they accept that over an infinite course of time, everything that can occur will, and that they will do everything imaginable eventually. This discovery kills their desire and hope, which is only fleetingly aroused by sensual experience. For them, _______________________________.

(a) every new experience is valuable
(b) time no longer has any relevance
(c) immortality is all they had hoped for
(d) rebirth was thought to follow death

14. Today saw the launch of New York's first ______________________.
Starting in London, with ads in five major subway stations, it will expand to Italy,
Ireland and Spain next week. New York's Mayor Bloomberg said it was necessary
to undo the harm done by a crackdown on illegal immigration, with harsh entry
requirements discouraging law-abiding visitors from visiting the city. "Current entry
requirements are making it harder for people from other countries to visit New York
and that's hurting businesses in this city," Bloomberg said.

(a) trial of a new security system for subways
(b) ads to help promote local restaurant businesses
(c) major international tourism marketing campaign
(d) touring fashion show with the city's top designers

15. During the nineteenth century, Western countries still made great efforts to learn the
Enlightenment ideals of freedom and individual liberty. Such ideals were clearly not
in accordance with the continuation of slavery and the enduring pursuit of oppressive
colonial practices. As a result, while optimism and faith in progress held out, numerous
impediments to reform, such as a resistance to cultural and racial equality, had to be
tackled. ______________________, by the close of the century, reform
movements had been launched that were aimed at stopping the slave trade, expanding
voting rights, and assimilating immigrants.

(a) Accordingly
(b) Nevertheless
(c) Meanwhile
(d) Besides

16. In spite of its success, the British film industry has suffered from a lack of government
investment for years. This has meant that, from the 1950s onwards, British film-makers
have been unable to compete with wealthy Hollywood studios and their extravagant
productions. Such adversity has forced them to focus on making films in genres that
usually do not require large budgets, such as horror and comedy, just to survive.
______________________, directors have frequently left for America,
lured by the promise of big film budgets and broader artistic horizons.

(a) Consequently
(b) Regardless
(c) Actually
(d) Instead

Part II **Questions 17—37**

Read the passage and the question. Then choose the option that best answers the
question.

17. As a small residential institution, New Forest Academy places great emphasis not only
on supporting students, but also on encouraging parental involvement in our school. The
Academy fosters wholesome communication between parents and school staff either
through video conferencing or face to face. We provide parents with updates of their
sons' progress via weekly email, and we have parent nights and alumni clubs parents can
join. New Forest Academy is a family affair.

Q: What is mainly being said about the New Forest Academy in the passage?
(a) It expects a strong commitment from students.
(b) It regards parental involvement as a priority.
(c) It has successful students due to its support.
(d) It hopes to reverse a decline in enrollment.

18. Learning to handle problems diplomatically is an essential skill for career success. In
meetings, for instance, you'll continuously hear unnecessary, irrelevant or downright
ridiculous remarks. You may feel you do not have to tolerate them and you may want
to tell the person across the conference room how silly his or her suggestions are. Resist
that urge. Keep in mind that your goal is not to create conflict. Limit your discussion
only to work issues. Your goal should be to advance your career by focusing on
producing solutions for the work at hand.

Q: What is the main idea of the passage?
(a) Make your views heard when you know you are right.
(b) Try not to say stupid things while at work meetings.
(c) Advance your career by choosing your words wisely.
(d) Do not criticize your superiors in the workplace.

19. Not everyone in Western culture considers beauty and attractiveness to be related only
to youth. A recent study indicates that African-American women place less emphasis on
youth as a factor of being beautiful compared to their Caucasian counterparts. According
to the study, 65% of African-American females claimed that they would get more
beautiful and attractive as they aged, and 22% maintained they would remain the same.
In contrast, most Caucasian females did not like the idea of getting old.

Q: What is mainly being said about African-American women in the passage?
(a) Most do not see aging as causing a loss of beauty.
(b) Most see beauty and youth as strongly linked.
(c) They age differently than women of other races do.
(d) They tend to live longer than Caucasian women.

20. Married couples, whose numbers have been declining for decades as a proportion of American households, now comprise a minority, according to new census figures. The American Community Survey for 2007, issued this month by the Census Bureau, found that 49.7%, or 55.2 million, of the nation's 111.1 million households consisted of married couples—with or without children. That is down from over 52% five years ago. However, this does not mean that marriage itself is in danger, since most Americans do eventually get married.

Q: What is the main idea of the passage?
(a) The number of marriages has been declining steadily in America.
(b) Less than half of American households comprise married couples.
(c) The number of couples in America appears to be on the decrease.
(d) More married couples in America are deciding not to have children.

21. The study of brain cells called neurons was frustrating for early scientists due to the size of the scale they were facing. Brain cells can differ in size, ranging from 4 microns (0.001mm) to 100 microns (0.1mm). As these sizes are at or beyond the limit of what can be observed with the naked eye, development in cellular neuroscience was inconceivable before the emergence of the compound microscope in the late seventeenth century. Even then, stumbling blocks remained. Scientists could not produce the thin slices of brain tissue—not much thicker than the diameter of the cells—needed for effective research.

Q: What is the passage mainly about?
(a) Problems in the early study of brain cells
(b) The unusually small size of brain cells
(c) Various sizes that brain cells can come in
(d) The troubled history of brain cell research

22. David Hume, considered one of the most important figures in Western philosophy, was born in 1711, in Scotland. He grew up during the Enlightenment, a period when rational thought was being applied to all aspects of life. Within this intellectual environment, he pursued the study of literature and philosophy and became well-known as an atheist. However, while it was a time of rationalism, religion still held sway over British society and people in authority did not look upon Hume favorably, sometimes preventing him from attaining prestigious positions because of his beliefs.

Q: What is the main idea of the passage?
(a) Hume was imprisoned in Britain for his atheistic opinions.
(b) Hume's philosophy was deeply influenced by the Enlightenment.
(c) Hume was praised for denouncing the religious culture in Britain.
(d) Hume's atheistic beliefs conflicted with the religious culture of his era.

23. It's that time of year again—time to get ready for the upcoming spring semester. Whether you are searching for the right textbooks for Accounting, History or Database Management, we've got all the answers you'll ever need! Avoid standing in long store lines. Get new or used college textbooks at Etexts.com, or sell back your old textbooks back to us. Win real cash-back deals to pay for your end-of-term festivities! For all your textbook needs, be sure to visit Etexts.com.

Q: Which of the following is correct about Etexts.com?
(a) It sells only old recycled textbooks.
(b) It specializes in science textbooks.
(c) It buys back used college textbooks.
(d) It donates books to needy colleges.

24. Each year on Easter weekend, our family goes on a camping trip with friends near a remote stretch of river in Victoria, Australia. It's a six-hour drive from the city. The last 20 kilometers to the camping site is an incredibly tricky stretch. We have to drive on a narrow rocky track, often descending a mountain with a steep drop on one side. If you ever run into another car on that narrow stretch of road, a lot of maneuvering is required to get past.

Q: Which of the following is correct according to passage?
(a) The family flies to Victoria every Easter.
(b) The road down to the campsite is narrow.
(c) The drive to the campsite takes two hours.
(d) The camping site is near a remote beach.

25. The Society of Will Writers has been assisting people with their wills for more than a decade in this region. The first step is consulting with one of our legal advisers, who is an underwritten member of the Society of Will Writers. The adviser will visit and offer you professional advice in the comfort of your own home on what kind of actions to take about your estate in the event of death. After your consultation, we can draw up your legal will for only $30 (tax included). Call us now for information on an adviser in your area.

Q: Which of the following is correct about the Society of Will Writers?
(a) It offers a funeral planning service.
(b) It provides legal advice on wills.
(c) It drafts your will for $30 plus tax.
(d) It requires clients to visit its office.

26. Articles should be forwarded to David Stuart, General Editor of *Arts and Artists*, at the mailing address provided on the top of this document. One printed copy of your article along with a cover letter is needed. Please be advised that rejected articles will not be returned to the authors. You may also mail in your articles electronically by email, but at present we only accept Word or Open Document format attachments. If you choose to submit via email, please include your cover letter within the body of the email. Thank you.

Q: Which of the following is correct about submitting articles?
(a) Any file format can be used for email submissions.
(b) All articles must be sent in hard copy.
(c) A single printed copy of an article is acceptable.
(d) A cover letter is not required with an email.

27. Parents living with children show a tendency to eat more fatty foods than those in child-free households, since the kitchens of households with children are more likely to be stocked with high-calorie foods like cookies, white bread, fries and processed meats. Parents purchase these junk foods because they do not have time to cook wholesome home-cooked meals, or are pressured by their children. Some parents are also affected by advertisements promoting the false belief that these foods are the only things children will eat. Once junk foods make their way into the house, adults are more prone to consume them.

Q: Which of the following is correct according to the passage?
(a) Adults without children are more likely to eat fatty foods.
(b) Children eat more high-fat foods than their parents do.
(c) Parents are sometimes influenced by misleading ads.
(d) Parents pressure children into cutting junk foods.

28. A troubling phenomenon called "learned helplessness" is becoming commonplace at nursing homes. Learned helplessness arises when every aspect of people's lives is controlled to the point where they perceive that their actions are of no consequence. The inability to distinguish when actions actually have an effect and the cessation of efforts to influence events eventually lead to depression. However, a recent study demonstrated that when nursing home residents are allowed to make small decisions, such as the timing of visits or caring for a plant, they are happier and suffer less from mental health problems.

Q: Which of the following is correct according to the passage?
(a) Learned helplessness is caused by severe depression.
(b) Frequent visits from family cure learned helplessness.
(c) Empowering nursing home residents makes them happier.
(d) Old people rarely suffer from depression when in nursing homes.

29.

> Hi Daniel,
>
> I wanted to say how pleased I am with your decision to forgo your move to New York and stay with our company. We would surely have been sad to see you leave. I hope staying with us will turn out to be the best choice for you, both personally and professionally. Great things are in store for this company, and I'm certain rewards will come to those who deserve them, like you. If you have any thoughts or concerns you wish to share, remember: I'm only a phone call away.
>
> Best,
> Ric Genkins

Q: Which is correct according to the email?
(a) Daniel was rewarded for staying on with his company.
(b) Daniel has started work for a company in New York.
(c) Ric believes more successes will come to the company.
(d) Ric was sad that Daniel had forgone moving to New York.

30. Ancient Greeks published writings for the public, such as treaties, dedications, accounts and even prayers, on stone. These writings suggest that the ancient Greeks had a high rate of literacy, even among common people. As historians point out, it would have been costly to carve messages into stone, and such expenditure would not have been worth it if many Athenian citizens could not read what was written. Also, many inscriptions end with a clause that translates as "so that all may know," which supports the historians' claim about general literacy.

Q: Which of the following is correct according to the passage?
(a) Only ancient Greeks from wealthier families could read.
(b) Citizens used inscriptions for personal correspondences.
(c) Public inscriptions included prayers and account records.
(d) Inscriptions were too expensive to be made for the public.

31.

> Dear Ms. Baxter,
>
> Having received your letter about your Chambers Mixmaster, it is heartwarming to learn that this appliance has been with your family for almost three decades. Regarding your request to purchase an additional model just like the one you own, I'm afraid the Mixmaster Double Blend you refer to is no longer in production. However, I can guarantee you that our current models are manufactured with the same high standards and feature many improvements over the older Mixmaster models. If you require any further information, please do not hesitate to let me know.
>
> Adrian Morris,
> Chambers Corporation

Q: Which of the following is correct according to the letter?
(a) Mr. Morris will send Ms. Baxter a new Mixmaster.
(b) Mr. Morris's company has stopped making Mixmasters.
(c) Ms. Baxter's Mixmaster model is a discontinued model.
(d) Ms. Baxter bought her first Mixmaster twenty years ago.

32. Since a new traffic law recently went into effect in Japan granting local police the authority to outsource the regulation of illegal parking, a brigade of enthusiastic traffic wardens has been patrolling the streets. Parking fines have jumped 30% compared to last year, the number of abandoned vehicles has dropped by 60% and traffic in crowded cities has never moved so smoothly. Yet there is one major problem: instead of getting motorists to use public transportation, parking enforcement has convinced many to simply remain at home—at a time when the government needs people to go out and spend money to revitalize the economy.

Q: Which of the following is correct about the new traffic law?
(a) It prohibited the outsourcing of illegal parking control.
(b) It has not been effective in freeing up traffic on the road.
(c) It resulted in a 30% reduction of parking fines.
(d) It has failed to persuade people to use public transit.

33. Welcome to Menlow's. You'll be amazed by our incredible selection of clothing for men, women and children. You can save from 20 to 60% daily on all of our apparel, including many of the same designer brands found in department stores and specialty boutiques! We have bargains even cheaper than the ones you'll find in outlet stores — and all this under one roof! Menlow's offers you the fashion you want for less. So why wait? Come and shop with us today!

Q: What can be inferred about Menlow's?
(a) It manufactures its own brand of clothing.
(b) It supplies clothes to department stores and boutiques.
(c) It offers high-quality clothes at reasonable prices.
(d) It exclusively houses high-end boutique apparel.

34. When the Avian Influenza was reported to be spreading rapidly among birds, concerns about a possible human pandemic rose. Health experts nationwide started asking how our country could prepare for such a pandemic. Stockpiles of Tamiflu and the development of an experimental vaccine were hailed as a good start, but researchers are still working on other remedies. A number of these could prove even more effective — provided that before the situation worsens, the small biotech companies developing them can successfully usher potential treatments through clinical trials and bring them to the market.

Q: What information will likely be given next?
(a) The ways that human beings can catch bird flu
(b) The kinds of vaccines now being used for bird flu
(c) The steps needed to develop potential bird flu treatments
(d) The measures countries are taking to prevent bird flu

35. In today's marketplace, creating a compelling presence on the web is no longer an option, but a necessity. Whether you're looking to create a new online site or to enhance an existing one, we at Genflex can give you that presence with the most up-to-date web design that attracts targeted visitors. We have been providing successful solutions to small businesses and entrepreneurs since 1997. So, if you want experience and know-how behind your web presence, contact Genflex today.

Q: What can be inferred about Genflex from the advertisement?
(a) It keeps abreast of the latest Internet trends.
(b) It offers website services that are among the cheapest.
(c) It is a fledgling company in the field of online technology.
(d) It plans to expand its clientele to include large businesses.

36. A massive extinction of 85% of the entire species on Earth happened 65 million years ago, making it the second largest mass extinction in our geological history. Commonly known as the End-Cretaceous or K-T extinction, it was likely caused by an asteroid impact off the coast of what is now Mexico. Most experts now accept this theory based on evidence of high concentrations of a rare element called Iridium connected with K-T aged rocks. Iridium is an element that is rare on Earth, but high concentrations of it can be found in extraterrestrial objects such as asteroids.

Q: What can be inferred from the passage?
(a) High levels of Iridium exist throughout the Mexican terrain.
(b) Dinosaurs went extinct due to Iridium poisoning.
(c) Chances of another asteroid causing extinction are slim.
(d) Iridium in K-T aged rocks came from an asteroid.

37. Jazz, a genre of popular music native to America, developed out of a series of increasingly complex playing styles. One of the earliest of these styles was ragtime, which peaked in popularity between 1899 and 1919. Its most influential composer was Scott Joplin, born in 1868 in Linden, Texas. Joplin wrote over 500 compositions, including *The Maple Leaf Rag*, which proved to be one of his most famous tunes.

Q: What will most likely be discussed next?
(a) The most famous ragtime compositions
(b) Jazz music and its place in modern culture
(c) The life and times of composer Scott Joplin
(d) Other early music styles that influenced jazz

Part III **Questions 38 — 40**

Read the passage. Then identify the option that does NOT belong.

38. Jinsun Lee is a world-famous dancer and choreographer. (a) Although she studied choreography in America, her specialty area is Asian dance. (b) One of the best-known Asian dances is the Dragon Dance, performed on festive occasions in China. (c) Ms. Lee's contribution to dance and choreography has been highly acclaimed not only domestically but also internationally. (d) She has performed in dance competitions and choreographed dance productions for both stage and TV.

39. Mars has long been an intriguing subject for research and speculation among astronomers. (a) Early telescopic observers reported what appeared to be signs of foliage on the Martian surface. (b) Other observers reported geometrical patterns that they suspected to be artificial canals. (c) Scientists thus speculated about the possibility of life on Mars and still do to this day. (d) Indeed, Science Fiction writers of the past wrote popular novels about Martians and life on Mars.

40. Horapollo was one of the last priests of the Ancient Egyptian religion in the 5th century AD. (a) He wrote the *Hieroglyphica*, an explanation of Egyptian hieroglyphs, which is based on real signs from hieroglyphic writing but is often wrong. (b) By the time Egyptian hieroglyphics were finally deciphered in the 19th century, his interpretations were universally dismissed. (c) The real breakthrough in the decipherment of Egyptian hieroglyphs was made by Champollion in the early 19th century. (d) But what makes Horapollo's book of continued interest is that it offers readers an archaic, mystical view of the universe.

This is the end of the Reading Comprehension section. Please remain seated until the proctor has instructed otherwise. You are NOT allowed to turn to any other section of the test.

서울대 최신기출 5

Listening Comprehension

Grammar

Vocabulary

Reading Comprehension

LISTENING COMPREHENSION

DIRECTIONS

1. In the Listening Comprehension section, all content will be presented orally rather than in written form.

2. This section contains 4 parts. In parts I and II, each passage will be read only once. In parts III and IV, each passage and its corresponding question will be read twice. But in all sections, the options will be read only once. After listening to the passage and question, listen to the options and choose the best answer.

LISTENING COMPREHENSION

Part I Questions 1—15

You will now hear fifteen conversation fragments, each made up of a single spoken statement followed by four spoken responses. Choose the most appropriate response to the statement.

Part II Questions 16—30

You will now hear fifteen conversation fragments, each made up of three spoken statements followed by four spoken responses. Choose the most appropriate response to complete the conversation.

Part III   **Questions 31—45**

You will now hear fifteen complete conversations. For each item, you will hear a conversation and its corresponding question, both of which will be read twice. Then you will hear four options which will be read only once. Choose the option that best answers the question.

Part IV   **Questions 46—60**

You will now hear fifteen spoken monologues. For each item, you will hear a monologue and its corresponding question, both of which will be read twice. Then you will hear four options which will be read only once. Choose the option that best answers the question.

GRAMMAR

DIRECTIONS

This part of the exam tests your grammar skills. You will have 25 minutes to complete the 50 questions. Be sure to follow the directions given by the proctor.

Part I **Questions 1—20**

Choose the best answer for the blank.

1. A: How many Korean students do you have in your class?
   B: Half of the students __________ Korean.

   (a) is
   (b) are
   (c) to be
   (d) being

2. A: Is it true that you sell stamps here?
   B: Yes, we __________ .

   (a) do
   (b) are
   (c) can
   (d) have

3. A: I must go now, but let's meet tomorrow again at the same time.
   B: Great. I look forward to __________ you then.

   (a) see
   (b) seeing
   (c) have seen
   (d) having seen

4. A: My business __________ quite a lot of money last year.
   B: That's great news.

   (a) made
   (b) makes
   (c) will make
   (d) is making

5. A: Do you know __________ to buy a big screen TV?
   B: No, I have no idea.

   (a) it will cost how much
   (b) how much will it cost
   (c) how much it will cost
   (d) cost how much will it

6. A: Do we need to go to the conference?
   B: I think we're __________ .

   (a) supposed
   (b) supposed to
   (c) supposed to it
   (d) supposed to be it

7. A: Why don't you buy both CDs?
   B: If I __________ more money, I probably would.

   (a) had
   (b) have
   (c) had had
   (d) will have

8. A: You have so many flowers in your garden!
   B: Actually, __________ .

   (a) used to be more there
   (b) there used to be more
   (c) were there more before
   (d) before more there were

9. A: Aren't you embarrassed to wear that hat?

    B: Not at all. I don't care about ___________ other people think.

    (a) that
    (b) who
    (c) what
    (d) which

10. A: What happened to your leg?

    B: I slipped and hurt it ___________ the picture on the wall.

    (a) hung
    (b) to hang
    (c) while hang
    (d) while hanging

11. A: What ___________ to talk to me about?

    B: It's about your relationship with Isabelle.

    (a) you were wanting
    (b) was it you wanting
    (c) was it that you wanted
    (d) it was that you wanted

12. A: Are you planning to study abroad?

    B: Yes, ___________ to go to Spain.

    (a) I decide
    (b) I'll decide
    (c) I've decided
    (d) I had decided

13. A: Why do we have to walk all the way to the store?

    B: Oh, stop complaining. It's not ___________ far.

    (a) just
    (b) such
    (c) very
    (d) rather

14. A: I have a headache and my chest hurts, Dr. Nickson.

    B: How long ___________ these symptoms?

    (a) will you experience
    (b) are you experiencing
    (c) were you experiencing
    (d) have you been experiencing

15. A: I'd like to know who is responsible for this failed project.

    B: I don't think we can lay the blame on ___________ individual.

    (a) single
    (b) the single
    (c) any single
    (d) another single

16. A: There's something wrong with this car.

    B: What makes you think ___________?

    (a) it
    (b) one
    (c) that
    (d) there

17. A: Are you working late again?

B: Yeah, ___________ finish my report yet, I need to stay longer and work on it.

(a) not be able to
(b) not was able to
(c) not had been able to
(d) not having been able to

18. A: The traffic will be heavy heading home at the end of this long weekend.

B: In that case, it'll be best ___________ an early start.

(a) make
(b) to make
(c) to be made
(d) being made

19. A: If you lend me $200, I'll return it tomorrow.

B: I find ___________.

(a) that hard believing
(b) hard to believe that
(c) that hard to believe
(d) that hard of believing

20. A: Excuse me, but where is St. Paul's Cathedral?

B: It's ___________ the other side of the river.

(a) in
(b) of
(c) on
(d) for

Part II   **Questions 21—40**

Choose the best answer for the blank.

21. The football players could not have lunch ___________ they came late to the cafeteria.

(a) yet
(b) while
(c) besides
(d) because

22. Occasionally, some advertised items ___________ be out of stock due to great demand.

(a) may
(b) need
(c) must
(d) should

23. Even though it took Lisa longer than she had ever imagined, she finally ___________.

(a) found her dream job
(b) her dream job found
(c) her job dreamed found
(d) found her job dreamed

24. One should look at all the options when ___________ an insurance policy.

(a) chose
(b) choose
(c) choosing
(d) to choose

25. The past ten years ___________ a dramatic improvement in Italy's wine-making technology.

(a) is seeing
(b) have seen
(c) has been seen
(d) are being seen

26. Absolute pitch is an exceedingly rare gift, found in as ___________ as one in 10,000 individuals.

(a) few
(b) little
(c) a few
(d) a little

27. Most employees ___________ as doing a good job and making a positive contribution.

(a) are wanting of the thought
(b) want to be thought of
(c) are thought to want
(d) want thought to be

28. People spend ___________ much time watching TV nowadays that they hardly have time to read books.

(a) even
(b) very
(c) far
(d) so

29. Former factories ___________ and the whole area was redeveloped.

(a) demolished
(b) were demolished
(c) were demolishing
(d) were being demolished

30. All the mothers looked worn-out, ___________ they had missed a night's sleep.

(a) as if
(b) unless
(c) whereas
(d) even though

31. ___________ brief and precious childhood is when we are older.

(a) Only we realize how
(b) How only realize we
(c) We only realize how
(d) We realize how only

32. The movie lacked intensity and left most viewers ___________.

(a) unmoved
(b) being unmoved
(c) to being unmoved
(d) have been unmoved

33. Recent studies have refuted the theory that Alzheimer's may begin in the brain, ___________ has until now been the prevalent assumption.

(a) that
(b) what
(c) which
(d) of which

34. In order to successfully make our popcorn by using a stove, it is essential that ___________.

(a) precisely follow all instructions
(b) follow all instructions precisely
(c) all instructions be followed precisely
(d) instructions be followed all precisely

35. Almost 6,000 enemy soldiers were killed, and about 4,000 more were taken ___________ in the fighting.

(a) prisoner
(b) a prisoner
(c) the prisoner
(d) the prisoners

36. No sooner ___________ than the candidates who were not picked started protesting the results.

(a) selected the finalists had been
(b) had been selected the finalists
(c) had the finalists been selected
(d) the finalists had been selected

37. If the Smith family ___________ a home prior to July 2000, they might have qualified for housing assistance.

(a) were not buying
(b) have not bought
(c) had not bought
(d) do not buy

38. Not one road sign ___________ to Fresno.

(a) of LA traffic was found directing
(b) was found in LA directing traffic
(c) found in LA was directed to traffic
(d) for traffic was found in LA directed

39. The famous short story writer was known to have come from ___________.

(a) a poor background
(b) the poor background
(c) each poor background
(d) every poor background

40. The new financial policy has contributed ___________ from double-digit percentage rates in the year 2000 to 5% in 2007.

(a) inflation to reduce
(b) to inflation reducing
(c) to a reduction in inflation
(d) to reducing of the inflation

Part III Questions 41—45

Identify the option that contains an awkward expression or an error in grammar.

41. (a) A: You seem to be pretty good at Chinese.
   (b) B: I studied it for quite a few years now.
   (c) A Maybe I should start learning it, too.
   (d) B: That'd be great. We could have conversations in Chinese!

42. (a) A: My son wastes too much time playing computer games.
   (b) B: Mine does, too. He is practically addicted to them.
   (c) A I'm thinking of banning from him using the computer.
   (d) B: But how? Computers are an unavoidable part of life now.

43. (a) A: Where did you put my books?
   (b) B: I put them in your study.
   (c) A But I don't see them anywhere in my study.
   (d) B: Try looking underneath the files for your desk.

44. (a) A: I can't believe you forgot your wife's birthday.
   (b) B: Well, I've been busy, and I didn't mark it on my calendar this year.
   (c) A But shouldn't you be able to remember it by now?
   (d) B: Yeah, I know. I'd better make it up to her with the expensive gift.

45. (a) A: It's not fair some siblings to get new clothes while others have to wear hand-me-downs.
   (b) B: Is that what's happening in your home?
   (c) A Unfortunately, yes, and my parents don't seem concerned about it.
   (d) B: Maybe they have their own reasons. They might be short of money.

46. (a) Pax Romana, or "the Roman Peace," was a 200-year period of relative peace and great achievements for Rome. (b) This period ended in AD 180 that Emperor Marcus Aurelius died. (c) He was succeeded by his 19-year-old son Commodus, who proved to be an unpopular ruler. (d) Commodus was finally killed in AD 193, but the Pax Romana never returned.

47. (a) The principles governed social conduct in Asian societies are fundamentally different from those of Western societies. (b) For Asians, social interaction must always be congenial, with behavior directed toward maintaining group harmony. (c) This so-called "situational centeredness" contrasts with the Western emphasis on individualism. (d) For example, Asian mannerisms and speech often express self-deprecation and deference to others, but these traits are seen as weaknesses in Western culture.

48. (a) DVD has become the film buff's favorite choice of format. (b) This is because of the many extra features the DVD format is allowed. (c) DVD movies often come with different language choices and commentaries by film experts. (d) Moreover, the storage capacity of DVDs makes it possible to include extra scenes deleted from the cinema version of a film.

49. (a) Neither corporal nor capital punishment have proved to be effective. (b) Statistics clearly show that the death penalty has failed as a deterrent. (c) Death sentences have not mitigated the crisis of teeming prisons, nor have they reduced the number of victims in our society. (d) They have only worked to stop criminals who have received the death penalty from committing other crimes.

50. (a) One of the greatest discoveries in science may be locating the genes that cause us to age. (b) If it is possible to understand these genes, then, theoretically, we may be able to counteract them. (c) We will then be able to slow down the physical and cosmetic effects of aging. (d) It is possible that our great-grandchildren ought to live to 150 and not look half that age.

This is the end of the Grammar section. Do NOT move on to the next section until instructed to do so. You are NOT allowed to turn to any other section of the test.

VOCABULARY

Part I   Questions 1—25

Choose the best answer for the blank.

1. A: Let's go for a drive in the countryside.

B: Yeah, that would be really _________.

(a) harmful
(b) stressful
(c) touching
(d) refreshing

2. A: Could you help me with moving?

B: No problem. Just let me know when you _________ me.

(a) help
(b) need
(c) gather
(d) remind

3. A: May I speak with Mrs. Crinkle?

B: I'm sorry, but she's not _________ to come to the phone.

(a) available
(b) applicable
(c) obtainable
(d) transferable

4. A: You did an excellent job on that report.

B: Thanks, that _________ a lot coming from you.

(a) shows
(b) means
(c) defines
(d) includes

5. A: Hi Janet, this is Karl. You called me earlier?

B: Oh, hi! Thanks for _________ my call.

(a) relating
(b) sending
(c) greeting
(d) returning

6. A: Did the presentation go well yesterday?

B: Yes, everything went very _________.

(a) fairly
(b) rightly
(c) eagerly
(d) smoothly

7. A: Hi, my name's Rick Collins. Nice to meet you.

B: Oh, hi. I've heard great things about you. Glad to meet you in _________.

(a) person
(b) individual
(c) friendship
(d) acquaintance

8. A: What's the bus _________ to the airport?

B: It's $10.

(a) tax
(b) bid
(c) rate
(d) fare

9. A: I tried to be straightforward during the meeting.

    B: But some of your remarks were ___________.

    (a) solid
    (b) blunt
    (c) envious
    (d) indifferent

10. A: Why won't this DVD play in this drive?

    B: That one only _________ CD-ROMs.

    (a) files
    (b) sorts
    (c) clicks
    (d) reads

11. A: I'm sorry you were forced to sell your house.

    B: Yeah, I just had no other _________.

    (a) choice
    (b) motion
    (c) presence
    (d) selection

12. A: Do you really want to see that play? I heard it's ___________.

    B: Let's go see a movie, then. That'll be more fun.

    (a) boring
    (b) implicit
    (c) exciting
    (d) engaging

13. A: How come you didn't buy sugar?

    B: I'm sorry. I didn't ___________ it on the list.

    (a) see
    (b) part
    (c) make
    (d) intend

14. A: I have so much to study for the test!

    B: Don't worry. You know the course ___________ a lot better than I do.

    (a) evidence
    (b) standard
    (c) material
    (d) concern

15. A: Are you going to make a contribution to the charity?

    B: Yes, I ___________ to donate $50.

    (a) granted
    (b) pledged
    (c) described
    (d) estimated

16. A: When will Ms. Marshall begin her term as Secretary of State?

    B: Her term has already begun. She was ___________ yesterday.

    (a) held on
    (b) stood up
    (c) sworn in
    (d) handed over

17. A: My car has been acting weird lately.

    B: Get it checked because ___________ cars cost you less in the long run.

    (a) well-refined
    (b) well-polished
    (c) well-furnished
    (d) well-maintained

18. A: I see you've implemented some of my suggestions for improvements.

B: Yes, I __________ most of them.

(a) adopted
(b) improved
(c) persuaded
(d) revitalized

19. A: Our tour starts early tomorrow at 5:30.

B: What? You mean we don't get to __________?

(a) sleep in
(b) slink off
(c) catch up
(d) check out

20. A: Those shoes look pretty __________.

B: Yeah. I expect them to last a long time.

(a) wearable
(b) valuable
(c) durable
(d) flexible

21. A: I can't believe that our executive got arrested.

B: Yes, she was caught __________ company funds.

(a) obtruding
(b) encroaching
(c) promulgating
(d) misappropriating

22. A: The information screen says the plane has arrived. Can you see it on the runway?

B: Yes, it's __________ to the terminal now.

(a) reaching
(b) running
(c) driving
(d) taxiing

23. A: How do I go to Shea Bank from here?

B: Head up this way. __________ on Maple Street for half a block, and it's on your right.

(a) Drag
(b) Turn
(c) Stay
(d) Stop

24. A: The situation is getting __________, don't you think?

B: Yes, I think we'd better call someone for help.

(a) grim
(b) irate
(c) bland
(d) genial

25. A: How old are you now?

B: I'm __________ 16.

(a) going on
(b) turning up
(c) passing onto
(d) moving through

Part II   Questions 26—50

Choose the best answer for the blank.

26. If you want to see lions hunting wildebeest, ___________ a trip to Africa and visit a wildlife park.

(a) dip
(b) pull
(c) take
(d) meet

27. ___________ rains yesterday caused severe flooding that left hundreds homeless.

(a) Bulky
(b) Heavy
(c) Chunky
(d) Weighty

28. Although a vast number of computer companies exist, only some of them ___________ the computer industry.

(a) profit
(b) dominate
(c) generalize
(d) investigate

29. The National Weather Service will ___________ a warning to leave beaches in the event of an approaching hurricane.

(a) issue
(b) attest
(c) admit
(d) reveal

30. A new generation of urban planners are ___________ suburbs to get people out of their cars and onto the sidewalks again.

(a) defining
(b) deferring
(c) designing
(d) depositing

31. Our children have the right to live in an environment ___________ from pollution.

(a) set
(b) cut
(c) free
(d) open

32. Pregnant women should avoid sports that ___________ the risk of a collision or a fall.

(a) witness
(b) handle
(c) follow
(d) carry

33. One possible ___________ to the hunger problem in poor countries is to rent out agricultural equipment.

(a) solution
(b) addition
(c) adjustment
(d) implication

34. Parents are welcome to bring their children to ___________ free public skating at the outdoor rink from 6 pm to 9 pm.

    (a) seek
    (b) hold
    (c) form
    (d) enjoy

35. After his ___________ performance, the critics agreed that Matthew Adams came short of the skills necessary to be a great concert violinist.

    (a) secluded
    (b) lackluster
    (c) acclaimed
    (d) delectable

36. Symptoms of drug addiction include feelings of anxiety often related to the need to ___________ more drugs.

    (a) secure
    (b) derive
    (c) release
    (d) restrain

37. The facilities in our restroom include a diaper-changing area where, for 50 cents, a machine ___________ one moist wipe and a fresh diaper.

    (a) displays
    (b) disposes
    (c) displaces
    (d) dispenses

38. Encouragement from superiors is vital to ___________ the morale of employees.

    (a) appraise
    (b) reserve
    (c) strike
    (d) boost

39. As a new manager, I was given the task of ___________ the areas in my department that needed improvement.

    (a) accusing
    (b) upholding
    (c) disheveling
    (d) pinpointing

40. The onset of World War II ___________ concern that Germany would eventually develop nuclear bombs.

    (a) prompted
    (b) assembled
    (c) segregated
    (d) underwent

41. The media frequently ___________ a sense of uneasiness among viewers with inaccurate reporting and bias.

    (a) arouse
    (b) inspect
    (c) suspend
    (d) separate

42. To ___________ confidentiality, please seal the envelop firmly and sign across the seal.

    (a) assert
    (b) assure
    (c) provoke
    (d) conspire

43. The driver was ___________ by the sight
of three large deer crossing the road and
quickly applied his brakes.

(a) delayed
(b) startled
(c) traced
(d) urged

44. A teacher can have a great impact on
children who are still at a(n) __________
age.

(a) deceivable
(b) formidable
(c) surmountable
(d) impressionable

45. Surfing the Internet certainly __________
children away from doing homework.

(a) sways
(b) swipes
(c) projects
(d) pressures

46. The UN General Assembly has grown
alarmingly ___________ from the
world's crises and thus often fails to
focus on the most compelling problems.

(a) distinct
(b) unstable
(c) beneficial
(d) disengaged

47. Most nations now ___________ that the
disappearance of forests worldwide is a
global problem that must be dealt with
immediately.

(a) detain
(b) function
(c) constitute
(d) acknowledge

48. During World War II, an ongoing
struggle ___________ between code
makers and code breakers on opposing
sides.

(a) reaped
(b) ensued
(c) pursued
(d) convened

49. In traditional theatrical dramas,
instrumental music, dances and masques
provided a pleasant ___________
between acts.

(a) banter
(b) interlude
(c) repertory
(d) periphery

50. David has been suffering from a(n)
___________ disease for several years
that has practically incapacitated him.

(a) flagrant
(b) tractable
(c) impinging
(d) debilitating

This is the end of the Vocabulary section. Do NOT move on to the Reading
Comprehension section until instructed to do so. You are NOT allowed to turn
to any other section of the test.

Reading
comprehension

DIRECTIONS

This part of the exam tests your ability to comprehend reading passages. You will have 45 minutes to complete the 40 questions. Be sure to follow the directions given by the proctor.

Part I　**Questions 1—16**

Read the passage. Then choose the option that best completes the passage.

1.　Is your computer spyware-free? Our NoSpies website can scan, disinfect and eliminate over 90,000 spyware programs from system devices, hard disks, compressed files and email folders. NoSpies is always up-to-date, so each scan is able to detect the latest spyware threats. You do not need to install any programs; just connect to our website. Once there, simply click to _______________________________.

(a) see all of your banking details online
(b) update your operating system's software
(c) download the latest music to your mp3 player
(d) check if your computer is infected with spyware

2.　Pireh Group, the operator of Pireh Hotels, conceded yesterday that the suicide bombings in London had reduced bookings at its hotels by 6% between July 7 and August 23. David Michaels, Pireh Group's chief executive, said that "the hotel relies heavily on visitors from abroad" and that "the attacks appeared to have negatively influenced overseas visitors." He added that it was too early to say whether visitor numbers would recover in September and October. "Pireh has suffered _______________________________ because of the bombs," Mr. Michaels said.

(a) a lot of damage to its buildings
(b) a significant decline in business
(c) more severely than other visitors
(d) very much over the winter period

3.　For centuries, Vikings have been envisioned as blue-eyed barbarians in horned helmets who conquered other lands and killed without mercy. However, in the past 20 years, archaeological investigations of Viking sites stretching from Russia to Newfoundland have revealed a more humane side to the Viking character. The evidence that has been uncovered contrasts sharply with prior accounts of Vikings, which were based on victims' reports and were thus one-sided. It gives us _______________________________.

(a) quite a different view of the Vikings
(b) a clue about the Viking Empire's size
(c) an idea of how the Vikings were conquered
(d) specific details about Viking attacks on villages

4. The discovery of the x-ray was _______________________. In 1895, a German professor of physics Wilhelm Roentgen was working in his darkened laboratory. His experiments centered on light effects caused by discharging electrical current in glass tubes. To Roentgen's surprise, he discovered that when his cardboard-shrouded tube was charged with electricity, an object across the room began to glow. While holding materials between the tube and screen to test what would take place, he came across the bones of his hand clearly visible, thus inadvertently witnessing the first human x-ray.

(a) a combination of scientific experimentation and luck
(b) one of the most important inventions in electronics
(c) not made without a series of setbacks and difficulties
(d) inevitable due to advances made in technology

5. Renowned German author Hermann Hesse was the grandson of Reverend Hermann Gundert, a Swiss-German linguist and missionary most renowned for _______________________. As a former missionary to India, Gundert was proficient in English, German, French and Italian and could also preach in Hindustani, Malayalam and Bengali. Most notably, Gundert was a scholar who dedicated his time and effort to composing works in the Indian language of Malayalam, including a translation of the Bible, a grammar guide and a dictionary.

(a) his groundbreaking studies on Eastern religions
(b) not having faith in Hermann Hesse's writing ability
(c) living a life of scholarly and religious devotion in India
(d) his multi-language fluency and his linguistic publications

6. Based on a novel by Emily Wheatbuck, *Hall of Mice* is a film about duty, lost love and self-preservation. Gayle Andrews craftily portrays Lola, a young English socialite of the Victorian Era in love with a boy next door. Lola's parents, however, have other plans and expect her to marry above her present situation to improve the family's standing in the community. Consequently, Lola finds herself forced to choose between obligations to her family and her true feelings. Don Allen, Lucy Lamb and Andy Paga also star in this classic tale of ________________________________.

(a) love versus family duty
(b) wisdom and human folly
(c) lust for power and money
(d) troubled marriage and divorce

7. One day, as I was looking through one of the local newspapers, I was struck by a sense of shame. It seemed to me that the standards of the mainstream media had slipped even further. About 40% of the newspaper had to do with various forms of entertainment, 30% had to do with sex, 20% with advertising, and the final 10% concerned political or local events. Most of the paper ________________________________. It had little to do with concerns of a serious nature.

(a) was filled with too many advertisements
(b) was about cheap thrills and pleasure seeking
(c) was critical of the government's latest policies
(d) was related to international rather than local news

8. Human beings have gone from claiming to be the pinnacle of creation to recognizing that there is little to distinguish them from other animals on the planet. It has been a progression from a self-centered and religious viewpoint to an objective and scientific one. We can no longer set our species apart by citing religion, intelligence or language, nor can we arrogate consciousness to ourselves without knowing quite what it is or how many other creatures have it. It is not possible for us to

________________________________.

(a) accept the flaws in evolutionary theory
(b) stand by while the environment suffers
(c) condone racism among human beings anymore
(d) claim superiority over all living things anymore

9. Often students who use English as a second language read English slowly and use their dictionaries frequently. This is one way of reading, but it is not always the most effective way. Language learners can benefit immensely by skipping unfamiliar vocabulary and just concentrating on the context and main ideas of a passage. It is not always good to interrupt your reading to look up definitions of unknown words in the dictionary. Remember, if you want to comprehend a sentence or passage, ________________________.

(a) try to learn new vocabulary each day
(b) you should try to read slowly and carefully
(c) it is not necessary to understand every word
(d) consulting diverse reference books is important

10.

Dear Mr. Alexis:

In the past, your firm has made generous donations to the Care Children's Society. The Society offers necessary daytime facilities for the young children of working mothers. It provides an available play space throughout the week and provides counseling services to families and single parents seeking assistance. We are certain your company will wish to continue to support our cause. For your convenience, we are enclosing a promissory card. Any amount you can donate this year would ________________________.

Sincerely,
Gerald T. Miller
Director

(a) be used to pay medical bills for the sick
(b) allow us to maintain our childcare services
(c) help our church to reach out to more people
(d) provide more scholarships for needy children

11. Many large American cities honor individuals who, while not always nationally famous, have contributed greatly to the histories of those cities. One example is Moses Cleveland, the man after whom the American city of Cleveland was named. Cleveland never visited the city that bears his name, but he negotiated with the natives to secure the city's site and was in charge of the survey team that laid the city out. So, even though he was not a major historical figure nationally, Cleveland was __________________________________.

(a) instrumental in negotiating with hostile natives
(b) a gifted historian on the subject of America's past
(c) famous among citizens of his hometown Cleveland
(d) a key figure in the history of a major American city

12. The federal Truth in Lending Act demands that lenders clearly express, in a set and predetermined way, the total amount of interest that is to be charged. Before the enactment of this legislation, lenders were not required to state the interest rate charged and could thus state the rate in a confusing way. The Truth in Lending Act requires the lender to disclose the interest using an annual percentage rate. Such statements makes "comparison shopping" easier when an individual is seeking credit. Both criminal penalties and civil recovery are available against those who fail to __________________________________.

(a) operate without a proper license
(b) offer loans to customers in clear need
(c) disclose their accounting practices
(d) reveal the interest terms to customers

13. Traditional vaccines work by introducing a weakened or benign form of a virus into a patient through an injection. This stimulates the immune system into taking protective action. DNA vaccines __________________________________. These vaccines involve the injection of part of the genetic code of a virus into a patient's muscle cells. The virus's genes are then reproduced inside the cells, simulating infectious organism proteins and causing the patient's immune system to respond. In this way, a DNA injection works to simulate what actually happens to our cells when we are infected by a harmful virus even more closely than traditional vaccines can.

(a) are better but not administered by a needle
(b) may lead to a new form of virus medication
(c) achieve similar results via a different method
(d) do not work as effectively as traditional vaccines

14. The implied warranty of merchantability is a merchant's guarantee that the products sold will do what they are supposed to do. It is an implied promise made each time a merchant sells any commodity that this commodity is fit for sale. For instance, if you sell an oven, you are promising that it is in good condition and will do its expected tasks. Otherwise, it is not fit for sale, and your implied warranty of merchantability would be breached. In such a case, the law demands you to provide a remedy so that ______________________________.

(a) customers may return to your business
(b) the buyer gets a working oven or refund
(c) malfunctioning parts are often identified
(d) the buyer admits his or her wrongdoing

15. Art should not be a possession but rather a passion both for the artist and the viewer. It should inspire us and communicate meaning. ______________________________, it is often the case these days that art is valued strictly as a commodity. Works of art are claimed as private property by avaricious collectors, rather than publicly displayed for their intrinsic merits. As a result of this commercialization, the meaning and real purpose of art are in danger of being lost.

(a) However
(b) Therefore
(c) In addition
(d) For instance

16. Papering a ceiling demands careful preparation. First, measure and mark off the side wall the width of your ceiling paper subtracted by approximately half an inch. Do the same at the opposite end of the ceiling. ______________________________, join these two marks with a builder's chalk line to mark where the edge of the first length of paper should go. Follow this line with caution while papering, or else your paper may curve, and too much curving could lead you to a point where you will be unable to line up the edges of the paper.

(a) Thus
(b) Then
(c) Instead
(d) Moreover

17. Many brightly-colored jungle animals use poisons that are either naturally found in their bodies or obtained from certain foods. They may use these poisons to capture prey. For example, venomous creatures, such as snakes and spiders, use powerful toxins to subdue prey that might injure them during a struggle. Alternatively, some animals use poisons to protect themselves from such predators. For example, some frogs have poisonous skin to prevent other animals from eating them.

Q: What is the main idea of the passage?
(a) Some animals protect themselves from poisons.
(b) Natural environment contains hidden dangers.
(c) Most poisonous creatures are brightly colored.
(d) Jungle animals use poisons in different ways.

18.

Dear Mr. Hillman,

Please accept our sincere apology for the mistake with your March 15 order, which we have now rectified. To accommodate our growing business, we have recently moved our inventory to a new warehouse. During the process of moving, some of our items were incorrectly labeled. Since receiving your letter, we have corrected this situation, and there will be no more mishaps such as the one you have experienced.

Regards,
Frank Tiller
Director of Shipping and Logistics

Q: What is the writer mainly trying to do in the letter?
(a) Advise Mr. Hillman of his overdue payment
(b) Explain his company's new inventory procedures
(c) Inform his boss of problems at the new warehouse
(d) Apologize for a mistake made with Mr. Hillman's order

19. Contrary to popular belief, the term "fairy tales" does not only apply to stories that have fairies in them. Rather, it is a term used to describe traditional folk stories in general. It comes from the French term "contes de fées," which was used in 17th-century France to describe a group of adult folk tales. "Contes de fées" simply translates into English as "fairy tales." Over time, the term "fairy tales" was used to describe similar tales created outside of France, such as those by the Brothers Grimm and Hans Christian Andersen.

Q: What is the main point of the passage?
(a) Fairy tales are not just stories for children.
(b) The French invented the idea of writing tales for children.
(c) Fairy tales were first written in France during the 17th century.
(d) The term "fairy tales" comes from a French phrase for folk tales.

20. For thousands of years, Australia's Aboriginals have lived according to ancient traditions and belief. Their central belief is called "Dreamtime," which is about how ancestral spirits created the world. These great spirits became part of the land they created, and as such, Aboriginals perceive the land as having spiritual powers. In a sense, "Dreamtime" is the religion or spiritual foundation upon which Aboriginals have built their laws, traditions and worldviews. That is why "Dreamtime," the land and the traditions of Aboriginal societies are all intimately linked. For Australia's Aboriginals, the past is still very much alive in the land of the present.

Q: What is the main idea of the passage?
(a) Australia's indigenous people still live by ancient customs.
(b) Australian Aboriginal culture is based on an ancient creation myth.
(c) Creation myths like "Dreamtime" are common in Australian society.
(d) Dreams of Australian Aboriginal people have evolved into their culture.

21. Start designing fashionable clothing today with Dazzle 3.0. With Dazzle 3.0, you have control over every aspect of your digital creation. Sexy or demure, liberal or conservative, you can dress your digital model in any way you choose. Dazzle 3.0 contains all of our basic 3D models, plus a large range of fashions and hundreds of accessories. You can dress your models in any way you like and put together your own fashions. Dazzle 3.0 has everything you need to start creating the next new look on your computer today.

Q: What is the advertisement mainly about?
(a) A new brand of fashion for young women
(b) Software for designing creative clothing styles
(c) Software that helps you make computer games
(d) A website that allows you to create digital people

22. Environmentalists protested at Navy headquarters on Wednesday, claiming that a widely used form of sonar to detect enemy submarines can be dangerous or even fatal to whales. According to a spokesperson for the environmentalists, the sonar is "capable of flooding thousands of square miles of ocean with dangerous levels of noise pollution." The protest is the second of its kind in six months, following an official refusal by the Navy to limit the peacetime use of experimental low-frequency sonar.

Q: What is the best title for the article?
(a) Protests against Navy for Harming Whales with Sonar
(b) Sonar Use Condemned by Top Navy Spokesperson
(c) Whale Protection Now Major Environmental Issue
(d) Navy Protests Decision to Restrict Sonar Pollution

23. Marseilles is located in the French region of Provence. Founded in 600 BC by Greek sailors from Phocaea, this great city, the oldest in France, contains a wealth of history and folklore. During the period of France's colonial expansion, Marseilles was the gateway to the Mediterranean and beyond. Today it is France's second largest city and has her largest commercial port. In many ways, Marseilles is the capital of southern Europe—cosmopolitan, exuberant and picturesque.

Q: Which of the following is correct about Marseilles?
(a) It was France's first colony.
(b) It is the oldest city in France.
(c) It was founded by French sailors.
(d) It has the second largest port in France.

24. In certain hot real-estate markets in America, speculation can become so profitable that people will deal contracts on condos before construction is even completed. The so-called "preconstruction market" in Miami is a fitting example. Recently, this market has witnessed some of the highest investor returns ranging from 200% to 400% within a year of the initial investment. Now, up to 80% of condo purchases in Miami are being carried out by people with no intention to ever live in their new condos.

Q: Which of the following is correct according to the passage?
(a) Realtors in Miami are currently earning higher-than-average returns.
(b) Miami has ceased to be the hottest real estate market in the US.
(c) Many condos are bought and sold solely for profit in Miami.
(d) Up to 80% of condos in Miami are reconstruction projects.

25. According to a Canadian study, the Red Delicious variety of apple contains higher levels of disease-fighting chemicals than other major varieties. It has long been known that apples, especially the skins, contain high levels of dietary antioxidants, which help neutralize cancer- and disease-causing molecules called free radicals. However, it was not known how apple varieties compared with each other in terms of antioxidants. The Canadian study has now determined that, of the eight popular apple varieties measured for antioxidants, Red Delicious apples have the highest antioxidant level—more than six times the level of other varieties.

Q: Which of the following is correct according to the passage?
(a) Apple skin has molecules that can cause cancer.
(b) Canadian apples are healthier than other varieties.
(c) Apple skins are a particularly good source of antioxidants.
(d) Red Delicious apples were found to be the most popular variety.

26. SteamHigh Carpet Cleaning is the best in carpet cleaning. We offer two different types of cleaning packages to suit your needs. Hot-water extraction (commonly referred to as steam cleaning) is our preferred and most popular method of carpet cleaning. But you may want one of our professionals to dry clean your carpets, which is the option customers select if they require a quicker and more affordable service.

Q: Which of the following is correct according to the passage?
(a) SteamHigh Carpet Cleaning offers three cleaning packages.
(b) Most customers prefer steam cleaning to dry cleaning.
(c) Hot-water extraction is cheaper than dry cleaning.
(d) Dry cleaning requires a team of professionals.

27. A 5% shift in retail spending away from the mall and department stores to the Internet is likely to have a significant impact on offline businesses. A recent survey by Jackson Brothers has predicted that a swing of such magnitude would be sufficient to bankrupt many offline retailers and lower the value of the real estate upon which their stores stand.

Q: Which of the following is correct according to the passage?
(a) Internet sales have surpassed those of department stores.
(b) The Internet is increasingly being used by wholesalers.
(c) A 5% retail swing could greatly affect offline retailers.
(d) Retailers are predicting a 5% swing in prices soon.

28. During North America's pioneering days, loggers led an unsettled life because jobs were short-term and they had to search for work continuously. Many stayed at a logging camp for only a few days or weeks. Their work was hard and long with only one day off on Sundays. Loggers worked 11 hours a day until their workday was reduced to 10 hours in 1910. After 1920, they worked 8 hours a day, five days a week. The pay was not high, but they would work even in rain, snow and freezing cold because there was one simple rule they all had to live by: if you do not work, you do not get any pay.

Q: Which of the following is correct according to the passage?
(a) Loggers worked 11 hours a day after 1910.
(b) Early loggers worked only four days a week.
(c) Loggers were once guaranteed a high income.
(d) Logging was not a secure job in the early days.

29. *You and Me* represents French-Canadian singer and cellist Cindy Belame's exploration of new musical territory. It is a first time collaboration with other singer-songwriters for Belame, and yet she gives us a deeply personal and introspective album. Although it is more rhythmic and less subtle than her previous offerings, it is a quintessential Cindy Belame album.

Q: Which of the following is correct about Cindy Belame's new album?
(a) She wrote all the songs on it by herself.
(b) It is more subtle than her earlier recordings.
(c) It uses new instruments for a unique sound.
(d) She made it in collaboration with other people.

30. Rather than being in a state of equilibrium, the surface of the sun actually "vibrates" like a struck bell. Robert Leighton first observed this in 1960, noting that portions of the sun's surface moved up and down by about ten kilometers every five minutes. More recently, helioseismologists, people who study the sun's vibrations, have discovered a variety of similar surface oscillations, some with longer durations and others that move across greater distances. Because oscillations are influenced by temperature, composition and motions deep within the sun, they yield insights into the conditions of the solar interior for helioseismologists.

Q: Which of the following is correct according to the passage?
(a) Solar pulsations occur at a constant rate on the sun's surface.
(b) Robert Leighton discovered that the sun makes a vibrating noise.
(c) The term "helioseismology" was coined by Robert Leighton in 1960.
(d) The sun's oscillations allow scientists to find out more about its interior.

31.

Dear Sean Stratton,

After considerable discussion at our recent directors' meeting, we have decided to proceed with the construction of new residence buildings at Belleview. You were previously notified that as Managing Director of our Boston office, you will be given the opportunity to lead the construction project at Belleview. As a strong emphasis on economics and work efficiency are desired, we have decided that you should take full charge of construction work expenses and approval of all said expenditures. If you have any questions, please contact me at your earliest convenience.

Walter Burns,
Chairman

Q: Which of the following is correct according to the letter?
(a) Sean Stratton has been relieved of his position as Managing Director.
(b) Sean Stratton has the task of overseeing the Belleview project's costs.
(c) Construction of the new Boston office will be managed by Sean Stratton.
(d) Contractual problems are being experienced at the Belleview building site.

32. The Uskoks were a group of Croatian Christians who fled their Balkan homeland to escape the advance of Ottoman Turks in the late 16th century. They migrated to a region known as Dalmatia, and from there fought back and committed acts of piracy against their Ottoman adversaries throughout the Adriatic Sea area. Powerful rulers of neighboring countries, such as Emperor Ferdinand I of Austria, supported these guerrilla attacks, trying to use the Uskoks as a buffer against Ottoman efforts to dominate the Adriatic.

Q: According to the passage, which of the following is correct about the Uskoks?
(a) They fled their native homeland when the Croats invaded.
(b) They were incited by neighboring rulers to attack the Turks.
(c) They were defeated by the Ottoman Turks in the 16th century.
(d) They took up piracy because they could not practice agriculture.

33. Welcome and thank you for visiting our SmallTeach website! We offer quality educational materials specifically designed for parents to use with pre-kindergarten children. Our materials provide hours of fun activities that you and your child can do together, all with an emphasis on learning. If you have any questions, suggestions or concerns, contact us at Info@smallones.com. Enjoy our website!

Q: Who is the announcement targeting?
(a) Parents who had childhood problems
(b) Parents with children in middle school
(c) Parents who have trouble with reading
(d) Parents with pre-kindergarten children

34. Pottery presents us with the best archaeological evidence of the movements of the
Greeks and the arrangements of their trade around the Mediterranean and Black
Sea basins. Vital sources of this proof have come from central and northern Italian
Etruscan cemeteries, as their tombs have revealed thousands of Greek vases. Because
comparatively few Etruscan manufactured products turn up in Greek archaeological
sites, it is widely believed that Etruria traded raw materials such as lump iron, lead and
bronze in exchange for Greek pottery and other finished goods.

Q: What can be inferred from the passage?
(a) The Etruscans only used Greek pottery for funerals.
(b) The Greeks were more powerful than the Etruscans.
(c) The Greeks were better craftsmen than the Etruscans.
(d) The Etruscans were involved in a war with the Greeks.

35. African-American children in the US face ridicule and ostracism by their peers if they
perform well in school. That is the finding of Harvard economist Roland Johnson,
who researched the relationship between academic performance and popularity among
children in public and private schools. "Acting white" is a derogatory term used by
African-American children to portray fellow black students who display behaviors
considered characteristic of Caucasians, such as getting good grades or reading books.
Johnson says this phenomenon could help clarify at least a portion of the persistent
black-white achievement gap in school and in later life.

Q: What can be inferred from the passage?
(a) The black-white achievement gap results from differing family backgrounds.
(b) Black students who do not excel in school are more popular than those who do.
(c) White students generally have more intelligence than black students.
(d) The school system in America is biased against black students.

36. The lingering effects of malnutrition on a large number of people in India continue to plague the nation, despite decades of agricultural innovation and poverty alleviation policies. Particularly affected are the most vulnerable members of society, namely women and children. The shocking statistics are that half of all children under four are malnourished, and 60% of women are anemic. What is more, mothers and daughters, especially in poor families, often forego food to give husbands and sons a larger share.

Q: What can be inferred from the passage?
(a) The majority of women in poor families are primary wage earners in India.
(b) India has experienced the highest malnutrition rates in the world for decades.
(c) Malnutrition in India is caused as much by cultural issues as by food shortages.
(d) The Indian government has done little in recent years to redress food shortages.

37. The 1889 Johnstown Flood was a disaster that hydrologists had attempted to prevent by building a series of canals that could divert flood waters from the city. Citizens thought the plan would work, but as they reeled from the loss of life and property damage, the myth of a truly flood-free town was dispelled. However, the city's flood protection program was at least partially effective, as it did mitigate the scope of the flood. Army engineers noted that had the city's system of canals not been in place, the waters would have reached at least 11 feet higher and caused much more damage.

Q: What can be inferred from the passage?
(a) Too many canals were built in the inner city.
(b) Prompt action could have reduced the damage.
(c) Preventive measures were not a complete failure.
(d) More cooperation was needed to prevent flooding.

38. Looking for mountain-fresh clean air in your own home? (a) Clea-air filter units are so efficient that they can filter particles the size of bacteria from the air. (b) These ultra-small particles must be prevented from entering the clean rooms of precision semiconductor fabricators. (c) The state-of-the-art technology used in these units, combined with ease of use, makes our filters ideal for home or office. (d) Buy one of our award winning filters today and enjoy the world's cleanest air.

39. How the story of *Frankenstein* was first conceived is one of the most famous legends in English literature. (a) One stormy summer night in 1816, Mary Shelley was among the guests of the poet Lord Byron at his villa in Lake Geneva. (b) Byron and P. B. Shelley are two titans in the world of Romantic literature. (c) After reading numerous ghost stories, Byron dared Mary Shelley and his other guests to write a horror story each. (d) Shelley invented a story that she eventually developed and later published as the novel *Frankenstei*n.

40. A knowledge of computers can improve a child's confidence. (a) Children find that mastering computers increases their self-esteem and makes them feel on a par with adults. (b) Feeling competent on a computer can also promote academic confidence as they get older. (c) Perhaps most importantly, computers can enrich family life. (d) Researchers have found, for example, that attitudes toward writing improve when students compose on a computer.

This is the end of the Reading Comprehension section. Please remain seated until the proctor has instructed otherwise. You are NOT allowed to turn to any other section of the test.

서울대 최신기출 6

Listening Comprehension

Grammar

Vocabulary

Reading Comprehension

LISTENING
COMPREHENSION

DIRECTIONS

1. In the Listening Comprehension section, all content will be presented orally rather than in written form.

2. This section contains 4 parts. In parts I and II, each passage will be read only once. In parts III and IV, each passage and its corresponding question will be read twice. But in all sections, the options will be read only once. After listening to the passage and question, listen to the options and choose the best answer.

Part I ## Questions 1—15

You will now hear fifteen conversation fragments, each made up of a single spoken statement followed by four spoken responses. Choose the most appropriate response to the statement.

Part II ## Questions 16—30

You will now hear fifteen conversation fragments, each made up of three spoken statements followed by four spoken responses. Choose the most appropriate response to complete the conversation.

Part III **Questions 31—45**

You will now hear fifteen complete conversations. For each item, you will hear a conversation and its corresponding question, both of which will be read twice. Then you will hear four options which will be read only once. Choose the option that best answers the question.

Part IV **Questions 46—60**

You will now hear fifteen spoken monologues. For each item, you will hear a monologue and its corresponding question, both of which will be read twice. Then you will hear four options which will be read only once. Choose the option that best answers the question.

GRAMMAR

Part I Questions 1—20

Choose the best answer for the blank.

1. A: What did the doctor say?

B: She advised me __________ smoking.

(a) quit
(b) to quit
(c) quitting
(d) will quit

2. A: Why are you taking so many English classes?

B: __________ I want to go to college in the US.

(a) If
(b) Once
(c) While
(d) Because

3. A: How long will construction on this building take?

B: I don't know __________.

(a) it will be when finished
(b) when will it be finished
(c) when it will be finished
(d) will it be finished when

4. A: Are there any foreign students at this university? I've only seen Koreans.

B: Sure. I heard around 10% of the students __________ foreigners.

(a) is
(b) are
(c) was
(d) were

5. A: __________ does this vase go?

B: Just put it anywhere. I'll move it later.

(a) Where
(b) When
(c) What
(d) How

6. A: Dr. Baker, Mr. Collins is here to see you.

B: OK, please __________.

(a) him show in
(b) show in him
(c) show him in
(d) him in show

7. A: Are you going home now?

B: Yes, I'm __________.

(a) about just leaving
(b) to leave about just
(c) leaving just about
(d) just about to leave

8. A: It seems like you're always reading history books.

B: Yes, history is __________.

(a) fascinating subject
(b) a fascinating subject
(c) the fascinating subject
(d) every fascinating subject

9. A: Would you like to go skiing this Saturday?

   B: But __________ on weekends?

   (a) crowded isn't it
   (b) crowded it isn't
   (c) isn't it crowded
   (d) it isn't crowded

10. A: Congratulations on passing the exam!

    B: Thanks. I never thought I'd do __________ well on it.

    (a) much
    (b) ever
    (c) that
    (d) as

11. A: __________ kind of coffee would you like?

    B: Cappuccino, please.

    (a) How
    (b) That
    (c) What
    (d) Of which

12. A: When are you going to ask Julie out on a date?

    B: __________ one of these days.

    (a) I will
    (b) I do
    (c) I'm going
    (d) I'm going to ask to

13. A: What's Jimmy doing these days?

    B: Well, he's still a student at Wilson University __________ in psychology.

    (a) to major
    (b) majored
    (c) majoring
    (d) is majoring

14. A: Did you go to the party last night?

    B: Yes, but I __________ have gone to see the movie with you instead.

    (a) will
    (b) would
    (c) should
    (d) need to

15. A: Oh, no! It's raining, and we don't have an umbrella.

    B: Well, we can only blame __________ for forgetting to bring one.

    (a) us
    (b) both
    (c) oneself
    (d) ourselves

16. A: Is that a stain on your shirt?

    B: Yeah, someone bumped into me when __________ juice.

    (a) I'm drinking
    (b) I was drinking
    (c) I've been drinking
    (d) I had been drinking

17. A: How was Dr. Grant's speech?

    B: Pretty lame. He talked about his theories, only a few __________ were valid.

(a) that
(b) which
(c) in that
(d) of which

18. A: So, did you find out where Natal is?

    B: Yes, it's situated __________ the Indian Ocean coast.

(a) to
(b) at
(c) in
(d) on

19. A: __________ of bananas is low now.

    B: Right, fifty cents a pound is a great price!

(a) Price
(b) Prices
(c) A price
(d) The price

20. A: You should've left your job last year.

    B: Yeah. If I had known then what I do now, I __________ definitely have quit.

(a) might
(b) would
(c) could
(d) must

Part II   **Questions 21—40**

Choose the best answer for the blank.

---

21. Today the Internet __________ quick access to a wealth of information.

(a) provide
(b) provides
(c) has provided
(d) have provided

22. When Typhoon Bilis __________ Taiwan, it caused much damage.

(a) struck
(b) strikes
(c) has struck
(d) was striking

23. Countries without natural resources have to import them __________ elsewhere.

(a) to
(b) by
(c) from
(d) around

24. Chemists must __________ before carrying them out in the laboratory.

(a) their experiments prepare carefully
(b) their experiments carefully prepare
(c) prepare their experiments carefully
(d) carefully their experiments prepare

25. The real estate agent told the couple not to worry about __________ a decision right away.

(a) make
(b) making
(c) to make
(d) being made

26. Heat added to ice at its melting temperature __________.

(a) causes it to melt
(b) causes to melt it
(c) causing it to melt
(d) is to cause to melt it

27. This morning two people were killed and four __________ in a gas explosion in downtown Chicago.

(a) injured
(b) injuring
(c) being injured
(d) were injuring

28. Magnetically levitated trains, or Mag-Levs, __________ smoke or exhaust.

(a) are not producing
(b) produce not any
(c) do not produce
(d) producing no

29. It is not clear why __________.

(a) the president has resigned
(b) has resigned the president
(c) has the president resigned
(d) that the president has resigned

30. Some great early works in Japanese literature __________ in the hiragana script by aristocratic women.

(a) writing
(b) written
(c) were writing
(d) were written

31. Some of __________ advances in health care have been made thanks to discoveries in physics.

(a) the most important recent
(b) important the most recent
(c) most of the recent important
(d) the recent of most important

32. Australia __________ as "a cultural sponge lying in the Pacific" because it takes in so many immigrants.

(a) was described
(b) will be described
(c) had been described
(d) has been described

33. Many people know about great works of literature, but seldom __________ to read them.

(a) they bother
(b) do they bother
(c) they will bother
(d) will bother they

34. The Internet Archive is building a digital library of __________ sites.

(a) Internet
(b) the Internet
(c) any Internet
(d) every Internet

35. When President Carter lost control of the American economy, __________ some three years of double-digit inflation, voters turned against him.

(a) produced
(b) producing
(c) to produce
(d) he produced

36. Yeast multiplies quickly even in dry storage, __________ foods containing yeast cannot be kept for very long.

(a) so
(b) for
(c) since
(d) although

37. While most are safe for consumption, __________ are as effective as advertised.

(a) all vitamin products not
(b) not all vitamin products
(c) vitamin products all do not
(d) all vitamin products do not

38. The doctor suggested that the patient undergo physical therapy __________ for six months.

(a) every other week
(b) other every week
(c) every week the other
(d) the week every other

39. Statistics show that more than half of all used cars __________ in an accident.

(a) are
(b) will be
(c) had been
(d) have been

40. Despite __________ to leave out the red pepper in the customer's dish, it got into his food and caused an allergic reaction.

(a) being instructed
(b) having been instructed
(c) the cook being instructed
(d) the cook having been instructed

Part III Questions 41—45

Identify the option that contains an awkward expression or an error in grammar.

41. (a) A: How much long do you think this humid weather will last?

(b) B: According to the forecast, it should be over by the weekend.

(c) A: I certainly hope so. It's draining all my energy.

(d) B: I know. I feel exactly the same way.

42. (a) A: Excuse me. Can you tell me what this is made of?

(b) B: Yes, of course. That purse is made of leather.

(c) A: Oh, is this the one who is advertised on sale?

(d) B: Yes, it is. It's 20% off the regular price.

43. (a) A: Are you OK? You looked like you haven't slept well lately.

(b) B: I haven't. I've been studying linguistics every night, and it's so hard.

(c) A: I can help you with that. For me, it's easy.

(d) B: Thanks. I really need help to pass the class.

44. (a) A: I feel so miserable. This stomach ache is killing me.

(b) B: You ought to have eaten something bad for lunch.

(c) A: Maybe. Come to think of it, the fish did taste weird.

(d) B: If that's the case, you'd better go see a doctor right away.

45. (a) A: It seems a number of cell phone users are ever increasing.

(b) B: Yeah, and so are the instances of brain tumor.

(c) A: Are you suggesting the two are related or something?

(d) B: Who knows? But it's probably more than just a coincidence.

46. (a) Drinking green and black teas may help people with Alzheimer's disease. (b) They act to some drugs in a similar way used for Alzheimer's patients. (c) That is, they inhibit the activity of an enzyme known as AChE. (d) In so doing, these teas improve cognitive functioning in Alzheimer's patients.

47. (a) While I was jogging yesterday morning, I witnessed a terrible accident. (b) From the woods, a deer suddenly ran out onto the road in front of a passing car. (c) The motorist braked but still knocked the animal over. (d) Stunned by the accident, the car parked not far off as the deer got up and staggered away.

48. (a) Located off Africa's east coast, Madagascar is world's fourth largest island. (b) Separated from mainland Africa for millions of years, it developed a unique ecosystem. (c) About 80% of the animals on the island are found nowhere else on Earth. (d) One of its most famous residents is the lemur.

49. (a) Please take a moment to complete the Parent Survey, which last undertook in the spring of 2004. (b) Your survey results will help us focus our short- and long-term planning efforts at our school. (c) Please be sure to return your survey by June 15, 2006. (d) For your convenience, we have enclosed a postage-paid return envelope.

50. (a) Disgraced trader Mark Rich was charged in 1989 with 51 counts of tax evasion and racketeering. (b) He faced a truly astonishing array of charges, but he escaped by fleeing to Switzerland. (c) If he did not, he would have been sentenced to years in prison. (d) But, despite his crimes, he has been living as a free man in Switzerland for many years now.

Vocabulary

DIRECTIONS

This part of the exam tests your vocabulary skills. You will have 15 minutes to complete the 50 questions. Be sure to follow the directions given by the proctor.

Part I   Questions 1—25

Choose the best answer for the blank.

1. A: Bye, Helen. I have to go see mother, now.
   B: OK. Please give her my __________.

   (a) hello
   (b) respect
   (c) regards
   (d) greeting

2. A: Good afternoon. What can I do for you?
   B: I need help in deciding what classes to __________ next semester.

   (a) fix
   (b) use
   (c) find
   (d) take

3. A: Everything looks delicious.
   B: I know. I'm having a(n) __________ time deciding which dish to order.

   (a) easy
   (b) hard
   (c) tense
   (d) super

4. A: Guess what! It's my birthday today.
   B: Oh, really! How are you going to __________ it?

   (a) party
   (b) celebrate
   (c) entertain
   (d) appreciate

5. A: How did the job interview go?
   B: It didn't __________ very well.

   (a) turn out
   (b) show up
   (c) go around
   (d) fall through

6. A: Why didn't you come to the picnic yesterday?
   B: Sorry I __________ it. I was sick.

   (a) failed
   (b) passed
   (c) missed
   (d) escaped

7. A: I think you should add more supporting details to your paper.
   B: OK, I'll do that. Is there anything else I can do to __________ things?

   (a) expand
   (b) promote
   (c) upgrade
   (d) improve

8. A: Let's go out for a few drinks tonight.
   B: OK, but let's not make it too __________.

   (a) lengthy
   (b) often
   (c) fast
   (d) late

9. A: Hello, I'd like to speak with the
    manager.
    B: Certainly, please __________.

    (a) stand
    (b) hold
    (c) link
    (d) call

10. A: I wish I could afford to buy that
    sweater.
    B: Why not? It's not __________.

    (a) ugly
    (b) cheap
    (c) terrible
    (d) expensive

11. A: I'm so glad I __________ my trip
    to Guam.
    B: Yes. Had you gone, you would've
    been caught up in that earthquake.

    (a) avoided
    (b) stopped
    (c) cancelled
    (d) prevented

12. A: Did you __________ your alarm
    clock?
    B: No, I left it at home.

    (a) pack
    (b) time
    (c) wrap
    (d) forget

13. A: Roger looks like he's gained weight.
    B: Maybe, but he's still in good
    __________.

    (a) shape
    (b) nature
    (c) energy
    (d) position

14. A: How can I get to Boston?
    B: __________ the next train at Union
    Station. It leaves in 15 minutes.

    (a) Travel
    (b) Catch
    (c) Offer
    (d) Pull

15. A: What can I do for you, ma'am?
    B: Well, my flight here was delayed
    and my __________ flight has
    already left.

    (a) joining
    (b) previous
    (c) connecting
    (d) associating

16. A: We only have $50 in the bank.
    B: What! How are we going to pay the
    __________ this month?

    (a) bills
    (b) costs
    (c) credits
    (d) receipts

17. A: I can hardly see the players from
    here.
    B: Here, you can borrow my __________.

    (a) optometry
    (b) binoculars
    (c) hourglasses
    (d) stethoscope

18. A: Why did you buy so many comic books?

B: They're just to __________ the time.

(a) pass
(b) delay
(c) waste
(d) break

19. A: I can't make it to the meeting tomorrow.

B: That's OK. I'll fill you in on the __________ later.

(a) clues
(b) details
(c) reasons
(d) thoughts

20. A: The new teacher's last name is the same as yours.

B: Yes, but we're not __________.

(a) close
(b) related
(c) familiar
(d) acquainted

21. A: What's the fastest way to get to the Hoskins Art Gallery?

B: Take Fifth Avenue. It's a(n) __________.

(a) inroad
(b) shortcut
(c) hyperlink
(d) throughput

22. A: Don't you think our teacher has difficulty expressing himself clearly?

B: Yes, his communication skills are rather __________.

(a) severe
(b) limited
(c) inexpressive
(d) inconceivable

23. A: Why are you rearranging the boss's files?

B: I'm just __________ instructions.

(a) doing over
(b) making out
(c) carrying out
(d) handing over

24. A: I doubt the kidnappers will actually get what they're asking for.

B: I know. The __________ is way too high.

(a) alibi
(b) wage
(c) ransom
(d) alimony

25. A: What should we do about finding a new name for our club?

B: Let's ask the members to __________ one.

(a) stick up for
(b) make up for
(c) catch up with
(d) come up with

Part II   **Questions 26—50**

Choose the best answer for the blank.

26. Our software is designed to ___________ your business needs.

  (a) make
  (b) allow
  (c) keep
  (d) meet

27. The first snowfall this season is expected as early as this weekend, which is quite ___________ for this time of year.

  (a) current
  (b) regular
  (c) abnormal
  (d) impossible

28. In surveys, many people report ___________ more cheerful on bright, sunny days than on dark, cloudy ones.

  (a) feeling
  (b) looking
  (c) sensing
  (d) sounding

29. All doors in the building must be ___________ secured after working hours.

  (a) hardly
  (b) tightly
  (c) closely
  (d) fixedly

30. After you put in your dirty ___________, the washing machine will display how much detergent is needed to clean your clothes.

  (a) attire
  (b) fabric
  (c) laundry
  (d) dressing

31. Exercise has many ___________: it strengthens the heartbeat, helps regulate blood sugar levels and increases blood circulation.

  (a) assets
  (b) profits
  (c) benefits
  (d) blessings

32. Until modern forms of transportation were invented, the mountains were ___________ to economic development.

  (a) flaws
  (b) locks
  (c) fences
  (d) barriers

33. All train passengers must have a(n) ___________ photo ID to purchase tickets.

  (a) true
  (b) real
  (c) valid
  (d) actual

34. An elected, representative government is a(n) __________ part of democracy.

(a) impartial
(b) essential
(c) singular
(d) popular

35. A new terrorist group has claimed __________ for yesterday's bombing.

(a) capability
(b) probability
(c) responsibility
(d) accountability

36. Through their paintings, artists often attempt to __________ complex thoughts in visual form.

(a) govern
(b) furnish
(c) repress
(d) convey

37. Salt is __________ in water, but sand does not dissolve in water.

(a) soluble
(b) solvable
(c) disposable
(d) dissociable

38. The Surgeon General warns that smoking causes lung cancer and may __________ pregnancies.

(a) decompose
(b) complicate
(c) disengage
(d) confound

39. The Education Board is pushing schools to __________ their grading systems so that the entire nation will have a uniform system of evaluation.

(a) evaluate
(b) measure
(c) calculate
(d) standardize

40. The Black Death of the 1300s was a(n) __________ that wiped out over a quarter of Europe's population.

(a) ailment
(b) upsurge
(c) eruption
(d) epidemic

41. Modern technology has changed the way we __________ the world around us.

(a) grieve
(b) receive
(c) perceive
(d) conceive

42. It is disgraceful that our children's test scores have dropped below the fiftieth __________ among their peers.

(a) ratio
(b) ranking
(c) percentile
(d) proportion

43. Some parents have such high __________ of their children that they are never pleased with their children's efforts.

(a) inflations
(b) expectations
(c) anticipations
(d) considerations

44. With the ___________ of TV channels following WWII, viewers had a wider variety of programs to choose from.

(a) implosion
(b) indulgence
(c) proliferation
(d) promulgation

45. Time seems to fly when you are having fun but seems to ___________ when you are bored.

(a) crawl
(b) flutter
(c) wobble
(d) tumble

46. The laborious delivery of my opponent's argument made it seem ___________.

(a) inimitable
(b) traversable
(c) transfusable
(d) interminable

47. Gun culture is so ___________ in the US that it ranks as one of the most heavily armed societies in the world.

(a) innate
(b) ingrained
(c) impetuous
(d) impertinent

48. When employees leave the company, they receive ___________ pay.

(a) severance
(b) settlement
(c) extraneous
(d) compensation

49. Piltdown Man, once credited as a missing link between humans and apes, was later discovered to be an elaborate ___________.

(a) facade
(b) decoy
(c) feint
(d) hoax

50. The biography explores how the writer's reserved lifestyle and need for ___________ are compromised by intrusive social demands.

(a) solitude
(b) rapport
(c) solicitation
(d) equilibrium

This is the end of the Vocabulary section. Do NOT move on to the Reading Comprehension section until instructed to do so. You are NOT allowed to turn to any other section of the test.

READING COMPREHENSION

DIRECTIONS

This part of the exam tests your ability to comprehend reading passages. You will have 45 minutes to complete the 40 questions. Be sure to follow the directions given by the proctor.

Part I   **Questions 1—16**

Read the passage. Then choose the option that best completes the passage.

---

1.   In *Anne Frank: The Diary of a Young Girl*, Anne writes that her father, Otto Frank, is an exceptional man, someone who always supports her and listens to her whenever she has any problems. For example, when Anne talks to her father about her first boyfriend, her father offers some well-balanced and sensible advice on boyfriends and the ways of the world, for which Anne is truly grateful. For Anne, Otto clearly was _______________________________.

   (a) her first true boyfriend
   (b) worried about the future
   (c) a friend as well as a father
   (d) someone she could not trust

2.   Scientists come to Greenland because it is a unique location for studying weather. Many of them study storm developments over the North Atlantic Ocean and provide vital information to ships in the area. Others do important research on _______________________________. This is because changes in Greenland can show scientists what is happening or about to happen to weather patterns around the globe.

   (a) what life is like for people in Greenland
   (b) how the weather in Greenland is changing
   (c) what natural resources exist in Greenland
   (d) how to improve Greenland's shipping industry

3.   As we grow into adults, everyone develops two relationships with our parents. One is based on the past. It comprises the recollections we have of growing up, of how our parents dealt with us and how we appreciated them. These memories can either be positive or negative. The second relationship, which is quite different from what things were like growing up, is the one we have with _______________________________.

   (a) the person that we marry
   (b) the teachers at our school
   (c) our parents in the present
   (d) our own children as parents

4. A small town in Colorado has decided unanimously to forbid smoking at bars and restaurants—even though there are no bars or restaurants. But the prohibition will go into effect as soon as someone actually opens a bar or a restaurant in Timnath, announced the town's board of trustees. As Mayor Donna Benson states, "We learned that ________________________, but we decided it was still a good idea to have in place for when it will be necessary."

(a) there was no reason to have the ban yet
(b) we might have to reverse the ban later
(c) our town is too small to ban smoking
(d) the ban is going to affect businesses

5. By the 4th century BC, most Italic people in central Italy had already been conquered by the more powerful Romans. But the Samnites, who lived in the remote upland valleys, fought back. Needing more space for their sheep, they expanded until their territory was dangerously close to Rome itself. It soon became clear that the struggle to dominate central Italy had narrowed down to two groups, ________________________.

(a) the Samnites and the Italians
(b) the Romans and the Samnites
(c) the Italic people and the Romans
(d) the upland and the lowland tribes

6. Do you want to repaint the interior of your home but can't decide which color or paint to use? Then, come to Benjamin Paints. You can use our Color Preview Studio display to help you choose the right paint color and the right kind of paint. And our friendly staff will be glad to provide you with helpful tips for finding the right finish. When you shop at Benjamin Paints, you are guaranteed to get good service. So, if you ________________________, contact your local dealer today.

(a) need help remodeling your home
(b) want to hire a professional painter
(c) plan to add new color to your home
(d) are looking for redecoration supplies

7. In factories, you often have a huge amount of one air pollutant, but in office buildings you might see low — but damaging — levels of more than one at the same time. Symptoms of this phenomenon may involve one or more of the following: coughing, headaches, dizziness, sore throats or deprivation of the ability to focus. Usually several people in your office will get these symptoms, which disappear when they are away from the office, simultaneously. If you show any of these symptoms, it is probable that

_______________________________________.

(a) you are catching some kind of flu
(b) you need to quit working in the factory
(c) your water filters need to be replaced
(d) your office has low levels of pollutants

8. SOS Shredding offers a cost-effective, easy and secure method for disposing of your company's confidential documents. With SOS Shredding, there is no need to purchase a shredder, no need for your employees to waste time shredding paper and no need to pay for the removal of shredded paper waste. SOS will take care of everything for you, and we guarantee that _______________________________________. Call today for a free estimate.

(a) your company's premises will be kept secure
(b) your computer data will be completely private
(c) your documents will be confidentially eliminated
(d) your packages will be delivered safely and on time

9. The company behind the online fantasy game EterniQuest has started punishing players for bending the game's rules to make money. The company decided to crack down on these players because the huge amounts of virtual cash transactions taking place in the game world were threatening to bring the EterniQuest economy to its knees. If left unchecked, there could have been a risk of hyperinflation that would have made it impossible for beginning players to compete. This just goes to show that some online game worlds have one thing in common with real life: they both

_______________________________________.

(a) are subject to the laws of economics
(b) rely upon political decision-making
(c) are characterized by violent warfare
(d) depend on strategies for survival

10. Hypothetically, if we were to take an infant from his own family and place him with a new family in a completely different cultural environment, his mental outlook and self-identity would develop differently. By involvement in a new cultural environment, the child will adopt certain other views as his or her own. This is because children's attitudes ________________________________.

(a) gradually change as they grow up
(b) develop independent of family upbringing
(c) are predetermined by their genetic makeup
(d) tend to be influenced by their surroundings

11. When it comes to development, we normally think first in terms of economic development satisfying our material needs. But could that be all there is to development? Should it be weighed solely in economic terms? It could be argued that development should be linked not only to material aspects, but also to social and cultural ones. For example, a developed society should possess an adept legal system developed through years of parliamentary action and judicial interpretation. In this sense, development would be seen as something ________________________________.

(a) in need of restructuring in coming years
(b) regarded as insignificant by economists
(c) linked to the effects of a slow economy
(d) that comprises many areas of a society

12. When Hernando Cortes and his Spanish troops of not even a thousand men blitzed into Mexico in 1519, the native population totaled roughly 22 million. By the end of the century, however, after a range of fatal epidemics to which the locals displayed no immunity, a mere 2 million had survived. This exceptionally high mortality rate forever changed the culture of Mesoamerica. It also put the Spanish among history's worst conquerors, the type who ________________________________.

(a) kill with their microbes as well as their swords
(b) take over other lands by first waging bio-warfare
(c) systematically alter the cultures of other people
(d) completely exterminate those that they conquer

13.

> Dear Editor:
>
> It was disappointing to read your newspaper's attacks on Mayor Gary Moss for speaking the truth and protecting the PTA from criticisms that seem to be politically driven. Sticking with the truth, even when it is unpopular or when it may not be "politically correct," should be encouraged rather than condemned. I have been following the public career of Mayor Moss for nearly four decades, and the only thing that you can criticize him for is not behaving like a typical bureaucrat and lying to safeguard political self-interests. The world would be a much better place if ___________________________________.
>
> Sincerely,
> Laura Edwards

(a) we had more public officials willing to speak the truth
(b) we had fewer politically motivated individuals like him
(c) newspapers would speak out against corrupt politicians
(d) organizations like the PTA would just stay out of politics

14. There has been much argument about when babies can first identify where a sound comes from. Although it was once believed that it only became possible late in their development, it is now thought that babies can localize sound as early as ten minutes after birth. Earlier observers only studied whether a baby could turn her head toward the source of a sound, a reaction that begins around the age of three months. However, a closer examination has revealed other telltale signs of reaction. A newborn baby may not be able to ___________________________________.

(a) differentiate his mother's voice from those of others
(b) identify which person is making the sound
(c) turn his head but rather his eyes
(d) immediately tell night from day

15. Beethoven had a very volatile personality. Even his friends had a hard time predicting when his temper would flare. By nature, Beethoven was impatient, irritable and intolerant. He would often misunderstand a facial expression and accuse faithful friends of disloyalty, or he would become angry for no apparent reason, then dismiss his friends for being untrustworthy. ____________________________, he would often write a letter the next day to apologize for his behavior.

(a) Finally
(b) Similarly
(c) However
(d) Therefore

16. Because of the interactive sophistication of computer games, beating a human opponent is seen as the ultimate measure of success for those trying to create an artificially intelligent machine (AI). Winning in the game of chess, for example, has been deemed an especially high benchmark for AI engineers over the years. This is because the game only has a handful of rules, and yet its complexity requires a great deal of intelligence to master. ____________________________, AI machines must be able to master that complexity to challenge and beat chess players of high intelligence. If they can do so, then the machines can be thought of as possessing true artificial intelligence.

(a) Thus
(b) Even so
(c) In addition
(d) At the same time

Part II   **Questions 17—37**

Read the passage and the question. Then choose the option that best answers the question.

17. About 65% of kindergartners in the US are in school five to six hours a day. That percentage represents a doubling of the number of full-day kindergartners since the early 1980s. Even just a decade ago, most kindergartners only went for the morning or afternoon. The academic demands of kindergarten also have increased for today's generation of young kids. Regarded now as the entry point of academic life, kindergarten is seen as a time of basic but substantial learning rather than as a soft step into first grade.

Q: What is the best title for the report?
(a) Full-day Kindergarten and Intelligence
(b) The Changing Role of US Kindergartens
(c) US Kindergartens: More Fun Than Ever
(d) The Decline of US Kindergarten Education

18. Many medical researchers believe that an overweight child will suffer from heart disease or Type 2 diabetes later on in life. But children who are obese develop other problems before this, problems that concern their mobility: specifically, fractures and joint pain. A study of 227 obese children and teens, led by Dr. Stanley Coleman at the National Institute of Diabetes, revealed that these youngsters were far more prone to suffer fractures than their ideal-weight peers. They also displayed more bone and hip joint abnormalities.

Q: What is the main idea of the passage?
(a) Overweight kids can develop diabetes and heart disease.
(b) More and more children and teens are getting fractures.
(c) Obese children and teens risk bone and joint problems.
(d) Diabetes can lead to mobility problems in children.

19. ARPP members can now save anywhere between 5 and 30% on acupuncture, massage, yoga, personal training and chiropractic services at gyms through the new ARPP Alternative Health and Wellness Network. ARPP membership cards are currently accepted for discounts at approximately 25,000 participating practitioners nationwide. To find out more—including the names of your local practitioners—call (888) 893-4639, or visit ARPP's website at www.arpp.org/alternatives.

Q: Which of the following is the best title for the advertisement?
(a) ARPP's New Discount Services Network
(b) 25,000 Participating Practitioners at ARPP
(c) New Services Available for ARPP Members
(d) The Benefits of Alternative Health Therapies

20. Amina Harun, a farmer in Africa, used to spend hours searching for a working pay phone she could use to call the markets and find the best prices for her fruit. Since the advent of cell phones, however, she has been able to call sellers and customers much more easily. Harun is one of an estimated 100 million of the continent's 906 million people who have learned the value of mobile phones, which comprised 74.6% of all African phone subscriptions last year. The cell phone industry, which barely existed 10 years ago, is now worth $25 billion.

Q: What is the main idea of the report?
(a) Cell phone use is on the increase in Africa.
(b) The cell phone industry is now worth billions.
(c) African farmers use cell phones for business.
(d) Cell phone usage in Africa is low.

21. Every year between 1-2% of the world's rainforests disappear. There are many reasons for this problem. Trees are cut down, often illegally, by unscrupulous loggers or by people who wish to clear more land to raise more cattle or grow more crops. Meanwhile, other areas of rainforest are polluted by mining activities; mining and logging companies also build new roads that penetrate into once inaccessible regions, leaving them open to more destruction. At this current rate of deforestation, some scientists estimate that 17,000 species of rainforest plants and animals become extinct every year.

Q: What is the main point of the passage?
(a) More scientific research is needed on deforestation.
(b) Human exploitation is causing the loss of rainforests.
(c) Too much pollution is damaging the Earth's rainforests.
(d) Rainforests around the world are being occupied by humans.

22.

> Dear Sir/Madam:
>
> I recently purchased a Pronkar XL sedan with automatic transmission. But after several months, I noticed that it became hard to shift from reverse to drive and from drive to neutral. I took the vehicle into the dealership for repair, and they said all of the models like mine made by your company had this problem and that it couldn't be fixed. You are a major carmaker. How could this happen? Please address this situation immediately, or I will be contacting my lawyer.
>
> Sincerely,
> Graham Stevens

Q: What is the main purpose of the letter?
(a) To ask a carmaker for a refund
(b) To criticize a dealership for not repairing a car
(c) To demand that a car problem be fixed at once
(d) To ask a carmaker to explain a mechanical problem

23. The world's oldest person on record, a Dutch woman, died on Tuesday at the age of 116. The woman, Hendrikje van Andel, was a former needlework teacher. She was born on June 29, 1890 and died Tuesday in her sleep at a nursing home in the northern Dutch town of Hoogeveen. According to her son, Johan van Andel, Hendrikje's secret to a long life was a daily meal of fish.

Q: Which of the following is correct about Hendrikje van Andel?
(a) She died at a nursing home.
(b) She died in her sleep at her home.
(c) She ate fish twice a day for her health.
(d) She taught needlework in Hoogeveen.

24. Putting together a family genealogy can be easy or hard depending on your ancestors. In general, the more successful they were, the easier it is to find information about them. If they were famous, tracing them is simple because there are probably newspaper records or other written accounts available with plenty of information. But if they were not successful, your best chance of tracing them is by going through old church records or government statistics.

Q   Which of the following is correct according to the passage?
(a) Tracing ancestors is easier if they were well-known.
(b) Government statistics provide information on old churches.
(c) No records were kept for ancestors who were not successful.
(d) Old churches have the best records for tracing one's ancestors.

25.

Dear Customer:

At Ice Mountain Gear Equipment, Ltd., customer safety is our top priority. For this reason, we are recalling our model Z-10 Ice Pick. We have discovered that a number of ice picks were manufactured with faulty heads. If you have bought a Z-10 Ice Pick recently, we strongly encourage you to check its six-digit code. If it has "110206" stamped into the head, then you are advised to return it. Tools not displaying this date code are not being recalled. You may return your product to: Customer Return Center, 2300 West Avenue, Salt Lake City, UT 67721.

With your safety in mind,
Gerald Cavanot
President, Ice Mountain Gear Equipment, Ltd.

Q: Which of the following is correct according to the letter?
(a) Picks without the 110206 code are not being recalled.
(b) Ice Mountain Gear is giving a refund for all Z-10 picks.
(c) The Z-10 Ice Pick has caused head injuries to customers.
(d) Picks with the six-digit code must be returned in person.

26. Ecooper.com is a new website that aims to serve as a concise guide to some of the most commonly violated rules of writing, grammar and punctuation. It is designed for writers of all levels and skills. You can explore basic definitions for grammar rules and use the reference section to find additional explanations and examples for further study. You can also look up grammatical terms in the glossary and browse many other writing resources on our site. Visit our website, and you will improve your writing in no time!

Q: Which of the following is correct about the website according to the advertisement?
(a) It has definitions and examples of grammar rules.
(b) It is designed for teachers of grammar and writing.
(c) It has links to other writing resources on the Internet.
(d) It is aimed at learners of English as a second language.

27. When scuba divers descend into deep water, their lungs absorb more nitrogen than usual, which diffuses from the lungs to the blood and from the blood to body tissues. Then, when the diver surfaces, it diffuses back from the tissues into the blood and from the blood into the lungs to be exhaled. This process is safe unless the return to the surface is too rapid. In that case, the nitrogen in the tissues and blood cannot diffuse out rapidly enough to be expelled through the lungs, and nitrogen bubbles form. These can cause severe pain, particularly around the joints.

Q: What happens to nitrogen when a scuba diver slowly ascends?
(a) It is exhaled in greater quantities.
(b) It diffuses from the blood into the lungs.
(c) It is absorbed into the blood and body tissues.
(d) It forms painful bubbles in the diver's body tissues.

28. Kiwi Wine Company is proud to announce that Monkey Bay is now America's top-selling New Zealand white wine. We created Monkey Bay to address the growing thirst of American wine lovers for New Zealand's zingy white wines. Its unique taste comes from the choice fruit we use from Marlborough's renowned Sunny Valley, where a cool maritime climate, sparkling sunshine and well-drained soils produce grapes with a rich tropical flavor, exquisite herbal tones and crisp acidity. Try Monkey Bay today and discover why it is number one.

Q: Which of the following is correct according to the advertisement?
(a) American wine drinkers like New Zealand red wines.
(b) New Zealand is renowned for its rich and crisp wines.
(c) Monkey Bay white wine is a top seller in New Zealand.
(d) Monkey Bay was originally created by an American company.

29. The movie *The Hunt for Red October* was based on a real case of mutiny, but it was not until recently that the true details of this tale have been revealed. The incident involved a Soviet naval destroyer, not a submarine, and the person who led the mutiny, Valery Sablin, did not intend to defect to the West but was instead hoping to launch a new Russian revolution. Sablin was a Leninist with an idealistic tendency who was disillusioned by the hypocrisy of his country's leaders and the huge inequalities that had arisen within the Kremlin walls.

Q: Which of the following is correct according to the passage?
(a) *The Hunt for Red October* was based on a real submarine incident.
(b) Sablin's plan was to spark political change in the Soviet Union.
(c) The intention of Sablin's crew was to defect to a Western country.
(d) Sablin was upset over his country's strict adherence to Leninism.

30. Most northern Italian cities were bustling centers of activity at the end of the 14th century. But the noise pollution generated by all this activity created problems. For one thing, people could not hear the tower bells that would indicate the time by ringing at specific intervals throughout the day. So, to solve this problem, authorities passed laws mandating silence. The Grocers' Guild of Florence, for example, forbade store owners from calling out to customers in other shops to entice them to come over to their stores.

Q: Which of the following is correct according to the passage?
(a) Shop owners in Florence were banned from advertising.
(b) The tower bells were being damaged by all the pollution.
(c) The chiming was meant to help residents keep track of time.
(d) Silence laws were passed to regulate the loud noise from bells.

31. Writers who produce wildly entertaining books are often not appreciated by the literary establishment. Miles Hathaway is one of them. But while his terrific new novel, *On the Loose*, lacks the high-brow qualities critics appreciate, it excels in every other respect. Hathaway writes with an offbeat sense of humor that leads to subtle revelations of character. In *On the Loose*, he captures the lively world of Nancy Melbourne as she experiences a series of minor social and professional failures but then finds happiness by radically changing the way she looks at life.

Q: Which of the following is correct about *On the Loose*?
(a) It is written by an author with a skill for characterization.
(b) It is about a woman who triumphs in her professional life.
(c) Its high-brow topics would not interest the general public.
(d) Its sophisticated sense of humor has been praised by critics.

32. On December 21, 1961, I landed at New York City's Idlewild Airport, kissing the ground after having returned from Afghanistan. What I had experienced there led to my becoming an activist in the American feminist movement. As a young bride in Kabul, I was an eyewitness to just how badly women are treated in some countries. I was mistreated, too, and just barely survived. I returned to weighing just 90 pounds, bruised both emotionally and physically. So, in a very real sense, my "Western" feminism was forged through experience, unlike so many other American radicals at that time.

Q: Which of the following is correct about the writer according to the passage?
(a) She lost 90 pounds during her time in Afghanistan.
(b) She became a feminist after living as a wife in Kabul.
(c) She left for Afghanistan from an airport in New York.
(d) She was deeply impressed by the feminist movement.

33. Dr. and Mrs. George King kindly request your attendance at a reception celebrating the marriage of Matthew Lucas King and Ellen Margaret Holt on Saturday, November 18, 2006, at Inverness Club, 4601 Dorr Street, Toledo, Ohio. Cocktails will be served from 6:30 pm and dinner is at 7:30 pm. No gifts or flowers, please.

Q: What is the purpose of the announcement?
(a) To organize a party
(b) To offer an invitation
(c) To book a dinner reservation
(d) To explain marriage arrangements

34. A disturbing trend is sweeping through corporate America. Disgraced executives, despite their dismal or even unlawful performances, are receiving lucrative severance packages. Bernard Moffat, who stepped down under pressure from his role as WorldOp Inc.'s chief executive, will receive $1.5 million annually for the rest of his life—even though the company is now bankrupt and involved in a scandal. Likewise, Jack Kelly, the senior accountant who left Yardley Telecom last month while at the center of several congressional probes, took about $32 million with him. The worry is that these examples are not uncommon.

Q: What does the writer of the article imply?
(a) Companies should honor their severance agreements.
(b) CEOs work hard to earn their large severance packages.
(c) High severance packages corrupt the behavior of CEOs.
(d) Severance packages for disgraced CEOs are unjustified.

35. One question that is perpetually raised in philosophy is this: "Is humankind inherently good or evil?" But it is probably safe to say that a person is not born inherently good or bad. Most people are born with the capacity for cooperation and love as well as the capacity for aggressive and hostile behavior. The question of which traits develop in an individual and grow to dominate in a person depends upon the individual's experiences in his or her environment. People develop a stance toward life out of life's stance toward them.

Q: What does the writer imply about human beings?
(a) They are genetically predisposed to exhibit certain traits.
(b) They require some form of religion in order to become good.
(c) With a proper environment, they are likely to develop good traits.
(d) Without early intervention, some are destined for aggressive behavior.

36. Your role as a leader is to inspire the people you lead, and help them overcome difficult situations. This is true no matter what your leadership task may be, whether it is teaching or leading a hike. For example, Sir Ernest Shackleton, who led an expedition in the Antarctic, told jokes and stories to help his men stay alive during a cruel winter. His humor inspired them to stay positive. This is only an example, and it does not matter how you help others overcome hardship, as long as it works.

Q: What does the passage imply about good leaders?
(a) They are humorous at all times.
(b) They enjoy having responsibilities.
(c) They do not have many weaknesses.
(d) They use their talents to motivate others.

37. In much of the world, the penalties for using cannabis are severe. But in 1976, the possession of small amounts was legalized in Holland. This radical move eventually led to even more leniency toward drug use in Dutch society. As a result, marijuana use has become widespread; now in Amsterdam, you can smoke marijuana at a local coffee shop offering cannabis varieties such as Moroccan Blue and Northern Lights. Just as advocates of decriminalization predicted, use of hard drugs, such as heroin and cocaine, has declined. This does not mean Holland's acceptance of soft drugs has come without a price. In public parks, children high on marijuana walk around like zombies, much to the dismay of parents and local officials.

Q: What can be inferred from the passage?
(a) Holland now has no civil penalties for drug trafficking.
(b) Drug legalization has made Holland more popular with tourists.
(c) Liberal marijuana laws can stop people from turning to harder drugs.
(d) The legalization of drugs was part of a radical social reform in Holland.

Part III **Questions 38—40**

Read the passage. Then identify the option that does NOT belong.

38. Across the length and breadth of China, dust storms are an annual event. (a) Between January and May each year, strong winds blowing from the northwest carry off millions of tons of fine soil from China's Gobi Desert. (b) Much of this dust gets blown to other parts of the country, while the rest is wafted high into the air and carried to other countries. (c) The Gobi Desert covers the northwest portion of China and part of Mongolia. (d) Dust from the Gobi Desert can actually end up being carried as far away as the United States.

39. Jamaica has a long history of violence and slavery. (a) From 1517 onwards it was increasingly populated by African slaves, who were made to work on sugar plantations. (b) By the end of the 18th century, over 300,000 slaves inhabited the island. (c) The plantations where these slaves worked produced phenomenal wealth, but only for the white owners. (d) Many former slaves wanted to run their own plantations.

40. Intellectual Property (IP) is a legal term that refers to patents, utility models, designs, trademarks, trade secrets and other copyrighted material. (a) The International Intellectual Property Alliance oversees copyright protection of all types of computer software, films, TV programs, music, books and other media. (b) Protection is automatic for some property, and it is unnecessary to make a formal application for protection. (c) However, formal applications must be made to register patents, utility models, designs or trademarks. (d) These are registered under Patent Law, Utility Model Law, Design Law and Trademark Law, respectively.

This is the end of the Reading Comprehension section. Please remain seated until the proctor has instructed otherwise. You are NOT allowed to turn to any other section of the test.

서울대 최신기출 1
Listening Comprehension **Scripts**

1

M Is Amy back in town?

W _______________

(a) Yeah, I just found out about it.
(b) No, I don't know what town.
(c) She just stepped out.
(d) I came in last.

2

W Want to have lunch together?

M _______________

(a) I'd really enjoy that.
(b) No, I'm heading over.
(c) Yes, I've eaten there.
(d) I'm not picky about food.

3

M My new apartment is a 20-minute walk from work.

W _______________

(a) I'll bring you one.
(b) That's not too bad.
(c) I'm sorry for the delay.
(d) Just work 10 more minutes.

4

W What do you think of this house that's for sale?

M _______________

(a) It's just down the street.
(b) It looks like a nice place.
(c) I don't know who owns it.
(d) Now is a good time to sell.

5

M Stetson Investments, how may I direct your call?

W _______________

(a) Phone me later.
(b) I don't know who called.
(c) Please send it right over.
(d) The sales division, please.

6

W Excuse me, where can I find a digital radio?

M _______________

(a) The sound is excellent.
(b) Feel free to listen to it.
(c) Go a little farther down this aisle.
(d) I can't find the right model, either.

7

M Hey, I just noticed a scratch on our car door.

W _______________

(a) It'll take a long time to heal.
(b) You should've known better.
(c) Accidents like that can be fatal.
(d) I'm afraid I made that this morning.

8

W Do you want to go to a soccer game with me?

M _______________

(a) Thanks, but I know nothing about soccer.
(b) Sure, let's watch it on my widescreen.
(c) Well, I forgot to rent the video.
(d) OK, I'll play soccer with you.

9

M Thanks for volunteering to help with my project.

W _______________

(a) You were a great help.
(b) You're welcome to do it.
(c) I appreciate your hard work.
(d) I just wish I could've done more.

10

W   Honey, that tie doesn't go with your suit.

M   ___________________________________

(a) But neither does this suit.
(b) OK. I'll have it cleaned.
(c) Hmm, I'll try another.
(d) I wear this suit often.

11

M   Is something wrong with your TV, Tina?

W   ___________________________________

(a) I'll watch TV soon.
(b) No, it's my only one.
(c) I'm sorry, but not yet.
(d) Well, it's been acting up.

12

W   I can't decide whether to move abroad this year or not.

M   ___________________________________

(a) Go over your decision one last time.
(b) Clearly you chose the right path.
(c) You can't change past mistakes.
(d) Take some time to mull it over.

13

M   How was the turnout at the meeting?

W   ___________________________________

(a) We mainly discussed staff issues.
(b) It was an excellent presentation.
(c) The audience seemed to like it.
(d) It was smaller than expected.

14

W   Well, another publisher backed out on my novella.

M   ___________________________________

(a) Maybe you can find another one to read.
(b) I'm sorry, but the loss is entirely theirs.
(c) Thanks, I'd be thrilled to look it over.
(d) Surely it'll be well-received.

15

M   I'm sorry I shouted. How can I make it up to you?

W   ___________________________________

(a) I just ask you not to do it again.
(b) I have quite enough already.
(c) I don't know how to go about it.
(d) Your approach was questionable.

16

W   Frank, why aren't you out of bed yet?
M   I'm still very tired!
W   Really? Why?
M   ___________________________________

(a) I'll get up soon.
(b) I already started.
(c) I'll make the bed.
(d) I went to bed late.

17

M   I'd like a single room, please.
W   I'm sorry, they're all booked.
M   Oh, do you expect any cancellations?
W   ___________________________________

(a) Not for tonight.
(b) That's correct.
(c) I'll stop them.
(d) I'll cancel it.

18

W   Hey, Tony! What have you been up to?
M   Oh, hi Sue! Nothing much.
W   I haven't seen you in quite a while.
M   ___________________________________

(a) Yes, it's been ages.
(b) We've grown to be close.
(c) You didn't change it much.
(d) Right. It didn't take that long.

19

M Is that the tip you're leaving our waitress?

W Yes. Isn't three dollars enough?

M Well, I think it should be more.

W _______________________

(a) True. It's a good deal.
(b) But the price changed.
(c) Yeah, let's order soon.
(d) I'll add another dollar, then.

20

W Excuse me, where is the fish market?

M Go straight and turn left at the traffic light.

W Oh, so is it just around the corner?

M _______________________

(a) They sell a lot of fish.
(b) No, several blocks down.
(c) I'm not sure where that is.
(d) Yes, in the other direction.

21

M Wow! I love your new hairstyle.

W Thanks. I got it cut yesterday.

M You look younger with short hair.

W _______________________

(a) I don't want to wear it that long.
(b) That's the style I want to try.
(c) That's what I was hoping for.
(d) I know. It's growing fast.

22

W Hi, it's Amy. Sorry for calling at this odd hour.

M That's OK. What's up?

W I had a rotten day and need a sympathetic ear.

M _______________________

(a) Don't worry. I'm almost there.
(b) Go ahead and tell me about it.
(c) It took you so long to answer.
(d) You're right. We'll get by.

23

M What's the trouble, ma'am? Your car broke down?

W Yes, officer. It stalled and won't start again.

M Let me have a look. Maybe I can figure it out.

W _______________________

(a) Oh, that would be greatly helpful.
(b) Thanks for fixing the problem.
(c) But that can't be the problem.
(d) I'll get going now.

24

W Have you ever been to Thailand?

M Yes, twice on vacation.

W Really? What was it like?

M _______________________

(a) About a six-hour flight.
(b) Kind people and fabulous beaches.
(c) I'd love to see you there next time.
(d) Good enough. You should try some.

25

M You look more relaxed these days.

W Yeah, it's a lot less stressful at work.

M Oh? How have things changed?

W _______________________

(a) The changes will be for the better.
(b) I'm sure you can find another job.
(c) The company hired more employees.
(d) The stress was getting worse over time.

26

W Thanks for telling me about that show on global warming.

M No problem. So, you caught it last night?

W Yeah, and now I wonder if it's too late to reverse the damage.

M _______________________

(a) No, it'll be a lot earlier than expected.
(b) Yes, going the other way sounds better.
(c) Yes, what you did was more than enough.
(d) No, we can still step up and do something.

27

M What a beautiful night for a walk along the
   pier.
W Really? It looks like it'll rain.
M No, it's just clouding over a little.
W ___________________________

(a) All right. I'll go get an umbrella.
(b) No way. I have a hunch it'll pour.
(c) I'm not up to the idea of hard work.
(d) There's got to be something else on.

28

W We should've hired the last candidate even
   though he was mediocre.
M Yeah, we're so shorthanded these days.
W I know. We're practically doing double shifts.
M ___________________________

(a) Recruiting has become routine.
(b) Training usually takes a lot of time.
(c) We worked really hard to get that raise.
(d) I hope we'll get some good applicants soon.

29

M I love what your decorator did with your
   apartment.
W Thanks. I got sick of the old décor.
M And the color combinations work so well.
W ___________________________

(a) Then maybe I'll rearrange them.
(b) No, I couldn't change the colors.
(c) Actually, I selected them myself.
(d) Yes, there are a few mismatches.

30

W We need to do more for the environment.
M I don't see how we can do more than we are
   doing now.
W Well, we don't always unplug appliances
   we're not using.
M ___________________________

(a) That's the benefit of recycling.
(b) I'm all for it if it'll make a difference.
(c) I thought they were off. I must have forgotten.
(d) That's not an environmentally friendly
    measure.

31

W Oh, no! I can't believe this!
M Why? What's the problem?
W I just realized I used indoor instead of
   outdoor paint on my fence.
M Is that really such a big deal?
W Yes, indoor paint doesn't stand up in rain or
   sun.

Q: What is the conversation mainly about?
(a) Using the wrong paint.
(b) Fixing a broken fence.
(c) A disagreeable color.
(d) A half-painted gate.

32

W David, can you sign this requisition form?
M But I'm no longer your team manager. Toby
   Dunn is.
W Yes, but he's out of the office until Thursday.
M Still I can't go signing things for him.
W I wouldn't normally ask, but this is urgent.
M I'm sorry, Jane. I don't have the authority.

Q: What is mainly taking place in the
   conversation?
(a) The woman is going over the requisition
    form.
(b) The woman is asking for the man's signature.
(c) The man is helping the woman with her work.
(d) The man is refusing to do extra work.

33

M Where is your next concert?
W I'll be playing in Boston.
M Will you have any free time?
W A bit. I'm using it to see some friends.
M Do they know you're coming?
W Yep. We have plans to go sightseeing
   together.

Q: What is the conversation mainly about?
(a) The woman's concert performance.
(b) The parts of Boston the woman likes.
(c) The woman's upcoming visit to Boston.
(d) The friends the woman plans to contact.

34

M   Please put your carry-on bag here to be x-rayed.

W   Sure, but my camera is in the bag. Will the film be affected?

M   Is it a standard camera and film?

W   It's just a disposable camera I bought.

M   Then there should be no problem.

Q: What is the woman mainly doing in the conversation?
(a) Purchasing a new camera.
(b) Checking the film she took.
(c) Asking about her film's safety.
(d) Packing her carry-on luggage.

35

W   Where's Roger? It's almost time for our presentation.

M   As far as I know, he hasn't arrived yet.

W   You're kidding! We can't do this without him.

M   He'll turn up. Maybe he just stopped for coffee.

W   Well, has anybody tried calling him?

M   Not that I know of. But I'll do that now.

Q: What is the conversation mainly about?
(a) Roger's unknown whereabouts.
(b) Roger's upcoming presentation.
(c) Past presentations given by Roger.
(d) Whether or not Roger was called in.

36

W   Someone gave me a hot tip on the commodities market.

M   Really? Is it anything you'd like to share?

W   Sure. Concentrated orange juice stocks are set to rise.

M   Interesting. But do you think it's possible?

W   Yes, and I'm going to buy now while the price is low.

M   Then I might buy some, too.

Q: What is the conversation mainly about?
(a) Sales of concentrated orange juice.
(b) Information on stocks that may rise.
(c) A warning against investing in stocks.
(d) An investment the woman profited from.

37

W   I'm not sure who should be the lead in our play.

M   Well, Janice's audition was very good.

W   But Sally is a better singer than Janice.

M   Only slightly. Janice is more suited overall.

W   But since it's a musical, shouldn't Sally do it?

M   No, I don't think she has what it takes to be the lead.

Q: What are the man and woman mainly doing?
(a) Planning auditions for a play.
(b) Replacing the actors in a play.
(c) Choosing an extra for a musical.
(d) Debating who should play the lead role.

38

W   Welcome to Ruby's Family Restaurant.

M   Hi, I'd just like a table for one, please.

W   Certainly. There'll be a ten-minute wait, though.

M   That's fine. I'm in no hurry.

W   I'll bring you over some juice to drink while you wait.

M   Thanks. I'd appreciate that.

Q: Which is correct according to the conversation?
(a) The man is dining with his family.
(b) The woman got the man a table.
(c) The man will wait to be seated.
(d) The woman will bring a soda.

39

W   Jim, that cough of yours sounds terrible.

M   I know. And it's getting worse.

W   Well, you ought to do something about it.

M   You're right. I've had it for over a week.

W   You should go and see a doctor.

M   Yeah, I think I'll make an appointment.

Q: Which is correct about the man according to the conversation?
(a) His cough has gotten better.
(b) His cough has lasted over a week.
(c) He went to see a doctor last week.
(d) He canceled a doctor's appointment.

40

M   Hello! You look familiar.

W   Oh, so do you. Have we met before?

M   Oh, yes! At Joanne Smith's housewarming party.

W   Yes, last month! It's Bob, right?

M   Yes, you've got a good memory.

W   I've always been good with names.

Q: Which is correct according to the conversation?

(a) The man does not recognize the woman.

(b) The woman held a housewarming party.

(c) The man and woman met last month.

(d) The woman forgot the man's name.

41

M   How was your trip to the art museum last weekend?

W   Exasperating. Hordes of people were there. It was so noisy.

M   That had to have been uncomfortable.

W   And there were too many kids running around.

M   Oh, no. That must've been a nuisance, too.

W   Yes, so if you're thinking of going, go on a weekday.

Q: Which is correct according to the conversation?

(a) The woman's museum visit was enjoyable.

(b) The man went to the museum with the woman.

(c) The woman was annoyed by children at the museum.

(d) The man is unsympathetic to the woman's complaints.

42

M   Well, I've chosen my courses for the semester. How about you, Diana?

W   Almost. I'm undecided between a history and a politics class.

M   What history class do you have in mind?

W   Medieval European History—Mondays and Wednesdays.

M   I'm taking that. Wouldn't it be better than politics?

W   Hard to say, but I might be joining you.

Q: Which is correct according to the conversation?

(a) The man cannot decide which class to take.

(b) The Medieval European History class is held on Fridays.

(c) The man prefers the politics class to the history class.

(d) The woman is unsure if the history class would be better.

43

W   Excuse me. I just checked out at 11, but I need to go back to the room.

M   Did you leave something there, ma'am?

W   Actually, I think I left my watch there.

M   I'll call housekeeping to check, then. What was the room number?

W   It was 2140. I hope it's still there.

M   I'm sure it is, ma'am.

Q: What can be inferred from the conversation?

(a) The man believes housekeeping will find the watch.

(b) The man is worried the room may be unavailable.

(c) The woman was late checking out of her room.

(d) The woman thinks her watch has been stolen.

44

M   Did you enjoy yourself yesterday?

W   My team lost, but I had a good time, anyway.

M   I heard you had a front-row seat.

W   Yes, we were right up near the action.

M   I wish I had been at the game.

W   Yeah. It's much better than watching it on TV.

Q: What can be inferred from the conversation?

(a) The woman watches a lot of TV.

(b) The man has no interest in sports.

(c) The man played in a sports match.

(d) The woman went to a sports game.

45

W   I really envy you going on business trips so often.

M   You envy me? It's not all fun and games.

W   But you get to go to new and interesting places.

M   Well, sometimes I envy your lifestyle.

W   Believe me, it's not so great working in an office all the time.

M   But you get to sleep at home every night.

Q: What can be inferred from the conversation?

(a) The woman is overloaded with work.

(b) The woman does not often go on business trips.

(c) The man wishes he did not have to work overtime.

(d) The man would like to find a more challenging job.

46

The average American family spends up to four hours a day watching TV. Do you want to waste precious time like that? If not, then turn to the Freedom Foundation. The Freedom Foundation is a volunteer organization that has helped millions of people turn off their TVs. Our two major campaigns, "Turnoff Week" and "More Reading and Less TV," help children and adults cut back on TV watching. Call 519-4433 now for more information!

Q: What is the advertisement mainly about?

(a) A school that teaches children reading skills.

(b) A television network operated by volunteers.

(c) An organization with a TV recycling program.

(d) An organization that promotes watching less TV.

47

I now want to turn to the aftermath of World War II. After the Allies defeated the Nazis, they were divided on how Germany should be treated. The Soviets wanted to stop the country from rebuilding. They also wanted Germany to pay large sums of money in reparations. Britain and the United States, however, saw that rebuilding Germany was important for world peace.

Q: What is the talk mainly about?

(a) How the Allies envisioned post-war Germany.

(b) How the Allies cooperated to defeat the Nazis.

(c) Why Germany's economic recovery was important.

(d) Why the Soviets demanded reparations from Germany.

48

Enjoy Lake Powell on your very own houseboat, but share the cost of maintenance with an elite group of owners. Our shared ownership program is ideal for friends, families and corporations who want to experience great vacations for years to come. From large luxury houseboats to small family-oriented houseboats—we have it all. Visit our Houseboat Park in Page, Arizona, for a personal tour, or call 1-800-572-5701 for an information packet.

Q: What is the advertisement mainly about?

(a) Restrictions on Lake Powell boat rentals.

(b) Resort packages around Lake Powell.

(c) Sharing ownership of a houseboat.

(d) Secondhand houseboats for sale.

49

In science news, Brazilian fire ants, which are capable of damaging crops and even killing small animals, have been spreading in the US and are on a destructive march through the southern states. But that could be about to change. Researchers plan to release a South American fly into the US to prey on the pests. These imported flies attack only fire ants, so they pose no threat to the ecosystem.

Q: What is the main idea of the news report?
(a) The US fire ant problem may soon be solved.
(b) Foreign ant species pose a threat to the South.
(c) Researchers warn of the dangers of imported flies.
(d) Fire ants have negatively impacted the US ecosystem.

50

I spoke earlier about how, for a great many American Jews, a sense of Jewish identity has been forged and nurtured by external enemies, who have defined Jews as victims through persecution. But unfortunately, even some Jews without a background of persecution are automatically taking on a victim identity instead of basing their sense of self on the strengths of the Jewish heritage. This has caused great worry among Jewish thinkers.

Q: What is the main idea about American Jews in the lecture?
(a) They falsely see themselves as victims.
(b) They are too little concerned with identity.
(c) They cling to victimization in forming an identity.
(d) Their identity is based on Judaism and Jewish history.

51

I now want to discuss another theory on global warming based on data from satellites that have been monitoring the Sun. Analysis of their data suggests that solar radiation received by Earth has been increasing in intensity over the last 24 years. Due to subtle solar changes, Earth has been receiving about 0.05 percent more radiation each decade. This increase, as opposed to human-made greenhouse gases, could possibly account for the climate getting warmer.

Q: What is the main idea of the lecture?
(a) Greenhouse gases are causing global warming.
(b) The sun may be responsible for climatic warming.
(c) Global warming may begin to increase dramatically.
(d) The Earth is subjected to varying intensities of radiation.

52

I'm sure everyone in the audience sees the need for our government to reduce the budget deficit by increasing taxes. If it doesn't, cutbacks will have to be made to health care, education and welfare programs. The way we are going, we cannot expect services to continue as they have been indefinitely. Imposing higher taxes, as part of the budget plan, is the only way to reduce the deficit without eliminating essential services.

Q: What is the main idea of the talk?
(a) Balancing the budget requires cutbacks in services.
(b) Raising taxes is grounded in unrealistic expectations.
(c) Maintaining services must come at the cost of a tax hike.
(d) Reducing the budget deficit is crucial for economic growth.

53

And now for local news. An 85-year-old Brooklyn man has suffered a punctured lung after being attacked with a knife. The man told police he was attacked on Dale Road at around one o'clock this morning. He fought with his attacker, who stabbed him in the side then ran from the scene. The victim is now in stable condition after surgery. Police are asking any witnesses to come forward.

Q: Which is correct about the victim according to the news report?
(a) He was attacked at gunpoint.
(b) He was attacked during rush hour.
(c) His attacker fled the scene of the crime.
(d) His attacker was apprehended by police.

54

Next, I would like to introduce a man who stands as an example of the great contribution immigrants can make to this country. Twenty years ago he became an illegal immigrant by jumping a border fence between Mexico and the US. He first worked on a farm, and from there, he went on to become one of the top neurosurgeons in the country. Currently, he is researching treatments for brain cancer. Ladies and gentlemen, please give a warm welcome to Alfredo Quinones.

Q: Which is correct about Alfredo Quinones according to the announcement?
(a) He migrated to the US illegally.
(b) He worked as a farm worker in Mexico.
(c) He is currently studying to be a surgeon.
(d) He recently found a cure for brain cancer.

55

In this part of the lecture, I want to talk about how kings became regarded as living gods in unified ancient Egypt around 3000 BC. While the god status gave them tremendous power, it was also a major burden. During that time, in order for kings to prove their "godliness" and therefore their ability to govern, they were forced to undergo rigorous physical challenges. If they failed the tests, they were deemed unfit to rule and were subsequently killed by priests in ritual sacrifice.

Q: Which is correct according to the lecture?
(a) Egyptian kings were seen as gods.
(b) Egypt was not unified in 3000 BC.
(c) Egyptian kings had to pass intellectual challenges.
(d) Egyptian priests commonly sacrificed themselves.

56

Good afternoon, everyone. Welcome to this year's first shareholder meeting for Visik Technologies. I have an exciting announcement: Visik's planned merger with Synon Communications has been given the go-ahead by our board of directors. If all goes as planned, we expect to gain assets in wireless technology and infrastructure worth around $45 million. Of course, this move is not without an initial outlay, but $15 million from commercial investors will offset that.

Q: Which is correct about Visik Technologies according to the talk?
(a) It recently bought Synon Communications.
(b) Its assets currently add up to $45 million.
(c) Its technological infrastructure will be sold.
(d) It has secured commercial investments.

57

In my view, ladies and gentlemen, fundamental reform of the health care system is necessary to provide proper health care for everyone. Not having a national health care system run by the government puts us at the mercy of a private insurance system that insures only the healthiest people and denies coverage to individuals with certain "pre-existing" conditions or even those who become ill. This is nothing short of outrageous.

Q: Which is correct according to the talk?
(a) The health care system has been reformed.
(b) A government health care system is in place.
(c) Private insurance companies seek out sick people.
(d) The current health care system is failing those who need it.

58

The next health myth I want to talk about concerns sports drinks. For decades, successful marketing has convinced the public that sports drinks are good for you. However, this is only true if you are exercising strenuously. For a hard workout of 30 minutes or more, sports drinks are OK. Otherwise, you don't need them. In fact, if you drink some of them while not exercising, it's just as bad as drinking soda.

Q: What is the speaker likely to talk about next?
(a) What to drink while working out.
(b) How sports drinks are similar to soda.
(c) Why exercising regularly is beneficial.
(d) When soda is better than sports drinks.

59

Teachers, I am going to give you your new class schedules for the spring semester now. Before registering any complaints, please keep the following facts in mind. First, every teacher must teach at least two conversation classes. Second, there are many teachers who have been assigned certain classes because they have special training in those areas—for example, debate. Following these criteria makes it very difficult to make any changes to schedules.

Q: What can be inferred from the announcement?
(a) The school administration assigns classes arbitrarily.
(b) Teachers have little control over their schedules.
(c) The classrooms may lack necessary equipment.
(d) Teachers can expect to have large classes.

60

We'll now look at an example of satire in Jonathan Swift's *Gulliver's Travels* by turning to where Gulliver describes life in his native England to the king of a country he visits. Gulliver is naive and much too honest in detailing the behavior of England's political and legal institutions and its ruling classes. He had hoped to convince the king of their merits. Ironically, however, the king deduces that the English must be the most wicked and detestable race of people to have ever existed on Earth.

Q: What can be inferred to be the target of Swift's satire?
(a) Kings who refuse to cooperate with other nations.
(b) English people who are critical of their own country.
(c) Faults and corruptions of the ruling classes in England.
(d) England's questioning of its role as a world colonial power.

서울대 최신기출 2
Listening Comprehension **Scripts**

1

M   Excuse me. Which way is Seoul Station?

W   _______________

(a) That's true, it is.
(b) Yes, you're right.
(c) It's straight ahead.
(d) The train goes there.

2

W   How would you like your eggs cooked, sir?

M   _______________

(a) I would, yes.
(b) No, not eggs.
(c) Sure, about three.
(d) Scrambled, please.

3

M   Passport, please. How long will you be visiting Mexico?

W   _______________

(a) Tomorrow morning.
(b) It takes about 5 hours.
(c) Only to see my relatives.
(d) I'll be staying two weeks.

4

W   I hear you're doing well in taekwondo class.

M   _______________

(a) I do try hard.
(b) Yes, I was there.
(c) Thanks for coming.
(d) I'm sure that's done.

5

M   I'm sorry about what I said. I hope you weren't offended.

W   _______________

(a) Yes, it does.
(b) No, not at all.
(c) Yes, it is, finally.
(d) No, I haven't seen it.

6

W   Mr. Bay, could you fax this contract to our Ohio branch?

M   _______________

(a) It's too far away.
(b) It's usually around now.
(c) I'll see to it that it gets done.
(d) He couldn't have done it yet.

7

M   Why are you afraid of spiders?

W   _______________

(a) No, I'd rather not be.
(b) I think everybody did.
(c) Please, don't be afraid.
(d) I don't know. I just am.

8

W   Have you finished reading that biography?

M   _______________

(a) Sure, I'd be happy to.
(b) He should finish it soon.
(c) No, I've only just started.
(d) That's where I last saw it.

9

M   Ouch! Be careful with that saucepan!

W   _______________

(a) Let's make dinner together.
(b) OK, pass it over and I'll see.
(c) Did I burn you? I'm so sorry.
(d) My apologies for taking so long.

10

W   I can't believe I failed my driver's test again.

M   ______________________________

(a) Now's as good a time as any.
(b) I'm sure you'll pass next time.
(c) Let's see what we can organize.
(d) Maybe my grades will improve.

11

M   I had a wonderful time with you tonight, Kate.

W   ______________________________

(a) OK, we'll set a date.
(b) Let's just wait and see.
(c) We should go out more often.
(d) Yes, it would be my pleasure.

12

W   Hello. This is Anne Davies. May I speak to Mr. Tucker?

M   ______________________________

(a) Yes, he'll be in touch.
(b) No, it's none of our concern.
(c) There was just one response.
(d) I'll have to ask him to call you back.

13

M   You seem very keen to volunteer here.

W   ______________________________

(a) I'll look forward to some help.
(b) I suppose it was a while back.
(c) I want to help out any way I can.
(d) I've already decided who to support.

14

W   Do you know when the Russian Ballet will be in town?

M   ______________________________

(a) The paper said next week.
(b) I'll definitely go to it, then.
(c) Great! I can't wait to see it.
(d) No, I've never been to Russia.

15

M   Has Tom been under a lot of pressure lately?

W   ______________________________

(a) That's why I let him finish it.
(b) I think he feels the same way.
(c) No, he's under too much pressure.
(d) Yes, he's struggling with a deadline.

16

M   Jenna, do you know much about sailing?

W   My dad used to take me. Why?

M   Can you teach me how to do it?

W   ______________________________

(a) It's not much farther.
(b) That'll be over soon.
(c) Sure, I can show you.
(d) No, I don't think he can.

17

W   That was the best movie I've seen in months.

M   Really? I found it boring.

W   No way! It was fantastic!

M   ______________________________

(a) There wasn't enough action.
(b) We ought to go and see it.
(c) It has been quite a while.
(d) That's a good idea.

18

M   Hi, Julie. I'm glad you could make it.

W   I've been looking forward to this party all week.

M   Let me introduce you to some friends.

W   ______________________________

(a) Great. I'd appreciate that.
(b) What a lovely introduction.
(c) I only just got here myself.
(d) Thanks, but I should get going.

19

W   I'm getting tired of waiting for Jerry.

M   He's only 15 minutes late.

W   But it feels like hours.

M   ______________________________

(a) I'm sure he'll understand.

(b) Sorry, I'll change it.

(c) No, it was earlier.

(d) He won't be long.

20

M Do you mind if I change the channel?

W Sure. Go ahead.

M There should be a movie on somewhere.

W _______________________

(a) Check channel 6.

(b) I haven't been there.

(c) It's my favorite show.

(d) Let's get tickets first.

21

W I can't believe you won't tip the waiter.

M Well, he wasn't very good. He got our order wrong.

W Still, we should leave something.

M _______________________

(a) OK, but not too much.

(b) Well, let's leave, then.

(c) I won't know until later.

(d) I don't deserve anything.

22

M Excuse me. Is this book out in paperback?

W No, it's only available in hardcover.

M When will the paperback be out?

W _______________________

(a) Not for 6 months.

(b) It is available here.

(c) We haven't run out yet.

(d) Just buy some more paper.

23

W Hi, you're Sally's brother, right?

M Yes, I'm Richard. How do you know Sally?

W We work together. I'm Ruth.

M _______________________

(a) I know. Ruth told me.

(b) I'm doing fine, thanks.

(c) Nice to meet you, Ruth.

(d) We don't work together.

24

M Hi, could you tell me what time the gym opens?

W We open at 6 am every morning.

M Even on weekends?

W _______________________

(a) It's closed at night.

(b) No, it's members only.

(c) I'm not here on weekends.

(d) Yes, every day of the week.

25

W We should really plan your mom's birthday party.

M I'm too tired. Can't it wait until tomorrow?

W It's only a week away. Let's at least pick a restaurant.

M _______________________

(a) Fine. We can do that.

(b) Thanks, that's great news.

(c) All right, we'll go that day.

(d) OK. That place sounds nice.

26

M Would you like to see an art show, Cynthia?

W I'd love to, but I'm busy for the next few days.

M The show is on all month. We can go anytime.

W _______________________

(a) I'm visiting family that day.

(b) Then I'll wait for you there.

(c) You could've told me sooner.

(d) Let's make it next week, then.

27

W Your apartment looks great.

M Thanks. I designed the interior myself.

W Really? You must have a gift for it.

M _______________________

(a) I know. The rent's cheap.

(b) No, I don't need anything.

(c) I just followed my instincts.

(d) Interior design wasn't my major.

28

M Hello, Monica. Please take a seat and we'll begin.

W Thanks. I'm glad to have made it to the interview stage.

M Good. Well, first off, what interests you about the job?

W ______________________

(a) I have the training to prove it.
(b) My strong organizational skills.
(c) I see it as something I could do well.
(d) Good management requires discipline.

29

W Good morning, Alpha Airlines. Can I help you?

M Yes, I'm calling because I've lost my ticket.

W OK. You'll need to come in and fill out an indemnity form.

M ______________________

(a) I don't have my ID with me now.
(b) All right, I'll drop by and do that.
(c) But I lost the ticket two days ago.
(d) Sure, just let me get a pen and paper.

30

M What did Bill say about our proposal?

W He was dead set against it.

M Despite the profit estimates?

W ______________________

(a) He continues to stand by us.
(b) Nothing I said made any difference.
(c) He insists on reversing our decision.
(d) He argued that it was a money-maker.

31

W Excuse me. Is this LCD TV on sale?

M Yes, but only if you pay in cash.

W I see. And what's the discount on it?

M This one is 25 percent off.

W That's a real bargain! I'll take it.

M Great. You won't be disappointed.

Q: What is mainly happening in the conversation?
(a) The woman is buying a TV.
(b) The man is returning his TV.
(c) The man is repairing appliances.
(d) The woman is asking for a discount.

32

W Are you ready for the conference in Paris?

M Not quite. I haven't booked a hotel yet.

W Why not? It's easy to do on the Internet.

M I know, but I couldn't find a nice one nearby.

W Well, keep searching. I'm sure you'll find something.

M Yeah, maybe I'll check online again tonight.

Q: What is the conversation mainly about?
(a) Buying plane tickets.
(b) A conference in Paris.
(c) Finding a hotel in Paris.
(d) Checking hotel prices online.

33

W Mr. Jones, do you have time for a meeting today?

M I'm free after 4. What's it about?

W I need to discuss a problem in accounting.

M I hope it's nothing too serious.

W It could be. I've noticed some major errors.

M Uh-oh. OK, I'll see you at 4, then.

Q: What is the conversation mainly about?
(a) Changing appointment details.
(b) Making accounting errors at work.
(c) Hiring someone to do the accounting.
(d) Scheduling time to discuss a problem.

34

M Hey Danielle, it's been a while. How's it going?

W To be honest, not so good. I'm really stressed out.

M Oh, I'm sorry to hear that. What's wrong?

W I'm giving a presentation to 500 people this afternoon.

M Wow, that sounds nerve-wracking.

W Yeah, I just hope I don't make any mistakes.

Q: What are the man and woman mainly discussing?
(a) The difficulty of giving a presentation.
(b) The woman's worries about giving a presentation.
(c) The stress caused by the woman's poor presentation.
(d) The man's disappointment at the woman's presentation.

35

M Susan, are you really quitting your job to have a baby?
W Yes, I'm putting my career on the back burner for now.
M But why not take maternity leave?
W Because I want more time off with the baby.
M Well, it could be hard to find another job later.
W That's a risk I'm prepared to take.

Q: What is the main topic of the conversation?
(a) The woman's newly-born child.
(b) The woman's desire for extra time off.
(c) The woman's decision to leave her job.
(d) The woman's rejection of maternity leave.

36

M Are you ready to go for a walk in the park?
W Yes, I think so. Just let me put my scarf on.
M Is that the coat you're wearing? I'd put on something warmer.
W Do you really think it's that cold outside?
M Yeah, the weather channel said today's even colder than yesterday.
W OK, wait a minute while I find a thicker coat.

Q: What are the man and woman mainly doing?
(a) Arguing over the weather outside.
(b) Discussing what to wear for a walk.
(c) Deciding which public park to go to.
(d) Going to the park for a morning walk.

37

W My engineering course is giving me problems.
M Why? What's the trouble?
W Math. It wasn't a problem in high school, but I'm struggling now.
M Well, it'll get easier as you go along, I'm sure.
W I guess, but I'm thinking of getting a math tutor to help me.
M That certainly wouldn't hurt.

Q: What is mainly happening in the conversation?
(a) The woman is asking about how to get a tutor.
(b) The woman is discussing her difficulties with math.
(c) The man is helping the woman with her assignments.
(d) The man is giving the woman advice about a math problem.

38

W So, how did the big date go last night?
M Don't even ask.
W But I thought you were really into Tina.
M I was, but she stood me up.
W You're kidding. Have you heard from her?
M Not even a text message.

Q: Which is correct according to the conversation?
(a) Tina did not keep her appointment.
(b) Tina sent the man a text message.
(c) The man forgot his date with Tina.
(d) The man was not interested in Tina.

39

W Good afternoon. How can I help you, sir?
M I have a reservation. My name's Edward Brown.
W Let's see... a double room for two nights?
M That's correct, yes. And is the room non-smoking?
W Of course. If you'll sign here, please, I'll give you your key.
M OK. Thanks a lot.

Q: Which is correct according to the
    conversation?
(a) The woman lost the man's key.
(b) The man is staying for two nights.
(c) The man needs to reserve a room.
(d) The woman has no vacancies in the hotel.

40

M Did Steve transfer here from another school?
W Yes, he did.
M Where did he transfer from?
W From MIT, in the States.
M Wow. Why would he leave such a great
    school?
W He said he found the coursework too difficult.

Q: Which is correct according to the
    conversation?
(a) The woman is unsure why Steve left MIT.
(b) The woman went to MIT with Steve.
(c) Steve is planning to transfer to MIT.
(d) Steve found MIT courses too hard.

41

W Wow! I like your glasses. Where'd you get
    them?
M I got a good deal on them last week at a
    store called Beautiful Sight.
W Oh, yeah. I think I've heard of it. Is it on
    Wilson Avenue?
M Yeah, that's it. It's kind of pricey but the
    frames are good quality.
W I might stop in there sometime and have a
    look.
M Well now's a good time because the sale is
    still on.

Q: Which is correct according to the
    conversation?
(a) The sale at Beautiful Sight is over.
(b) The man bought a new pair of glasses.
(c) The woman has been to the Beautiful Sight
    store.
(d) The woman is not interested in shopping for
    glasses.

42

M John's speech at the protest rally was
    absolutely brilliant.
W I thought so too. How did he think all of that
    up on the spot?
M He didn't, although it did sound pretty
    spontaneous.
W What do you mean? He wasn't reading from
    any notes that I could see.
M He wrote and memorized it all beforehand.
W Well, either way, it was impressive.

Q: Which is correct according to the
    conversation?
(a) John gave a speech at a fund-raiser.
(b) John drafted his speech before giving it.
(c) John asked the man to write his speech.
(d) John referred to notes throughout the
    speech.

43

M Jennifer, do you take vitamin supplements?
W I don't think they're necessary, and besides,
    they're really expensive.
M But I just read an article that says we should
    be taking them.
W You sound like a salesman. I hope you're not
    trying to sell me any.
M Don't be ridiculous. I'm simply interested in
    maintaining good health.
W Well, I don't think you need them if you eat
    right in the first place.

Q: What can be inferred from the conversation?
(a) The man is a medical professional.
(b) The man majored in nutritional sciences.
(c) The woman has most of her meals at home.
(d) The woman does not take vitamin
    supplements.

44

W   Jeff, did you get a document called "Meeting" attached to an email?

M   Yes, as a matter of fact I did. How did you know?

W   I got one too, but don't try to open it. It's a virus.

M   Oh, too late. I already tried. But it wouldn't open.

W   Yeah, mine was like that as well. You'd better do a virus scan.

M   Will do. Thanks for letting me know.

Q: What can be inferred from the conversation?
(a) The woman sent the man the document.
(b) The man has not been to a meeting recently.
(c) The woman's computer got infected by a virus.
(d) The man is embarrassed about opening the attachment.

45

M   I really like Senator Peter's views on the economy.

W   Are you serious? He only cares about big business.

M   But he can save the economy by helping businesses create jobs.

W   That's only what he says in his campaign. He hasn't done it yet.

M   I think he really will, though. That's why I'm voting for him.

W   Yeah, well, I've heard all this before. I'll believe it when I see it.

Q: What can be inferred from the conversation?
(a) The man works as an advisor to the Senator.
(b) The man wants funding for a small business.
(c) The woman is skeptical of the Senator's ideas.
(d) The woman enjoys attending political conferences.

46

As I mentioned earlier, groundwater pollution is a big problem, and numerous factors contribute to it. Manufacturers pour pollutants into rivers, or fail to fix leaky pipelines and underground storage tanks. Some pollutants enter city sewers, contaminating municipal areas. Groundwater near mines is often tainted by chemicals used in the processing of ore. Sources of groundwater pollution are numerous, but one thing is clear. We must do more to prevent it.

Q: What is the lecture mainly about?
(a) The most serious contributor to water pollution.
(b) The various sources of groundwater pollution.
(c) The groundwater pollution problem in cities.
(d) The consequences of polluting waterways.

47

After narcotics, rare animals are the second most lucrative illegal export from South America to the US. A Brazilian hyacinth macaw sells for $10,000, and a woolly monkey goes for $50,000. The result of this illegal trade is that endangered birds and animals are disappearing rapidly from South America's rain forests, making them tragic victims of what has become a $10 billion annual trade.

Q: What is the main idea of the talk?
(a) Buying an exotic animal is dangerous.
(b) Birds and animals are becoming extinct.
(c) Animal smuggling is now a huge industry.
(d) South American rain forests are endangered.

48

May I have your attention, please! There's going to be a fire drill this afternoon and it will be timed to find out how long it takes for all of you to evacuate. Please follow the procedure we've practiced in the past. I expect you all to behave yourselves and act in an orderly fashion. You should follow your group leader out of the building, and gather at the back of the playground.

Q: What is the main purpose of the
announcement?
(a) To urge the students to follow the rules.
(b) To inform the students of a new school rule.
(c) To notify students to gather in the playground.
(d) To prepare students for an upcoming fire
drill.

49

What I want to talk about now is the effect China's economic development is having on the West. China's growth has led to a drop in the cost of certain products in the West and has provided enormous investment opportunities. On the other side, though, numerous manufacturing jobs have been lost to Chinese competition. As this competition intensifies, calls for protectionist policies will increase and some countries may decide to block free trade.

Q: What is the main topic of the lecture?
(a) Reasons why trade restrictions will affect
China.
(b) Civil unrest caused by China's inexpensive
products.
(c) Growing tension between China and Western
nations.
(d) How China's growth has impacted Western
economies.

50

When attempting to promote change in an organization, it is advantageous to encourage others to participate in the process. You can do this by informing them of the benefits of change. Then let them know that the change cannot be brought about without them being involved in the process. Also, remember that passion and enthusiasm can be contagious. Demonstrate how committed you are to making change happen, and others will be inspired.

Q: What is the main point of the speech?
(a) It is easy to make changes within an
organization.
(b) Part of achieving change is motivating others.
(c) A good leader empathizes with employees.
(d) Strategic planning can deter change.

51

Last week I mentioned that Einstein's theory of relativity was initially received coolly because people could not grasp the concepts. In the world of science this kind of reception is not an unknown phenomenon. For example, many scientists in the Middle Ages had their work renounced as heresy because it contradicted the teachings of the Catholic Church. And while we think we live in a more enlightened age, skepticism can still be inhibiting.

Q: What is the speaker's main point?
(a) Scientists' theories often encounter initial
resistance.
(b) Einstein had to wait years for his ideas to be
accepted.
(c) Scientists in the Middle Ages worked under
church law.
(d) Religious institutions did not support
scientific theories.

52

The mayor's surprise announcement that he will resign has sent shockwaves throughout the city. A spokesperson from the mayor's office said that the mayor is resigning for personal reasons, and he declined to elaborate further. However, observers cited a pending investigation by the Federal Department of Veteran's Affairs as being behind the move. The mayor has been accused of receiving military disability payments under false pretenses.

Q: What is mainly being said about the mayor in
the news report?
(a) He is quitting because of a war injury.
(b) He has resigned amid accusations of fraud.
(c) His surprise resignation has confused
everyone.
(d) His military disability payments were
miscalculated.

53

Hello. Thank you for calling the Market Place Mall. We are currently closed. Our shopping hours are from 9:30 am to 9:30 pm, Monday through Saturday, and 9:30 am to 6:00 pm on Sunday. The Market Place Mall is located off exit 17 on Interstate 75 and has over 300 specialty stores all under one roof. If you would like to speak to our after-hours service representative, press 1. Thank you.

Q: Which is correct about the Market Place Mall according to the announcement?
(a) It is open 24 hours a day.
(b) It is located on Interstate 17.
(c) It has reduced hours on Sunday.
(d) It has about 300 specialty restaurants.

54

And now for the weekend weather from Channel 10's weather desk. On Saturday, you can expect showers and thunderstorms across a broad front from the Great Lakes and eastern Plains right up to the Rio Grande. Showers and storms are likely throughout this corridor on Sunday, too. Meanwhile, a high pressure system off the southern Atlantic coast is expected to bring warm, dry weather to an area extending from the Ohio Valley up to northern New York State.

Q: Which area will have wet weather according to the weather report?
(a) The Ohio Valley.
(b) The eastern Plains.
(c) The South Atlantic.
(d) The State of New York.

55

Are you interested in improving the world? Regent University can give you a head start. Join over 2,300 dedicated men and women currently at Regent pursuing graduate degrees in diverse disciplines such as education, law, government, business, journalism, psychology, counseling, and communications. These leaders of the future will soon be making a difference in the world along with the thousands of Regent alumni already in positions of influence. Enrollments close November 1. Don't miss out—enroll at Regent now.

Q: Which is correct about Regent University according to the announcement?
(a) It offers graduate degrees.
(b) It will soon offer law programs.
(c) It has just under 2,000 students.
(d) It is primarily a business school.

56

The belief that birth order affects personality, intelligence, and achievement is common in Korea. Some researchers claim that this is true, especially with regard to personality traits. However, for the most part these claims are not supported by scientific evidence, and many psychologists dispute them. Psychologists point out that myriad other influences in a person's life, such as genetics and social experiences, affect personality and intelligence far more significantly than birth order.

Q: Which is correct according to the lecture?
(a) Intelligence is primarily determined by birth order.
(b) The influence of birth order is largely discredited.
(c) The effects of birth order can last for a lifetime.
(d) Birth order affects a person's genetic make-up.

57

British and Filipino researchers have found a new bird species on a remote island at the northern end of the Philippines archipelago. The bird is a type of rail, and was discovered by an expedition team that was surveying birds, mammals, reptiles, and amphibians on Calayan Island, one of the Babuyan Islands. The bird was named the Calayan rail, after the island on which it was found. Though new to science, it is not new to Calayan Island locals, who call the birds "piding."

Q: Which is correct about the Calayan rail according to the speaker?

(a) It was found on one of the Babuyan Islands.

(b) It is named after a tribe on Calayan Island.

(c) It is not new to island locals, who called it a rail.

(d) It was unknown to humans until researchers found it.

58

Ladies and gentlemen, I am honored to receive the J. J. Peabody Award for Social Sciences Research. My work among the aboriginal tribes of Central Africa has always been rewarding for me, but this recognition from my peers shows me just how much my work is appreciated by others. This award highlights the critical importance of anthropological research in preserving the cultures of people who have historically been undervalued and overlooked. Furthermore, the generous payment accompanying the award will help fund and nurture future endeavors.

Q: What can be inferred from the speech?

(a) The speaker has been working in Africa for a short time.

(b) The speaker believes traditional cultures should be preserved.

(c) The speaker will embark on studying ethnic groups in modern cities.

(d) The speaker feels that anthropological research funds in Africa are adequately funded.

59

The next novel I'd like to talk about is *Ruthless*, by John Ruggles. As I've mentioned, his previous works impressed me greatly. In those, he creates worlds of believable characters and situations through which he pursues a social commentary on contemporary life. I anticipated more of the same in *Ruthless*, but was regrettably disappointed. Very little in *Ruthless* is contemporary. It's a historical novel, and thus represents a change in direction for Ruggles. However, it's a change many fans like me may wish he hadn't made.

Q: What can be inferred from the review?

(a) The great success of the novel, *Ruthless*, is predictable.

(b) Most of Ruggles' novels suffer from unbelievable characters.

(c) *Ruthless* has a narrative style that defies literary convention.

(d) Fans of Ruggles are likely to be disappointed by his latest novel.

60

Last year was a very good year for this company. We experienced growth in all aspects of our business. The main reasons for this were the dramatic decrease in the price of raw materials and the excellent market conditions in South America. Consequently, profit was 20 percent over our initial projections. The growth in our transportation sector is particularly noteworthy, considering that it has been relatively flat for the last three years. We feel that we have now turned the corner, and we expect next year to be even better.

Q: What can be inferred from the speech?

(a) The speaker has never visited South America.

(b) The speaker had predicted it would be a bad year.

(c) The company will sell off its transportation sector.

(d) The company profits from enterprises in South America.

서울대 최신기출 3
Listening Comprehension **Scripts**

1

M   Don't forget to lock your car door.

W   ___________________________

(a) OK. I'll drive.
(b) Oh, I almost forgot.
(c) It's quite a new car.
(d) That will come later.

2

W   Would you like to be dropped off here?

M   ___________________________

(a) Thanks anyway.
(b) I'll wait over there.
(c) Yes, Friday would be best.
(d) No, at the next corner, please.

3

M   Could you tell me where the shoe department is?

W   ___________________________

(a) I believe that's out of stock.
(b) This is women's clothing.
(c) It's on the fifth floor.
(d) I wear a size six.

4

W   Sorry for being late, but traffic was backed up for an hour on the highway.

M   ___________________________

(a) No problem. I heard about it on the radio.
(b) Right, we could've set another time.
(c) I saw you driving by yesterday.
(d) I hope it won't be necessary.

5

M   Hello, Mrs. Jones. It's a pleasure to meet you.

W   ___________________________

(a) And you too.
(b) It's a lot of fun.
(c) It's always nice.
(d) It must have been.

6

W   How could you lose a tennis match against Roger?

M   ___________________________

(a) Right, I met him once.
(b) But I found another one.
(c) Well, he's a good player.
(d) I hope it's OK to play against him.

7

M   Is Mr. Johnson here? I need to give him this file right away.

W   ___________________________

(a) I don't think so but ask him later.
(b) In that case, he can find out for you.
(c) Give it back to me when you're done.
(d) He's out, but I'll make sure he gets it.

8

W   Do you think it's safe to shop online?

M   ___________________________

(a) I don't like shopping myself.
(b) Only if it's a well-known site.
(c) Sure, but don't stay out too late.
(d) It depends if there are any deals.

9

M   I'm sorry for not attending the meeting.

W   ___________________________

(a) All right. It won't happen again.
(b) Well, try not to miss it next time.
(c) Don't worry. I'll keep that in mind.
(d) Yeah, it's too bad you can't arrange it.

10

W I'm coming down with a fever.

M ___________________________

(a) Try to win it over.
(b) I'll meet you there, then.
(c) I'll come up with an idea.
(d) You should take something for it.

11

M Hey, did our team win the soccer game?

W ___________________________

(a) No, I lost them.
(b) They did, 6 to 2.
(c) Well, I already knew that.
(d) They also played last night.

12

W I can't wait for tonight's movie special.

M ___________________________

(a) Tell me when you're ready.
(b) That makes two of us.
(c) I think it's still on.
(d) That's a pity.

13

M Do you have experience with database applications?

W ___________________________

(a) I lost some important data.
(b) Actually, they're my specialty.
(c) I submitted my application yesterday.
(d) Yes, I've experienced the same problem.

14

W Hello, I'm calling for Ken Bishop, please.

M ___________________________

(a) Sorry, he hasn't asked for you yet.
(b) Well, he's too busy to see you today.
(c) You'll have to announce that yourself.
(d) You just missed him, but I can take a message.

15

M You always complain about not having enough money.

W ___________________________

(a) I've heard a similar complaint.
(b) You never have anything to do.
(c) You'd be better off investing later.
(d) There are always unexpected expenses.

16

W Where are you from?

M I was born and raised in Portland, Oregon.

W I heard it's a beautiful city.

W ___________________________

(a) It's not that well-known.
(b) Sure, I'll find out for you.
(c) My parents still live there.
(d) Yes, the mountains are very scenic.

17

M Hi Gina. Good to see you.

W Hi, James. How have you been?

M Pretty busy. What about you?

W ___________________________

(a) I can take care of myself.
(b) You can visit me anytime.
(c) It doesn't matter. I'm fine.
(d) Things are much the same.

18

W I was in a car accident on the way to work.

M That's terrible. Are you OK?

W Yeah, but my car is a wreck.

M ___________________________

(a) Wow, I can't believe you caused it.
(b) I don't remember what car it was.
(c) Well, at least you're all right.
(d) I should drive it home, then.

19

M I'd like to book a dental appointment.

W OK, have you been to our dental clinic before?

M No, this is my first time.

W _______________

(a) It's not going to hurt.

(b) Well, I was here last month.

(c) Then, please fill out this form.

(d) I've been looking at it carefully.

20

W How come the accounts report isn't on my desk?

M I'm sorry, but I haven't finished it yet.

W But the deadline was yesterday.

M _______________

(a) I think you put it away.

(b) It couldn't have been that bad.

(c) It should've been delivered to you.

(d) I just need to finalize some details.

21

M Hi, Jessica. It looks like you could use some help.

W Oh, hi, Bill. Yes, I guess I bought too many things.

M Here, let me help you with those bags.

W _______________

(a) Thanks. I appreciate it.

(b) Well, I've got spare bags.

(c) That's OK. I'll move them.

(d) Sure, you can take over anytime.

22

W I heard you had some bad news over the weekend.

M Yes, my grandmother passed away.

W I'm sorry to hear that. Had she been ill?

M _______________

(a) Yes, but she's much better now.

(b) No, she was just passing through.

(c) I hope to find out how she's doing.

(d) She'd been in the hospital for months.

23

M Jane, do you want the window seat?

W I don't really care. Why?

M I can sleep better by the window.

W _______________

(a) OK, you take it, then.

(b) Tell me which one it is.

(c) I can always take that ride.

(d) I'd prefer to be sitting, thanks.

24

W I think I should drop this art class.

M No way. Why would you want to do that?

W Because I'm no good at drawing.

M _______________

(a) Yeah, it's a great class.

(b) I find it relaxing as well.

(c) But you're better than me.

(d) You should take a class, then.

25

M I'm glad we have a four-day weekend.

W Me, too. Do you have any plans?

M I'm going to visit my parents. And you?

W _______________

(a) I'd rather not, but thanks.

(b) I'll be driving to the coast.

(c) Same here. I'll see you there.

(d) I don't have to work, anyway.

26

W I'd like to return these skincare products.

M What seems to be the trouble with them, ma'am?

W They caused me to break out in a serious rash.

M _______________

(a) We accept either cash or credit card.

(b) I see. You may be allergic to them.

(c) I wasn't aware that we had them.

(d) But that'll make us suffer more.

27

M Have you noticed that sound our car has
been making?

W Yes. It seems to be getting worse. We should
do something about it.

M What if I just take it to a mechanic tomorrow?

W ________________________

(a) Good idea. I'll drive it to work, then.

(b) The weekend would be a better time.

(c) It might be easier if I just called a cab.

(d) Sure, but tomorrow works better for us.

28

W Why did so few people come to the
museum's opening?

M Because it didn't make the headlines,
I suppose.

W Why do you think it was overlooked?

M ________________________

(a) No one got a chance to look it up.

(b) Too many reporters were in the way.

(c) The museum is closed for renovations.

(d) I guess other stories were of greater interest.

29

M My boss is being really difficult nowadays.

W What's wrong with him?

M He gets upset with every little thing that
happens.

W ________________________

(a) That must be hard to deal with.

(b) I heard that it already happened.

(c) Don't get upset about every little thing.

(d) I wonder if we can reach an agreement.

30

W Marco, I can hardly hear you on this phone.

M Oh really? We must have a bad connection.

W Yeah, you'll have to speak louder.

M ________________________

(a) Maybe it'd be better if I called you back
instead.

(b) Sorry. I didn't mean to talk down to you.

(c) The volume doesn't go any higher.

(d) OK, I'll explain it more explicitly.

31

M Wow, the air show was terrific!

W What was your favorite part?

M The acrobatic displays!

W I bet they were noisy.

M Yeah, but they made the show more exciting.

W Did you take lots of pictures?

M Yes, especially of the acrobatics.

Q: What is the conversation mainly about?

(a) An air show the man visited.

(b) The man's latest pictures.

(c) The man's hobby.

(d) Noisy air shows.

32

W Thanks for fixing that sink.

M No problem. You shouldn't have any more
leaks now.

W I wish the other plumber had fixed it properly.

M Well, he probably wasn't very experienced.

W Yeah, I guess so.

M Just call me if you ever need plumbing done.

W I will. Thanks again for your help.

Q: What is the woman mainly doing in the
conversation?

(a) Interviewing a new plumber.

(b) Arranging to get a sink fixed.

(c) Criticizing the man's workmanship.

(d) Thanking the man for repairing her sink.

33

W Hey, what are those pictures of?

M Oh, they're photos of my son's birthday
party.

W He looks excited. How old is he now?

M He just turned 3.

W It looks like he enjoyed the chocolate cake.

M Yeah, it was a fun day for him.

Q: What are the speakers doing in the
conversation?

(a) Talking about their children.

(b) Planning a child's birthday party.

(c) Watching the man's son eat cake.

(d) Looking at some birthday photos.

34

M   How long have the Fensters lived in this town?

W   They've been here for ages.

M   Yes, but how long exactly?

W   They were among the first families who settled in the town.

M   So, they must've been here for at least a century.

W   Yes, that's right.

Q: What is the conversation mainly about?
(a) How long ago the town was established.
(b) How to trace the history of the Fensters.
(c) How the Fensters came to settle in the area.
(d) How long the Fensters have lived in the town.

35

W   We're going out for lunch. Want to come?

M   I would, but I have a lot of work to do.

W   Oh, come on. We'll be back soon.

M   Hmm. How long is it going to take?

W   We're going to a restaurant nearby, so not long. Come on!

M   OK. You twisted my arm.

Q: What is the woman mainly doing in the conversation?
(a) Inviting the man out to lunch.
(b) Asking the man if he had lunch.
(c) Urging the man to finish his work.
(d) Suggesting which restaurant to go to.

36

W   What do you think about the government's cutbacks?

M   As usual, they'll affect the poor the most.

W   Yeah, but something had to be done to curtail the national debt.

M   But why should the poor have to suffer?

W   I don't know. It's a bad situation.

M   Well, there must be a better solution.

Q: What is mainly being discussed?
(a) Why the government cannot create economic growth.
(b) Why the suffering of the poor cannot be easily solved.
(c) How the poor are disadvantaged by government cutbacks.
(d) How much debt the government has accumulated so far.

37

M   So, what did you think of the movie, Rachel?

W   I loved the whole thing. It was just so well acted, don't you think?

M   Yeah, except for the guy who played the villain.

W   Oh, you didn't like him? I thought he was good at being creepy.

M   Yeah, he was, but I think he overdid it a little now and then.

W   I didn't feel that at all. I thought he nailed the part.

Q: What is the main topic of the conversation?
(a) The performance of an actor in a movie.
(b) The degree to which an actor seemed creepy.
(c) Why the acting in a movie so intrigued the woman.
(d) Why the woman was happy with the movie's success.

38

W   Thank you for looking after my plants.

M   Oh, it was no problem at all.

W   You did a great job. They look wonderful.

M   I didn't do much—just watered them.

W   Well, anyway, I appreciate it.

M   I know you'd do the same for me.

Q: What did the man do for the woman?
(a) He planted her garden.
(b) He bought some plants.
(c) He took care of her plants.
(d) He gave her some flowers.

39

M   Hello. Is your restaurant open for brunch on Saturdays?

W   Yes, brunch service begins at 10 a.m.

M   Can I make a reservation for four, please?

W   Sorry. We don't take reservations for the weekend.

M   Then, if we just came in on Saturday, would there be a long wait?

W   Not before 11. After that, it's about a 30-minute wait.

M   OK. Thank you.

Q: Which is correct according to the conversation?
(a) Brunch service begins at 11.
(b) Saturday is busiest before 11:30.
(c) Brunch is served only on weekdays.
(d) Reservations are not accepted for weekends.

40

M   Have you read the two books you bought last month?

W   I've finished one of them.

M   Which one, the historical novel?

W   No, the other one—the romance.

M   How was it? Any good?

W   No, nothing special. I wouldn't recommend it.

Q: Which is correct according to the conversation?
(a) The man read a historical novel.
(b) The man bought the woman some books.
(c) The woman has just read a romance novel.
(d) The woman recommended one of her books.

41

W   You look stressed out, Mike.

M   I am. I have two exams tomorrow, but I'm not ready.

W   Well, it might do you good to take a break.

M   You can't be serious! I'm behind my study schedule as it is.

W   But taking time out occasionally can help you study better.

M   You really think so?

W   Sure. It's worked for me so far.

Q: Which is correct according to the conversation?
(a) The man is prepared for his tests.
(b) The man has to take exams tomorrow.
(c) The woman is worried about tomorrow.
(d) The woman recommends studying together.

42

M   Karen, can you make it to my house-warming party?

W   When are you having it?

M   Next Friday. It starts at 6, and I'll be serving dinner at 8.

W   Will you be making your famous Chicken Cordon Bleu?

M   That'll be just one of the dishes I'll prepare.

W   That sounds great! Count me in.

Q: Which is correct according to the conversation?
(a) The man changed the date of his party.
(b) The woman will take the man out for dinner.
(c) The woman wants to attend the man's party.
(d) The man will not make Chicken Cordon Bleu.

43

M   I've heard good things about this restaurant.

W   Yes, they have quality meat, and the chef is outstanding.

M   What do you recommend?

W   I'd go for the filet mignon.

M   Is it expensive?

W   A little, but it's a good deal for what you get.

Q: What can be inferred from the conversation?
(a) The woman is a professional chef.
(b) The woman rarely eats meat dishes.
(c) The man has never been to the restaurant.
(d) The man would rather eat somewhere else.

44

M Excuse me, how much longer will the flight to Dallas be delayed?

W We haven't heard anything yet, sir. I'm sorry.

M Can you book me on another flight to Dallas? I have to get there by 6 today.

W There is a 1:15 flight, but that has a brief stopover in Chicago.

M I don't mind. I'll take that. Are there any seats?

W Let me check... Yes, I will reserve one for you right now.

Q: What can be inferred from the conversation?
(a) The woman has overbooked the 1:15 flight.
(b) The woman is annoyed by the man.
(c) The man has a meeting in Chicago.
(d) The man will get to Dallas on time.

45

M Hello, is this Ms. Cynthia Jones?

W Speaking. How can I help you?

M I have a package to deliver to your home.

W But I'm at work now. Can you leave it with my apartment manager?

M I'm sorry, I need your signature.

W Well, that's going to be difficult.

M We can deliver after hours, say, around 7 p.m.

W That'll be fine. Thank you.

Q: What can be inferred from the conversation?
(a) The woman finishes work before 7 p.m.
(b) The apartment manager will keep the package.
(c) The man is not sure where Cynthia Jones lives.
(d) The package will be delivered to the woman's workplace.

46

On behalf of Diamond Star Cruise lines, I'd like to welcome aboard all passengers. We want to make your cruise as enjoyable as possible. So if you have any concerns or questions, do not hesitate to ask any of our crew. We will be leaving port in about 30 minutes. Once underway, all passengers are invited to a complimentary welcoming party on the Caribbean deck. Once again, welcome aboard.

Q: What is the main purpose of the announcement?
(a) To explain what the ship's crew needs to do.
(b) To welcome all passengers taking the cruise.
(c) To advertise a party being held for everyone.
(d) To inform that the ship will leave in 30 minutes.

47

In this segment of our program, we'll look at dining when traveling in Argentina. When in Argentina, you have to get used to the idea that adults seldom sit down to dinner before eight o'clock. Sometimes they have dinner as late as nine or ten. Common dishes for the evening meal feature beef and various kinds of pasta, but there are also vegetable dishes available. And of course, Argentine wine, which is world-famous, is served at almost every meal.

Q: What is the topic of the talk?
(a) The importance of beef to Argentines.
(b) Kinds of world-famous Argentine foods.
(c) Characteristics of Argentine dining culture.
(d) The reason why Argentines eat dinner late.

48

This Political Science 101 course is designed to introduce students to American government and politics by way of examining government institutions and public policy. During the course, I will discuss why each institution is organized the way it is and how its organizational structure shapes public policy. I will also focus on the concept of representation.

Q: What is the Political Science course mainly about?
(a) An examination of different organizational structures.
(b) An introduction to the US government and politics.
(c) An in-depth look at America's political history.
(d) An analysis of political practices in America.

49

By the year 2030, 25% of all animal species may be extinct. There are several reasons for this, but I'll now discuss the main ones. First, millions of animals die every year because of human pollution. Second, hunting—whether for sport, food or animal products—is threatening the survival of many animal species. And third, the ever growing need for land and resources by human populations is reducing the size of animal habitats such as jungles, fields, and forests.

Q: What is the main idea of the talk?
(a) Animal species are under threat due to human activities.
(b) There is no specific reason why animals go extinct.
(c) Human beings are harmful to the environment.
(d) Hunting is a major cause of animal extinction.

50

I always stress to new interns like you that a good bedside manner is essential for doctors when seeking to diagnose a patient. Approaching patients amiably encourages them to be completely honest. Remember, if your patient feels uncomfortable or gets the sense that you are not genuine or likable, he or she may withhold pertinent information or perhaps even lie about their symptoms.

Q: What advice is mainly given by the speaker?
(a) Be friendly with patients for better diagnoses.
(b) Make rounds often to provide better treatment.
(c) Try to diagnose patients with a minimum of fuss.
(d) Good bedside manner will make you a popular doctor.

51

As I mentioned at the beginning of my lecture, Wittgenstein's early philosophy states that we cannot talk precisely about things that humans deem highly significant, such as truth, beauty, goodness, or the meaning of life. Wittgenstein felt that only observable phenomena, which science demonstrated as real, could be discussed. He saw language as a helper to science, able to verbalize what science presented. But later on, Wittgenstein recognized the limitations of his ideas and stated that language could not always mirror what science revealed.

Q: What is the best title for the lecture?
(a) Wittgenstein's Early Thoughts on Language.
(b) Wittgenstein's Philosophy of Scientific Language.
(c) Wittgenstein's Changing Conception of Language.
(d) Wittgenstein's Beliefs about the Limitations of Science.

52

My discussion of German writer Johann Wolfgang Goethe will begin with his first novel *The Sorrows of Young Werther*, which caused a sensation when first published in 1774. It was widely read and praised and made Goethe famous. But what was its appeal? Well, written in the early Romantic period, it described the feelings of a young generation that was starting to embrace the values of Romanticism. The book represented the revolt against established values and a desire for higher ideals, self-expression and individualism.

Q: What is mainly discussed about *The Sorrows of Young Werther*?
(a) The emotional depth of Goethe's writing.
(b) The characteristics of Romanticism it portrayed.
(c) The sensation it caused throughout Germany in 1774.
(d) The impact it had as a novel representative of Romanticism.

53

Residents were awoken in the early hours of Sunday morning by a deadly tornado tearing across 40 miles of Indiana and Kentucky. Seven people were killed and more than 50 were injured by the tornado that officials estimate was about three-quarters of a mile wide and 20 miles long. Three horses stabled at the Ellis Park horse track in Kentucky were also killed. The tornado was rated a severe F3 on the Fujita scale, with winds ranging from 150 to 200 mph.

Q: Which is correct according to the news report?
(a) More people got injured than killed.
(b) A horse track in Indiana was destroyed.
(c) Tornado winds were well over 200 mph.
(d) No loss of life resulted from the tornado.

54

I will begin my discussion on crime fiction with the works of Patricia Highsmith. She is probably best remembered for her series of novels about the character Tom Ripley, the first being *The Talented Mr. Ripley*. This novel is a masterpiece of crime fiction and probably her most bizarre creation. Tom Ripley is the typical Highsmith protagonist, an antihero who is psychologically complex and whose dubious sense of morality allows him to commit acts of evil with little apparent cost to conscience.

Q: What is often found in Patricia Highsmith novels?
(a) People who commit crimes without feeling much guilt.
(b) Complex analyses of psychological disorders.
(c) Characters that uphold strong moral values.
(d) Crime stories based on actual events.

55

As an introduction to the diversity of life in deserts, let's look at Death Valley in America. Just from the name itself, you could probably come to the conclusion that Death Valley is a desolate place. Indeed, it initially seems to be a barren place with not a living thing in sight. However, despite its name and your first impression, Death Valley is not just an empty wilderness of sand and rock. Many plants and animals thrive there.

Q: Which is correct about Death Valley according to the talk?
(a) It is not a safe place to visit.
(b) It is more diverse than was once thought.
(c) It supports a variety of plants and animals.
(d) It is famous because of its name and reputation.

56

And now for local news. The trial of Lance White, accused of kidnapping toddler, Angela Burns, took another twist today when the court refused to admit as evidence photographs that the prosecution claims were taken just prior to the abduction. An expert in the field of photography testified that the photographs produced by the prosecution were possibly computer enhanced. Justice Percy Granger adjourned the trial until the photographs are determined to be genuine or not.

Q: Which is correct according to the news report?
(a) Defendant Lance White was pronounced not guilty.
(b) Resumption of the trial is pending an investigation.
(c) Photographs proved that Angela Burns was kidnapped.
(d) The photographs were taken right after the kidnapping.

57

In our effort to reduce training costs, all of you managers will now be required to compile employee skill inventories. Human Resources asks that you submit these inventories within the next six weeks. In the future, we hope to reduce the cost and time it takes to train employees by using existing resources more effectively and restructuring our training regimens. We encourage you to submit any ideas you may have to help us realize this goal.

Q: Which is correct according to the talk?
(a) New employees will be trained within six weeks.
(b) Managers need to restructure their training programs.
(c) Managers need to itemize the skills of their staff members.
(d) Human Resources has to submit inventories to management.

58

Honorable members of the council, five years ago, the Zenith Town Council formulated the Zenith Community Plan, of which one objective was to build a fire substation in Zenith. Five years have passed and little progress has been made. I'm disappointed that the Council has barely done anything to make the Zenith fire substation a reality. Although so many problems still remain, including funding, we must find a way to move ahead.

Q: What can be inferred from the talk?
(a) The Council will reconvene at another time.
(b) The Council has been negligent with council funds.
(c) The fire substation will be unnecessary before long.
(d) The fire substation is unlikely to be completed very soon.

59

Do you want to leave your old job and get more out of life? Well, here's where to start! At Lansing Technical Institute we offer certification in a number of high-growth fields such as Biomedical Engineering, Database Management, and Finance. With over 300 areas of certification, Lansing has plenty of choices to put your life on a new course. Call 1-800-LANSING now to receive a free information package.

Q: Who would benefit most from the institute in the advertisement?
(a) Office workers who want to get a promotion.
(b) People who want to change their career paths.
(c) Professionals who want to take up a new hobby.
(d) Technicians who want to learn about high-growth fields.

60

I'm not here to criticize capital punishment itself but the lack of certainty associated with it. Subject to an imperfect legal system in which error abounds, can the state ever be sure that it is not taking the life of an innocent individual? In some cases, we have seen new evidence emerge which exonerates those on death row, often years after the trial. As long as capital punishment remains legal, we cannot be absolutely sure that the innocent will not be executed.

Q: What can be inferred from the talk?
(a) The speaker once supported capital punishment.
(b) The speaker wants capital punishment abolished.
(c) The speaker personally knows a victim of wrongful execution.
(d) The speaker believes capital punishment does not reduce crime.

서울대 최신기출 4

Listening Comprehension **Scripts**

1

M Hello, can you tell me where the post office is?

W __________________

(a) In the letter box.
(b) Sure, I'll tell you when.
(c) Just around the corner.
(d) First, go to the post office.

2

W We should check our luggage in at that other counter.

M __________________

(a) Check over the luggage.
(b) OK, then, enjoy your trip.
(c) Yes, there's a shorter line.
(d) I'll arrive late to the airport.

3

M I don't see anywhere to park along this road.

W __________________

(a) Then try one of the side streets.
(b) There's no park around here.
(c) We'll get a ticket otherwise.
(d) Careful not to miss the turn.

4

W Thanks for helping me move.

M __________________

(a) Yes, I'm fine, thank you.
(b) You're welcome to have it.
(c) No problem. I was happy to.
(d) I don't know which house it is.

5

M So, did you end up buying a new bicycle?

W __________________

(a) I cycle to keep fit.
(b) I just fixed my old one.
(c) I was thinking that, too.
(d) I don't have the same brand.

6

W Sorry, I'm late. There was a fire in my apartment building.

M __________________

(a) You'll be safe here.
(b) Oh, I hope no one was hurt.
(c) I'm sorry you feel that way.
(d) Then, you'd better put it out.

7

M I think I'll major in journalism.

W __________________

(a) I think you're a fine journalist.
(b) Good idea, since you write well.
(c) So, I hear you're doing well in college.
(d) Congratulations on graduating with honors.

8

W Hello. I'm calling to speak to someone in customer complaints.

M __________________

(a) Please take a message.
(b) Certainly, I'll transfer you.
(c) No one has complained yet.
(d) Sorry, the customer has left.

9

M I feel like curry for dinner. How about you?

W __________________

(a) That sounds good.
(b) I'll pack us a snack.
(c) I would do that, too.
(d) I didn't feel anything, no.

10

W Do your children watch a lot of television?

M ________________________

(a) In fact, they prefer the other one.
(b) Actually, it's unclear who saw it.
(c) Sure, they're like most kids.
(d) OK, I'll turn it off.

11

M I'm sorry I haven't been able to spend more time with you, honey.

W ________________________

(a) I do wish your job were less demanding.
(b) That's a very considerate offer.
(c) You've spent far too little on me.
(d) I'm sure he didn't know.

12

W Shall we have lunch now or later?

M ________________________

(a) Yes please, I'm starving.
(b) No, I think it's happening later.
(c) Well, I'm not hungry right now.
(d) All right, that sounds like a good idea.

13

M Oh, hi Jessica. I haven't seen much of you lately.

W ________________________

(a) I'll stop by later, then.
(b) I've been in the hospital.
(c) I didn't expect to, either.
(d) I'd love to visit your place.

14

W Animal rights protesters take things too far these days.

M ________________________

(a) No, it's a little further on.
(b) I agree, they should do more.
(c) Some tend to go to extremes.
(d) Action should be taken to release them.

15

M I can't be bothered with all of this housework.

W ________________________

(a) Sorry, but I didn't realize I was late.
(b) We'll have to tackle it sooner or later.
(c) You'll just have to turn it in incomplete.
(d) Sure, this house could use some repairs.

16

W Do you need a hand moving into your office?
M Oh, yes, if you don't mind.
W Not at all. I'll carry these files over.
M ________________________

(a) It will be my pleasure.
(b) Those aren't in my office.
(c) That'll be a big help. Thanks.
(d) I wouldn't do that, if I were you.

17

M Good morning, Dean's Office.
W I'd like to speak to Dean Jefferson.
M May I ask who's calling?
W ________________________

(a) This is her daughter, Diane.
(b) I'm sure it's Dean Jefferson.
(c) She'll be getting back to me.
(d) I'm calling about our meeting.

18

W What are you up to these days, Mike?
M I'm taking a computer course at night school.
W Great! How is it?
M ________________________

(a) It's been quite difficult.
(b) I found it on the Internet.
(c) At an institute downtown.
(d) It took me a couple of hours.

19

M The train should have arrived by now.
W Yeah, it's ten minutes late.
M That's bad. We'll miss our connection.
W ________________________

(a) We barely made it, I know.
(b) It'll be on time, I'm positive.
(c) Don't worry, I don't miss it at all.
(d) Maybe, if it's not here in five minutes.

20

W   It's been a wonderful conference.
M   Yes, it was excellent this year.
W   And hopefully it'll be just as good next year.
M   ___________________________

(a) We should decide soon.
(b) I have no doubt it will be.
(c) This year it'll be in London.
(d) I thought it was just as good.

21

M   Hi Julie. How've you been?
W   Oh, hi! I've been keeping busy.
M   Really? What have you been doing?
W   ___________________________

(a) A lot has been done already.
(b) It's been a long time, I know.
(c) I started my own business, actually.
(d) I've been working on it in the evenings.

22

W   Excuse me. Do you have these trousers in a size 10?
M   Yes, but not in blue.
W   Then, what colors do you have?
M   ___________________________

(a) We have blue and black.
(b) Only brown in that size.
(c) Blue trousers suit you.
(d) Just try a smaller size.

23

M   I see you haven't done your homework yet.
W   I'll do it in a little while.
M   But when exactly?
W   ___________________________

(a) I'll be there in a minute.
(b) After this TV show's over.
(c) That was done before 7:30.
(d) I haven't been home for a while.

24

W   I'm glad James wasn't voted student body president.
M   Me too. He would have been terrible.
W   Anyway, Tim will do a great job.
M   ___________________________

(a) You think so? I think he's just as bad.
(b) Really? Let's ask around first.
(c) Yes, I'll try harder next time.
(d) So, he'll get my vote.

25

M   I thought I saw you get off a bus near our office.
W   Right, I didn't drive in today.
M   Why not? You normally drive to work.
W   ___________________________

(a) I didn't come in that way.
(b) I caught a later bus, in fact.
(c) I'm sure it was me you saw.
(d) I couldn't get my car started.

26

W   Can we still meet for dinner at 7 tonight?
M   I hope so, but I might be working late.
W   Then just give me a call when you find out, OK?
M   ___________________________

(a) Then I'll be there, absolutely.
(b) Once I'm finished, I'll leave.
(c) Sure, I'll tell you first thing.
(d) OK, I'll see you then.

27

M   Why did you tell Susan I was annoyed at her?
W   Well, you were, when she canceled your date.
M   Yeah, but that doesn't mean you go off and tell her.
W   ___________________________

(a) But she told me to come and tell you.
(b) Then, if you're not going to do it, I will.
(c) It wasn't like that. It kind of just slipped out.
(d) No, I'm telling you. I tried to make it sound official.

28

W When is the staff meeting?
M We're starting at 4:30.
W And is everyone expected to attend?
M _________________________

(a) I expect we'll reschedule.
(b) We're looking forward to it.
(c) They don't have much to say.
(d) I was told it's for the entire staff.

29

M My stocks just won't go up.
W I don't think the market will improve for a while.
M Would you suggest I sell them?
W _________________________

(a) For the moment, don't return them.
(b) On the contrary, hang onto them.
(c) You might invest in stocks.
(d) I don't know what I'll do.

30

W Where'd you take this photo, in Italy? It's beautiful.
M Yeah, that's a shot of a street in Rome.
W It's great how you got these lighting contrasts.
M _________________________

(a) Yes, my patience really paid off.
(b) Thanks. I've been expecting them.
(c) There was no photographic evidence.
(d) You can borrow them later if you like.

31

M Well, have a good trip to Atlanta.
W Yeah. I'd better get on the bus.
M Bye and good luck. I'll miss you.
W I'll miss you, too.
M Come back again soon!
W I will, soon. I promise.

Q: What is the man mainly doing in the conversation?
(a) Saying farewell to a friend.
(b) Planning to leave Atlanta.
(c) Ending a long friendship.
(d) Paying a friend a visit.

32

W Did you just hear the weather forecast?
M No. What did they say?
W Heavy snow this afternoon.
M Hmmm... That will mean heavy traffic after work.
W You'd better wear your other winter jacket.
M Good idea. I will.
W And don't forget your umbrella.

Q: What are the man and woman mainly doing in the conversation?
(a) Preparing to face bad weather.
(b) Deciding what to wear to work.
(c) Leaving work during heavy traffic.
(d) Complaining about the cold weather.

33

M Grand Palace Hotel. How may I help you?
W I would like to make a reservation.
M Just one moment. When will you be staying?
W From the 20th to the 23rd of this month.
M So, you'll be staying three nights.
W That's correct. It's for three nights.

Q: What is the woman mainly doing in the conversation?
(a) Calling a travel agent.
(b) Asking for room service.
(c) Booking a room at a hotel.
(d) Making a reservation for dinner.

34

W Hey, Justin. Did you know Robert is in the hospital?
M No. Is it serious?
W It may be. His heart is beating irregularly.
M Oh, what's causing that? Do they know yet?
W Well, apparently it runs in his family.
M That's terrible. I do hope he gets better soon.

Q: What is the conversation mainly about?
(a) A tragedy that has befallen a friend's family.
(b) The reasons why a friend has a bad heart.
(c) The medical treatment a friend is getting.
(d) A friend's hospitalization and symptoms.

35

M   Would you like to go to the Cloverdale Bar tonight?

W   Why? What's happening there tonight?

M   A friend of mine is playing in a band.

W   How much does it cost to get in?

M   Oh, don't worry. I've got free tickets.

W   Then, count me in.

Q: What are the man and woman mainly discussing?
(a) Going out for live music.
(b) Performing at a local bar.
(c) Getting free tickets to a show.
(d) Spending the weekend together.

36

M   Do you think we should hire the last applicant?

W   He did carry himself well during the interview.

M   True. And he has a strong résumé as well.

W   But the salary he asked for… that's a problem.

M   It's certainly more than we can afford to pay.

W   Well, let's make an offer on reduced terms.

M   OK. And if he accepts it, we've found our man.

Q: What are the man and woman mainly discussing?
(a) An applicant's performance during a job interview.
(b) Higher salaries being demanded by new applicants.
(c) Securing the services of a promising new applicant.
(d) Difficulties managers face trying to fill job vacancies.

37

M   BETA Corp shares have gone through the roof.

W   Yeah, we should've bought them when we had the chance.

M   But how could we have predicted the jump?

W   Don't ask me. Only insiders could have known.

M   Well, at least our employee shares haven't fallen.

W   Yeah, but that's a small consolation.

Q: What are the man and woman mainly doing in the conversation?
(a) Discussing the company's financial decision.
(b) Regretting the effects of a financial setback.
(c) Deliberating on buying shares at a low price.
(d) Musing about the loss of an investment opportunity.

38

M   Did you get that email I sent you?

W   An email from you? No, I didn't.

M   Are you sure? I sent you an update on the project last week.

W   That's strange. I check my email every day.

M   Well, I'll just send it to you again.

W   That's probably a good idea.

Q: Which is correct according to the conversation?
(a) The man sent several emails to the woman.
(b) The woman did not get the man's email.
(c) The woman receives a lot of junk mail.
(d) The man writes email every day.

39

M   Welcome to Tasty Burgers. What can I get for you?

W   A burger, fries and a lemonade, please.

M   Sorry, but we're out of lemonade.

W   OK, then Coke will do.

M   Will there be anything else?

W   No, that's it, thanks.

Q: Which is correct according to the conversation?
(a) The woman wanted lemonade.
(b) The Coke will be free of charge.
(c) The woman does not drink Coke.
(d) The customer must wait for fries.

40

W Bill, let's drive to the airport together tomorrow, OK?

M Yes, good idea.

W We'll take my car, and I'll drop it off at airport parking.

M OK, but let me pay half the parking costs.

W No need. It's paid for by the company, remember?

M Oh, yeah. I forgot about that.

W So, let's meet at the office at 8 am.

M OK. See you then.

Q: Which is correct about the man and woman?
(a) They will take the man's car.
(b) They will meet at the airport.
(c) They will split the cost of parking.
(d) They will travel together to the airport.

41

M I heard you were in a car accident. Are you OK?

W Yeah, I'm OK. Some guy just rear-ended me.

M Is your car damaged much?

W The rear bumper was damaged, but it's not serious.

M But you'll have to get it repaired, won't you?

W In fact, it's at the garage now.

Q: Which is correct according to the conversation?
(a) The man helped repair the car.
(b) The woman will not repair her car.
(c) The man backed into a car at the garage.
(d) The woman was not injured in the accident.

42

W Hello. I've come to pick up my dry cleaning.

M Do you have your receipt with you?

W Yes, just a minute... Oh, I can't find it.

M Then, can you tell me your phone number?

W Yes, it's 333-5946.

M Thanks. I'll just search our database for your number.

W I'm sorry for the inconvenience.

M That's OK. I found your number. I'll go and get your coat.

Q: Which is correct about the woman?
(a) She got a new phone number.
(b) She misplaced a dry cleaning receipt.
(c) She forgot to pick up her dry cleaning.
(d) She brought the wrong receipt with her.

43

M In tennis, you don't bend your elbow that way.

W Oh, I know that. You don't have to tell me.

M But you don't seem to be doing it right.

W What makes you such an expert?

M Well, for one thing, I've been playing longer than you.

W That doesn't mean you know everything.

Q: What can be inferred about the woman?
(a) She admires the man's tennis ability.
(b) She is irritated by the man's comments.
(c) She is worried that her playing bores the man.
(d) She hopes to convince the man of her dedication.

44

M Sarah, will I be getting a raise this year?

W I can't say. A committee reviews those matters each year.

M Do you know when that will happen?

W Well, there's usually a committee meeting in March.

M And you're certain salary increases will be discussed?

W Yes, they always have been before. That much is certain.

Q: What can be inferred from the conversation?
(a) The man will be promoted in March.
(b) The man will be attending the committee meeting.
(c) The woman is not receiving higher wages next year.
(d) The woman is aware of the procedure for a salary review.

45

W Look at this bag. It's gorgeous! I've got to have it.

M But it looks expensive. How much is it?

W Only 400 dollars.

M That much for a handbag? Are you kidding?

W No, and I think I'm going to buy it.

M Unbelievable! Will you really spend that much on a bag?

W Why not? You only live once.

Q: What can be inferred from the conversation?
(a) The man feels discouraged about the woman.
(b) The woman has a poor sense of fashion.
(c) The woman is hoping to impress the man.
(d) The man rarely buys any luxury bags.

46

In order to reduce pollution in the environment and congestion on Britain's roads, June 14th has been designated as National Carpool Day. Take this day as a chance to share a car with your friends, family and colleagues. Once you try car sharing, you will realize that cost, convenience and environmental benefits soon outweigh any excuse not to carpool. You can also register at www.liftshare.org to look for other members who are traveling your way and find out details of special events taking place on National Lift Share Day.

Q: What is the advertisement mainly about?
(a) A special national holiday in Britain.
(b) A nationally organized carpooling day.
(c) A plan to make carpooling more lucrative.
(d) A new kind of British public transportation.

47

I'd like to talk about an ongoing debate within educational psychology concerning the benefits of certain music on intelligence. According to two studies that challenge previous research on this topic, a Mozart sonata won't make listeners any smarter. Researchers concluded that listening to Mozart before an IQ test had no significant effect on results. This contradicts a 1993 study which showed subjects temporarily gained up to nine IQ points after listening to Mozart. The findings spawned an industry of supposedly mind-enhancing recordings.

Q: What is called into question by the speaker?
(a) The relationship between IQ and musical ability.
(b) The methods used in a renowned 1993 study.
(c) The positive effect of music on intelligence.
(d) The tactics of mind-enhancing recordings.

48

We have an aging infrastructure in this nation, and we are not doing our share to maintain it and replace it. The politicians are clearly to blame. Maintaining a sewer system is hardly an exciting political issue, and years of neglect with respect to funding and the consequent lack of maintenance across the nation have left many of the country's engineering systems unprepared to handle future problems. America's older cities are really modern-day Pompeiis—they are within the range of volcanoes of infrastructure failures.

Q: What is the speech mainly about?
(a) Corruption in America as compared to that of Pompeii.
(b) Financing infrastructure renewal in older American cities.
(c) American cities threatened by possible volcanic eruptions.
(d) Old American cities facing the danger of infrastructure failures.

49

A silver dollar dating back to 1804 and minted as a gift to the Sultan of Muscat was expected to garner record-breaking bids of up to $2 million at an auction Monday. Transferred as part of a secret mission to the Middle East by an emissary for American President Andrew Jackson, the silver dollar was a gift for the Sultan of Muscat—currently known as Oman—after a new trade deal was signed. However, bids fell short of meeting the reserve price, and the silver dollar was not sold.

Q: What is the news report mainly about?
(a) The value of a rare silver dollar.
(b) Rare coins minted in the Middle East.
(c) The auctioning of a famous silver dollar.
(d) A gift once given to the Sultan of Muscat.

50

I'm sure many of you know that coffee has been blamed for many health problems. However, researchers are now saying that a few cups of coffee a day might help prevent gallstones. In a recent study, men who drank two to three cups of caffeinated coffee a day had a 40 percent lower risk of gallstones than non-coffee drinkers. The risk is reduced because chemicals found in caffeinated coffee lower the cholesterol in bile that can result in gallstones.

Q: What is the main idea of the talk?
(a) Coffee can help prevent gallstone formation.
(b) Health benefits of coffee are debatable.
(c) Coffee effectively dissolves gallstones.
(d) Caffeinated drinks should be avoided.

51

Your assignment for this semester is to write a literature review. In order to do this, you will need to survey academic papers, books and other sources related to today's class discussion topic. Afterwards, you'll be asked to provide a summary and critical evaluation of each work. Basically, you will be giving an overview of significant literature published on the topic. As mentioned in the syllabus, the deadline for the assigned task is May 2nd.

Q: What is the main assignment according to the professor?
(a) To critique an essay on literary criticism.
(b) To summarize today's class discussion topic.
(c) To write an overview of published materials on a given subject.
(d) To read scholarly articles for an upcoming in-class discussion.

52

Congratulations, everyone, on a successful completion of the project. I'm certain you all have mixed feelings of triumph and sadness after finishing a project of such magnitude. That's natural. These are the things that define us as people, and losing them can leave us feeling empty inside. But this debriefing is all about keeping the momentum going. Think about what you have achieved and how you have changed in the process, and build on it. Accept all the mixed emotions you have and use them to move forward.

Q: What is the talk mainly about?
(a) Having confidence in the outcome of a project.
(b) Learning to cope with various project hurdles.
(c) Handling a series of project grievances.
(d) Moving on after a demanding project.

53

Class, we'll now discuss the destruction of the Temple of Jerusalem, which took place when the Roman Army, led by Titus, besieged the city. Why the Romans destroyed the Temple is a matter of conjecture. Some scholars assert that Titus wished to rid the Empire of Judaism. On the other hand, Flavius Josephus, who witnessed the event, portrayed Titus as wishing to save the Temple from uncontrollable troops committing personal revenge. This account, however, is full of contradictions and many historians question its historical accuracy.

Q: Which is correct according to the lecture?
(a) The Temple was most likely destroyed by unruly soldiers.
(b) Titus erected the Temple to commemorate his victory.
(c) The report that the Romans destroyed the Temple is uncertain.
(d) Some question the validity of Flavius Josephus's account.

54

After much consideration, we are pleased to announce the winner of the Fulton Story Competition. The judges selected *Half-Baked* by Justin Beagle for its humor, clarity and insight. Justin will receive $5,000 and his story will be printed by Spineless Books in a collection of short fiction. Justin Beagle teaches writing and cultural studies at Emerson College and is hard at work on his first novel. Justin, please come up and accept your award.

Q: Which is correct about Justin Beagle?
(a) His story won for its original plot.
(b) His novel is a continuation of *Half-Baked*.
(c) He is currently attempting to complete a novel.
(d) He is a student of cultural studies at Emerson College.

55

And now for the local forecast. Tonight in Tuscaloosa, it will remain partly cloudy and you can expect isolated thunderstorms later in the evening. A low of 64 Fahrenheit is likely and a high of 88 Fahrenheit is expected tomorrow. It will be clear in the morning; however, the afternoon will be variable with cloud cover and scattered thunderstorms. So, if you're heading out, don't forget that umbrella!

Q: Which is correct according to the weather report?
(a) Skies in Tuscaloosa will clear in the evening.
(b) Several days of stormy weather are expected.
(c) Temperatures will fall below 60 Fahrenheit tonight.
(d) Thunderstorms are predicted for tomorrow afternoon.

56

What our company needs is not just highly skilled, well-educated workers. We need team players. We should hire people, not just on their reputation on paper, but on how well they will work with our team. After all, there are plenty of experts in the field, but how many will fit into our company culture? We have to change the way we recruit people. So, when you're interviewing, start by asking yourself, "Is this the kind of person I would like to work next to?"

Q: Whom does the speaker want to recruit according to the talk?
(a) Better-educated team recruiters.
(b) Employees with specific experience.
(c) More highly skilled experts in the field.
(d) Workers who fit into the company culture.

57

Sarcoidosis is an immune system disorder that chiefly attacks the lungs, eyes or skin. Though it generally causes no more than severe discomfort, it can sometimes lead to serious organ damage. In fact, it causes death in about 10 percent of patients diagnosed. There is no cure, and treatment options are limited. However, for most sufferers, treatment with corticosteroids can somewhat ease symptoms. But for a significant number of others, unfortunately, this is not the case.

Q: Which is correct about sarcoidosis according to the lecture?
(a) It damages the body by attacking the immune system.
(b) Corticosteroids have proven to be an effective cure.
(c) About 10 percent of the population will come down with it.
(d) Contracting it could eventually prove to be fatal.

58

Assyria was a mighty kingdom, but it was conquered by Babylon. Babylon was a great empire, but it was subdued by Persia. Persia was subsequently conquered by Alexander the Great. That's the history of the ancient world. One kingdom comes along, prevails in battles and builds a huge empire. It lasts for a while, until another empire comes to power. However, this one was much bigger and mightier, and was to last much longer. The empire I'm going to talk about today grew to be bigger than even that of Alexander.

Q: What will the speaker most likely do immediately following this talk?
(a) Introduce a powerful empire that lasted for a long time.
(b) Talk about the empire founded by Alexander the Great.
(c) Compare the Assyrian, Babylonian and Persian Empires.
(d) Illustrate the order of the ancient empires on a chart.

59

I've summoned all the executives to this meeting because I have an important announcement to make. As you are aware, over the past two quarters our airline's operating expenses have skyrocketed while our earnings have fallen. As a result, it was decided at a company board meeting yesterday that we'll start offering low-priced flights to attract more business. It's a move we've been contemplating for some time. We'll name our proposed new service Fast Jet and will soon offer it nationwide.

Q: What can be inferred about the airline from the talk?
(a) It has long debated changing its name.
(b) It will have to reduce the number of its jets.
(c) It does not have a large fleet of passenger jets.
(d) It expects to profit from a higher volume of customers.

60

On today's tour, you will see one of Edward Hopper's most famous paintings, entitled "Nighthawks." It depicts an all-night café in which uncommunicative customers are illuminated in the pitiless glare of electric lights. The atmosphere of the painting communicates a strong sense of loneliness and solitude, making it quintessentially modern and one of Hopper's strongest pieces.

Q: What can be inferred from the talk?
(a) Hopper's "Nighthawks" was the first piece of art dubbed "modern."
(b) Customers and diners figure prominently in Hopper paintings.
(c) Hopper's work is relatively unknown and underappreciated.
(d) Modern art frequently addresses themes of isolation.

서울대 최신기출 5

Listening Comprehension **Scripts**

1

M How much is a one-way bus ticket to San Francisco?

W _______________

(a) About 1,500 kilometers.
(b) It takes about five hours.
(c) It's eighteen dollars and fifty cents.
(d) I wouldn't recommend San Francisco.

2

M I became a father yesterday.

W _______________

(a) I think the baby is due soon.
(b) I've never met your father.
(c) You must be very happy.
(d) I'll see you tomorrow.

3

W What did the teacher just say?

M _______________

(a) I'm not quite sure.
(b) You can tell him so.
(c) You can say that again.
(d) I hope to be in his class.

4

M Oh no! I forgot to bring my credit card.

W _______________

(a) Don't worry. I have some cash.
(b) I wonder if they accept cards.
(c) The bill is on the table.
(d) OK. I'll keep the card.

5

W Can you come to my birthday party this weekend?

M _______________

(a) Let me check my schedule.
(b) You're welcome any time.
(c) I had one already, thanks.
(d) He says he can't come.

6

W I think we've already met. It's Jerry Smith, isn't it?

M _______________

(a) Actually, it's Jeff, not Jerry.
(b) Sure, we can meet later.
(c) I know the Smith family.
(d) That's all right.

7

W Your mid-term grades weren't very good.

M _______________

(a) It's difficult to note.
(b) I'll do better next time.
(c) I'll have an answer for you.
(d) You can't cram for the test.

8

M So, why did you come to see me?

W _______________

(a) I didn't know where you were.
(b) I need some advice from you.
(c) Let's meet in my office.
(d) I came here by subway.

9

W Hey, look at that glass skyscraper over there!

M _______________

(a) OK, I'll go for it.
(b) I'd look over there.
(c) Be careful with the glass.
(d) Wow, it's simply amazing!

10

M Do you enjoy hiking?

W _______________

(a) OK, I'll think of something.
(b) Yes. I love the outdoors.
(c) It won't take long.
(d) I'll try that again.

11

W Do you think it's worth getting this old jacket altered?
M _______________________________

(a) Everything's mixed up.
(b) I'll have to ask you to fix it.
(c) I don't think it's mended properly.
(d) You'd be better off with a new one.

12

M Would you like anything in your tea?
W _______________________________

(a) Well, it's not my favorite.
(b) I don't drink tea that much.
(c) I'll take only a teaspoonful.
(d) Sugar, if it isn't any bother.

13

W One of your eyes is bloodshot. What's wrong?
M _______________________________

(a) I need your help putting in eye drops.
(b) I don't know. I should go see a doctor.
(c) I've never had problems with eyes.
(d) I can find out the results for you.

14

M How do I look in this suit? Should I buy it?
W _______________________________

(a) I'd use a different fabric.
(b) I'd grab it, if I were you.
(c) That sure was a great buy.
(d) Sure, you can try on other suits.

15

W Could you put me through to Mr. Baker?
M _______________________________

(a) My call has been cut off.
(b) Yes, I can take a message.
(c) Let me show you to his office.
(d) Sorry, but he's on another line.

16

M What do you do for a living?
W I run a small business.
M What kind of business?
W _______________________________

(a) In New York City.
(b) Three years ago.
(c) I sell cosmetics.
(d) It's my job.

17

W Excuse me, but which subway line goes to City Hall?
M It's line number one.
W Thanks. And how do I get to the platform?
M _______________________________

(a) I'll be back soon.
(b) Take those stairs.
(c) I'm taking the bus.
(d) It leaves in ten minutes.

18

M The woman at check-in said I can't take two carry-on bags on the plane.
W Why not?
M She said it's too much luggage for one person.
W _______________________________

(a) You can have mine.
(b) OK, have a good trip.
(c) Glad you could make it.
(d) Then, I'll carry one for you.

19

W How did your play go last night?
M It was a disaster.
W What happened?
M _______________________________

(a) The ticket line was long.
(b) Everyone seemed interested.
(c) I couldn't remember any of my lines.
(d) Luckily nothing happened last night.

20

M You look stressed out.

W It's because I have to finish this report by 5.
   Can you help me?

M Sure. What should I do?

W ___________________________

(a) You can check these figures.
(b) I have nothing to report.
(c) You were a great help.
(d) Take a break anytime.

21

W Smells good. What're you cooking?

M Avocado soup. Have you ever tried it?

W No, that's new to me.

M ___________________________

(a) Really? Here, try some.
(b) It's hard to find avocados.
(c) Sorry. There isn't any left.
(d) I've never heard of it, either.

22

M So, what brings you to the hospital today?

W My throat is very sore.

M Do you have any other symptoms?

W ___________________________

(a) I didn't ask.
(b) It started last night.
(c) Mostly when I swallow.
(d) I've been coughing a lot.

23

W Dan, is that you? I didn't recognize you.

M Hi. Yeah, I've lost a lot of weight since we
   last met.

W You sure have. You look great.

M ___________________________

(a) I don't think it's hard to take.
(b) You have to agree that it's true.
(c) Thanks. I work out regularly these days.
(d) Well, you haven't changed at all, either.

24

M I wish store clerks would leave me alone
   when I'm shopping.

W They're only doing their job.

M But when they hover around me, I feel like
   leaving the store.

W ___________________________

(a) I think they just stepped out.
(b) It's impolite to talk back to people.
(c) I guess they can be annoying at times.
(d) You could ask the store clerk to show you
    around.

25

W We need a new refrigerator.

M But there is nothing wrong with the one we
   have.

W It's an outdated model.

M ___________________________

(a) The electricity bill was high.
(b) You should buy a smaller one.
(c) It'll go well with our new interior.
(d) You can't buy a new one for that reason.

26

M When are you going to Brazil for your
   holiday?

W Next month.

M What made you want to go there?

W ___________________________

(a) I planned it all by myself.
(b) I'm so worried about the trip.
(c) I wanted to visit some relatives there.
(d) I've always wanted to live in a warmer
    climate.

27

W How was your weekend?

M Good. I didn't do anything exciting, though.

W Was it at least relaxing?

M ___________________________

(a) I wasn't very tired.
(b) I had to come back to work.
(c) I suppose you could say that.
(d) I couldn't enjoy the rest of it.

28

M   Are you stopping by Hawaii on your way to LA?

W   I won't be doing that, no.

M   Why not? It'll be an inexpensive way to see the island.

W   ___________________________

(a) I was hoping you'd cover the expenses.

(b) I know, but I can't spare the extra days.

(c) I promise I'll take you there next time.

(d) Yeah, I think it'll be a great getaway.

29

W   I'm sorry for having made you work extra hours.

M   That's all right. It was fortunate I didn't have plans.

W   I assure you nothing like this will happen again.

M   ___________________________

(a) That's a relief to hear.

(b) That's all I could do, then.

(c) I should've seen it coming.

(d) Nothing's further from the truth.

30

M   How about having spaghetti for lunch?

W   Sure, but is there a good Italian restaurant around here?

M   Yes, just around the corner.

W   ___________________________

(a) What are we waiting for? Lead the way.

(b) That's the one I was telling you about.

(c) Your timing couldn't have been better.

(d) Let's get together some time.

31

M   I can't find my cellphone.

W   Did you try calling it?

M   Yes, but I couldn't hear it ringing.

W   When did you last use it?

M   Maybe at the bus stop.

W   You might have left it there, then.

Q: What is the man's problem?

(a) He has lost his cellphone.

(b) He forgot his cellphone number.

(c) He does not know which bus to take.

(d) He cannot get his cellphone to work.

32

W   Directory assistance.

M   Could you give me the number for Amco Dynamics?

W   Amco Dynamics... I'm sorry, but I don't have a listing for that.

M   Is there anything for Amco, then?

W   There are Amco Industries and Amco Designs.

M   It could be the latter. I'll try their number.

W   Certainly, please hold.

Q: What is the man doing in the conversation?

(a) Finding the phone number for a company.

(b) Making an appointment with a secretary.

(c) Getting directions to a company office.

(d) Confirming the location of a business.

33

M   Do you want to watch the soccer game with us tonight?

W   Who's playing?

M   It's England versus Argentina.

W   That should be an exciting game.

M   Yeah. We're going to watch it around eight at the Downtown Bar.

W   OK. I'll see you there.

Q: What are the man and woman mainly discussing?

(a) What the soccer match will be like.

(b) When the man is going to watch the match.

(c) Which is the best bar for watching a soccer match.

(d) Whether the woman will join the man to watch soccer.

34

W   I didn't see you at Mark's party.

M   I was there for a little while, but I had to leave early.

W   That's too bad. My friend and I were looking for you.

M   Really? What for?

W   I wanted to introduce my friend to you.

Q: What are the man and woman mainly talking about?
(a)   How they did not see one another at the party.
(b)   Why the woman wanted to go to the party.
(c)   How much they enjoyed the party.
(d)   Why the man left the party early.

35

W   When are you organizing a clean-up around the office?

M   I asked everyone to start after lunch.

W   Isn't that a bit late? The CEO will visit at around 2.

M   I think we'll have enough time.

W   You won't get everything done, in my opinion.

M   Really? Well, yeah, I guess an earlier start is safer.

Q: What are the man and woman mainly discussing?
(a)   When the CEO will be visiting the office.
(b)   What the woman intends to do after lunch.
(c)   Why the man needs to collect his belongings.
(d)   Whether an office clean-up should be done sooner.

36

M   The guy downstairs is making a lot of noise again.

W   You should go and talk to him.

M   I've tried that before, but it didn't work.

W   Then, why don't you just bang on the floor?

M   But I don't want to resort to that.

W   Then, call Management. He's way too loud.

Q: What is the main topic of the conversation?
(a)   What to do about a noisy neighbor.
(b)   What it is like to live near a noisy neighbor.
(c)   Why banging on the floor is not a good idea.
(d)   Why the man does not want to confront his neighbor.

37

W   I finally got a promotion!

M   That's wonderful. Did you get a raise, too?

W   Not only that, but also my own office.

M   Wow, I'm so proud of you.

W   Thank you. I'm just happy that my hard work has paid off.

Q: What is mainly happening in the conversation?
(a)   The woman is complaining about the job.
(b)   The man is asking the woman about her pay raise.
(c)   The woman is announcing a well-earned promotion.
(d)   The man is congratulating the woman on a project she did.

38

W   Your son speaks French really well. Is your wife French?

M   No, but she studied it in college.

W   So, she taught your son?

M   Yes, she always speaks to him in French at home.

W   And do you do that as well?

M   Not me. I can't speak French at all.

Q: How did the man's son become fluent in French?
(a)   By using French at home.
(b)   By teaching other people.
(c)   By studying it in college.
(d)   By going to a private institute.

39

M   Oh, are you still working on our presentation?

W   Yes, I'm just making some final touches.

M   But why? When I last looked, everything seemed fine to me.

W   I wanted to make things flow a little smoother.

M   OK, then, if you think it needs it, why not?

Q: Which is correct according to the conversation?
(a) The man's presentation is nowhere near completion.
(b) The woman cannot find materials for the presentation.
(c) The man is worried about the work the woman is doing.
(d) The woman wants to improve the presentation material.

40

M   Welcome to Toronto. How can I help you?
W   Hi, I need to book a hotel room downtown for a convention.
M   Where is the convention being held?
W   At the Community Lodge.
M   In that case, I'd suggest the Cherriet. It's close to the Community Lodge and has rooms for $95 per night.
W   OK, can you give me their number? I'll call them.

Q: Which is correct according to the conversation?
(a) The man is accompanying the woman on the trip.
(b) The woman is staying in Toronto for two nights.
(c) The Cherriet is near the Community Lodge.
(d) The Community Lodge is expensive.

41

W   You'll surely pass your exam this time.
M   I don't think so.
W   But you've been studying, haven't you?
M   A little. But I don't often have the time.
W   Is there a way to give yourself more time?
M   I get home from work late, so I don't see how.
W   What about weekends?
M   I don't get a lot of time then, either.

Q: Why does the man think he may fail his exam again?
(a) Because he has not been studying at all.
(b) Because he does not study on weekends.
(c) Because he is not sure he can finish on time.
(d) Because he does not have enough time to study.

42

M   I'm afraid I can't make it tonight.
W   I suppose you're busy again.
M   I know we planned to go out, but...
W   I know, I know. You're held up at the office, and you can't come.
M   I'll make it up to you, tomorrow.
W   Oh, really?
M   Yeah, we'll have a nice dinner out, and we'll go to the movies.
W   Somehow, I don't believe you.

Q: Which is correct according to the conversation?
(a) The man is going to go home early.
(b) The man cannot book dinner for tomorrow.
(c) The woman has already set the dinner table.
(d) The woman is doubtful of the man's assurances.

43

W   Are you OK? Let me help you up.
M   Thanks. I didn't see that puddle of water on the floor.
W   You had a nasty fall. Are you sure you're OK?
M   Yes, no harm done, except I got wet.
W   You're lucky. It could have been worse.

Q: What can be inferred from the conversation?
(a) The woman helped the man back on his feet.
(b) The woman spilled water on the floor.
(c) The man got injured from a fall.
(d) The man tripped on a wire.

44

M   I'm going to the store. I'll be back soon.
W   Wait. You might as well pick up a few things.
M   I wasn't going to go for long. I just have to get an extension cord.
W   Couldn't you pick up some minced garlic and rice?
M   Do we really need them today?
W   Yes, for dinner. If you get them, it'll save me a trip.

Q: What can be inferred from the conversation?
(a) The man has to make another trip to the store.
(b) The man is reluctant to do any extra shopping.
(c) The woman is planning to go to the store with the man.
(d) The woman does not want to go shopping with the man.

45

W   Now, Mr. Jackson, why do you wish to sue the city?
M   Well, my wife tripped and fractured her ankle on Green Street yesterday.
W   And why do you feel the city is responsible for your wife's accident?
M   She tripped on a big crack in the sidewalk.
W   Well, it's true that the city is responsible for the condition of sidewalks.
M   Right. That's why my wife should not have to pay the medical bills.

Q: What can be inferred from the conversation?
(a) The man and his wife live on Green Street.
(b) The woman works in a government medical center.
(c) The man will organize someone to fix the sidewalk.
(d) The man's wife may not have to pay her medical expenses.

46

Now that everyone in the class has been given a field workbook, I urge you to make full use of it. You can learn more that way. You should not be worried about it getting grubby or dirty. The idea of having a field workbook is for you to take notes out in the field. So, use it at every opportunity. Always take your field workbook with you when you go out into the field.

Q: What is the instructor's main point?
(a) Do not leave your field workbook at home.
(b) Make maximum use of your field workbook.
(c) Keep your field workbook in good condition.
(d) Do not worry if your field workbook gets dirty.

47

While some breakfast cereals claim to be healthy, not all of them are. Most breakfast cereals are made with processed sugars and refined white flour. Even with reduced sugar content, they are still high in simple carbohydrates. Therefore, they are as bad for you as high-sugar cereals. That's why it's very important to check the label. A healthy cereal is one that is made with whole grains and has low sugar content. If it does not say that on the label, it is probably not healthy for you.

Q: What is the main point of the talk?
(a) Most breakfast cereals are good for your health.
(b) Healthy people prefer sugar-free breakfast cereals.
(c) Simple carbohydrates are healthier for you in the long run.
(d) People need to check whether their cereals are healthy to eat.

48

We have yet to find a real cure for avian flu. With this in mind, prevention is our best defense against what could become a human pandemic. If this disease cannot be properly controlled, millions of people could be killed within months. Thus, our priorities ought to be given to controlling the spread of the disease.

Q: What is the main idea of the talk?
(a) Prevention is the key to controlling the spread of avian flu.
(b) Avian flu is unlikely to spread as fast as everyone thinks.
(c) Without a cure for avian flu, millions of people could die.
(d) People tend to exaggerate the danger of avian flu.

49

For many seniors, a driver's license enables them to stay independent as they grow older. However, some sections of the community are now calling for mandatory reexamination of senior citizens' driving skills, following a series of accidents involving seniors over the past few months. One suggestion was that drivers over 70 years old should pass a driving test each year in order to have their driver's licenses renewed.

Q: What is the main idea of the news report?
(a) Senior citizens ought to practice their driving skills more.
(b) People have blamed senior citizens for a series of road accidents.
(c) Senior citizens regard a driver's license as a symbol of independence.
(d) Senior citizens' driving skills should be reassessed regularly to ensure road safety.

50

Seeking a way to transform your old home movies into digital movie magic? Look no further than the new CV-500 desktop system, which comes in the standard version with a 500GB partitioned memory, cutting-edge sound system and movie editing functions. The hardware package comes with two hi-fi digital camcorder links, a detachable capture device and a 22 inch LCD monitor. Movie Manic, Sounds-Off and Day-Vid software packages are also included, providing you with the capability to edit and burn your own movies like a professional.

Q: What is mainly being advertised?
(a) A movie editing software package.
(b) Digital camcorders with capture devices.
(c) A computer system for editing home movies.
(d) Extra memory to enhance movie editing capability.

51

In this Urban Studies lecture, you'll often hear me mention "urban sprawl," or the process of cities spreading out and rural lands being taken over for development. Be aware that from the standpoint of urban planning institutions, the style of development is very important. But for those concerned about the effects of sprawl on the natural environment and agricultural resources, the amount of land urbanized is more important. Either position is valid in achieving different, although not necessarily mutually exclusive, goals.

Q: What is the main topic of the lecture?
(a) The loss of rural land is often the result of poor urban planning.
(b) The fight to stop urban sprawl requires two main approaches.
(c) Urban sprawl is bad for agriculture and the environment.
(d) There are two different perspectives on urban sprawl.

52

While great attention has been paid to the role of doctored videos and pictures in recent campaigns, such media manipulation is nothing new to the democratic process. Even Lincoln published a now iconic campaign photograph of himself featuring his head on the fuller-bodied Southern politician John Calhoun's body. It's been a part of politics since photography began, and it won't go away. So, as political science students, never forget that in political campaigns images are routinely altered to advance a point of view.

Q: What is the speaker's main point?
(a) Politicians have long used media manipulation.
(b) Media manipulation is becoming progressively pervasive.
(c) People are becoming increasingly skeptical of political rhetoric.
(d) Lincoln's reputation for being honest may not be well-deserved.

53

Aloha. Welcome to the Kilauea Visitor Center. The island of Hawaii offers many attractions, from lush tropical rainforests to waterfalls to white sandy beaches, but nothing is as spectacular as the Hawaii Volcanoes National Park. It has one of the world's most active volcanoes, the Kilauea Volcano. The best time to view this natural wonder is at dawn or dusk, when the unearthly glow of molten rock is visible through cracks in the earth.

Q: Which is correct according to the announcement?
(a) Hawaii's main attraction is its white sandy beaches.
(b) Kilauea is the world's largest remaining active volcano.
(c) Kilauea Volcano is best viewed around dawn and dusk.
(d) Hawaii Volcanoes National Park is as popular as the waterfalls.

54

The movie *Back to Dust* will not appeal to everyone. If you want to watch excessive violence and see the good guy win against impossible odds, this movie is for you. However, don't expect much high production value. The acting is deplorable, the effects are fake, and the storyline consists of excuses to stage fight. Frankly, if you are looking for a smart realistic drama, you should avoid this movie.

Q: Which is correct about the movie *Back to Dust* according to the review?
(a) It is based on a fictional novel.
(b) It contains scenes with strong violence.
(c) It has a storyline that follows historical facts.
(d) It features a good guy who is clever at disguising himself.

55

Representatives of Oregon's tuna fishing industry announced today that the industry is in crisis because the migratory tuna it depends on have proved harder to catch this year. The tuna used to follow warm currents from Alaska, south along the Pacific coast to Mexico. But global warming is melting northern glaciers, producing cold water currents along the Oregon coast and driving the fish deeper and farther offshore, making them much more difficult to catch. The same pattern is likely to occur next year.

Q: What do we learn about Oregon's tuna fishing industry from the news report?
(a) Oregon's tuna fishing industry has collapsed.
(b) The temperature of Oregon's coastal waters has risen.
(c) Tuna deviated from their usual migration route this year.
(d) Tuna migration has not been affected by global warming.

56

You have reached the National Credit Bureau's safety line. If you would like to initiate an investigation, please follow the directions of this automated system. You will need the following information: your nine-digit identification number and your ten-digit telephone number. After you have entered your information, a representative of the Bureau will contact you within two weeks. To enter your personal information now, press the pound key.

Q: Which is correct according to the message?
(a) You must press the pound key after you enter information.
(b) Submitted information will be processed within two weeks.
(c) A Bureau representative will visit you to begin an investigation.
(d) You must call the National Credit Bureau for investigation results.

57

We will begin our study of the immune system's response to a dangerous organism or virus with the initial phase, identification. Our immune system recognizes a harmful cell by looking for telltale signs on its surface structure. These identifying signs are called antigens. Foreign cells—whether bacteria, viruses or allergens—all have distinctive antigens that set them apart from our own cells, and when our immune system finds cells with these antigens, it attacks them.

Q: Which is correct according to the lecture?
(a) Antigens prevent organisms from causing infections.
(b) Bacteria and viruses attack the human body with antigens.
(c) Our immune system detects bacteria and viruses by way of antigens.
(d) Antigens are produced during the initial phase of our immune response.

58

Good afternoon. It is truly a great pleasure for me to welcome our guests from abroad to the opening of our new factory. Today's event is the result of eighteen months of great effort and collaboration between our two companies. I am positive that this is just the beginning of a lasting and mutually beneficial relationship. At this time, let me introduce to you the president of our company.

Q: What can be inferred from the talk?
(a) The two companies have the exact same president.
(b) One company is planning to buy out the other company.
(c) One of the two companies is relocating to a foreign country.
(d) Two companies are expecting to benefit from a new relationship.

59

It is the City Council's decision that the rock band XTC will not be allowed to perform at any venue within city limits. The band has a history of problems, and the city does not feel it can assume liability for allowing this band to perform in our city. Our legal counsel suggests that we adhere to this position to avoid setting any precedent that will adversely affect the city in the future. This decision is a popular one, judging by the thousands of letters of support we have received.

Q: What can be inferred from the council's announcement?
(a) The council has a history of legal problems with XTC.
(b) The band XTC may put on a concert in the city at a later date.
(c) Most letters sent to the council were written by elderly people.
(d) Other controversial bands will also be prevented from performing.

60

It has been estimated that during the 16th and 17th centuries several thousand "crypto-Jews," or "secret Jews," emigrated from Spain and Portugal to the Indies. Although ethnically Jewish, they had been forced to convert to Catholicism, which meant that they had to practice their religion in secret. For them, the Indies offered religious freedom and an improvement of their material circumstances. These reasons were enough for them to emigrate.

Q: What can be inferred about the "secret Jews?"
(a) Most had abandoned their traditional religion.
(b) Many suffered under poor conditions in Spain.
(c) They eventually became the majority in the Indies.
(d) They converted to a different religion in the Indies.

서울대 최신기출 6
Listening Comprehension **Scripts**

1

M I'm so glad exam week is finally over.
W ___________________________

(a) I can't wait.
(b) Let's do it later.
(c) Thank you again.
(d) Me too. It's been a long week.

2

M Hello, may I speak with Mr. Roberts, please?
W ___________________________

(a) Thanks for calling.
(b) Hi, nice to meet you.
(c) Please tell him to call back.
(d) Sure. Just a moment, please.

3

M How would you like your eggs?
W ___________________________

(a) No, I don't need to.
(b) Scrambled, please.
(c) Fried rice is best.
(d) About two a day.

4

M What do you prefer to be called?
W ___________________________

(a) Call me anytime.
(b) Just call me Jenny.
(c) Tom's already here.
(d) I can't remember now.

5

W Congratulations on your new job!
M ___________________________

(a) Thanks. I'm so excited!
(b) I should look for a job.
(c) Maybe I'll get over it.
(d) I hope you're right.

6

W How did you finish your term paper so quickly?
M ___________________________

(a) I'd be glad to help you.
(b) I got it from the library.
(c) My sister typed it for me.
(d) The deadline is tomorrow.

7

W Sorry I'm late. My alarm didn't go off this morning.
M ___________________________

(a) I didn't change any settings.
(b) It's too early in the morning.
(c) Please don't let it happen again.
(d) Don't worry. I'll work tomorrow.

8

M Hi, I have a dinner reservation under the name Allen.
W ___________________________

(a) OK. I'll book that for you.
(b) I know. You're quite right.
(c) Sorry, but we can't take it.
(d) Certainly, please follow me.

9

M Would you mind living in a studio?
W ___________________________

(a) I like living in a big city.
(b) I'm moving next weekend.
(c) Not if it's near the university.
(d) There's one next to my house.

10

M   Let's meet at Central Park.

W   _______________________________

(a) But it might be too crowded.
(b) I can't. I'm busy at that time.
(c) Maybe it's at another location.
(d) The meeting's been postponed.

11

M   Do you have time for a chat?

W   _______________________________

(a) OK. I'll share it with you.
(b) Yes. Let's make it a date.
(c) Well, enough for a short one.
(d) No, I'm not doing anything now.

12

M   I'm sorry I gave you such a hard time.

W   _______________________________

(a) But it was very easy.
(b) Well, I'm sorry for asking.
(c) It was silly of me to say so.
(d) That's all right. I understand.

13

M   I'm afraid I sounded too mean at the meeting.

W   _______________________________

(a) I don't remember ever saying that.
(b) Well, it didn't come across that way.
(c) I thought it went on for too long, too.
(d) Yeah, you haven't seen the worst of it.

14

M   Do you take a lot of cream in your coffee or just a little?

W   _______________________________

(a) OK. Just go ahead.
(b) A spoonful will do.
(c) It's one or the other.
(d) Yes, absolutely. Thanks.

15

M   The company my father started is going out of business.

W   _______________________________

(a) It's a company matter as far as I know.
(b) I look forward to doing business with him.
(c) That's unfortunate. It seemed so promising.
(d) It should make his business much more profitable.

16

M   So, you're from Marysville? Where's that?
W   It's a town in Kansas.
M   Oh, I see. Is it a large town?

W   _______________________________

(a) Of course, I agree.
(b) No, it's not any smaller.
(c) It's near the capital city.
(d) It has about 3,000 people.

17

M   How long have you been studying Korean?
W   About a year.
M   That's amazing because your Korean is so good!

W   _______________________________

(a) Thanks for the compliment.
(b) Yes, what a surprise!
(c) But I'm not Korean.
(d) Don't mention it.

18

W   I hear you play a lot of tennis these days.
M   That's right. It's great fun.
W   How often do you play?
M   _______________________________

(a) Almost every day.
(b) I play with a friend.
(c) At the courts nearby.
(d) Maybe some other time.

19

M I have some bad news.

W Really? What is it?

M Our landlady is going to raise the rent again.

W _______________________________

(a) I don't want to rent it.

(b) I'm tired of going that way.

(c) I thought we'd already paid it.

(d) Oh, no! What are we going to do?

20

W Has everyone arrived?

M Well, everyone except Kevin. He never comes on time.

W It really annoys me when he does that.

M _______________________________

(a) Don't worry. I'll help you.

(b) I know. It bothers me, too.

(c) Be quiet, or he'll hear you.

(d) I have a good excuse this time.

21

M When will you go see the doctor?

W I went to the hospital yesterday.

M Already? So, what happened?

W _______________________________

(a) Medical insurance is expensive.

(b) I was told I might need surgery.

(c) I went to the one near my house.

(d) I've been having this pain for weeks.

22

W Hi, I came to pick up my pants.

M Oh, I'm sorry, but they're not ready yet.

W Didn't you say you'd have them shortened by today?

M _______________________________

(a) Sure, I'll have it done.

(b) Well, I'd like a refund.

(c) I'll try my best next time.

(d) I did, but I've been extra busy.

23

M My grandmother is coming to visit us.

W Really? Is your grandfather coming, too?

M No, just my grandmother. She's flying in tomorrow.

W _______________________________

(a) I'm sure she can find us.

(b) What time will she arrive?

(c) In that case, I'll take a taxi.

(d) I hope you have a good flight.

24

M Excuse me. How can I get to Finley Station?

W Take line 2 from Central Station.

M Do I need to transfer?

W _______________________________

(a) No, it's on the same line.

(b) Take the subway instead.

(c) The decision is up to you.

(d) Sure, I'll drive you to the station.

25

M Why are you going to the consulate?

W I have to apply for a visa.

M Oh, is yours about to expire?

W _______________________________

(a) It might be a long wait.

(b) It'll only take a few hours.

(c) It's only good till June 10th.

(d) I'll be traveling as a tourist.

26

W Hello. Can I be of assistance?

M Yes. I need some info on accommodations.

W Do you want to stay near this airport or downtown?

M _______________________________

(a) A hotel nearby is what I'd prefer.

(b) My permanent residence will be in Seoul.

(c) I'm here on official government business.

(d) The company branch is located downtown.

27

M   I'm not sleeping well these days.

W   Really? Do you know why?

M   It could be because I've been drinking a lot of coffee.

W   _______________

(a) You should go to bed earlier.
(b) I don't like caffeinated drinks.
(c) Probably. Try to drink less, then.
(d) I bought you some sleeping pills.

28

W   What's in these pots?

M   Oh, just some tree seedlings.

W   But they're so small. They don't look like trees at all.

M   _______________

(a) I'm not good with plants.
(b) Maybe they need more water.
(c) They will, once they've grown.
(d) Actually, there are different kinds.

29

M   We waste so much paper in this office!

W   I agree. And it all ends up in the trash.

M   Why don't we start recycling?

W   _______________

(a) No, it's too late to start now.
(b) Fine. I'll dump out the garbage.
(c) OK. Let's get a bin for paper only.
(d) Yes, let's subscribe to a daily paper.

30

M   Honey, can you see the drugstore yet?

W   It's on the left corner, right beside the theater.

M   Ah, yes. There were so many signs. I couldn't see it.

W   _______________

(a) Well, the streets are so crowded.
(b) I know. They're all over the place.
(c) I'm afraid I don't see any sign of it.
(d) Which medicine are you looking for?

31

W   Something's wrong with my golf swing. I keep slicing to the right.

M   You need to turn your arms a little more as you swing.

W   You mean like this?

M   Right. That should fix the problem.

W   Oh, OK. Thanks.

Q: What is the man helping the woman to do?
(a) Get a better golf club.
(b) Improve her golf swing.
(c) Hit the golf ball harder.
(d) Stand correctly as she swings.

32

W   How much will it cost to send this package by air to Malaysia?

M   Let me weigh it. Um..., it'll cost about $37.

W   Wow, that's expensive! Is there a cheaper way to send it?

M   You can send it by surface mail for $22.75.

W   I'll do that, then.

Q: What is the woman trying to do?
(a) Pick up a package.
(b) Fly economy class.
(c) Mail a parcel cheaply.
(d) Pay for a store purchase.

33

M   I bought this coat today. What do you think?

W   Looks great, except it seems a little small.

M   You really think so?

W   Yeah, a larger size would've been better.

M   OK. I'll go exchange it tomorrow.

W   But the style and color look nice.

M   Yeah. I'll just get a bigger size.

Q: What is the woman mainly telling the man?
(a) He needs to replace an old coat.
(b) He bought the wrong size coat.
(c) His coat does not look good.
(d) His coat is out of fashion.

34

M   Good morning, Sue. Did you do anything over the weekend?

W   Nothing special. And you?

M   Well, I finally got myself a motorcycle.

W   Oh, you actually got one!

M   Yeah, but I bought it used.

W   Did you get a good deal?

M   I think so. It was cheap but in good condition.

Q: What is the main idea of the conversation?
(a) The man sold his used motorcycle.
(b) The man finally bought a motorcycle.
(c) The man rides a motorcycle on weekends.
(d) The man has a motorcycle in good condition.

35

M   Do you see those two huge dogs?

W   Yes. They don't seem to be with anyone.

M   And they may be dangerous, especially to children.

W   We'd better do something about it.

M   Right. Let's call animal control.

Q: What is the conversation mainly about?
(a) Reporting stray dogs.
(b) Taking care of children.
(c) Searching for dogs that are lost.
(d) Looking at dangerous animals at the zoo.

36

W   So, are we still on for lunch tomorrow?

M   Sure. Is 12:30 still all right with you?

W   Let's make it 12:45.

M   OK. Do you have a particular restaurant in mind?

W   No, but how about something spicy, like Mexican or Thai?

M   Thai sounds perfect.

W   Great.

Q: What is the conversation mainly about?
(a) Arranging a lunch appointment.
(b) Promising to go out on a blind date.
(c) Cooking a spicy Thai meal for lunch.
(d) Changing the place of a lunch appointment.

37

M   This summer is unbearably hot. I'm sweating so much.

W   Yeah, it's hard to get used to.

M   No kidding. I have trouble sleeping at night as well.

W   That's why I leave my air-conditioner on all night.

M   I don't even have one, so I'm really suffering.

W   Well, hopefully the heat wave will end soon.

Q: What is the main topic of the conversation?
(a) Ways to get to sleep at night.
(b) Sweating too much from the heat.
(c) Sleeping with the air-conditioning on.
(d) The uncomfortable weather conditions.

38

M   What do you feel like eating tonight, Maggie?

W   Oh, I don't know. Chicken?

M   But we had that yesterday.

W   Then, what do you suggest?

M   I was thinking of pasta or seafood.

W   Let's cook some pasta, then. It'll be easy.

Q: What will the couple have for dinner?
(a) Pasta.
(b) Chicken.
(c) Seafood.
(d) Hamburgers.

39

W   Oh, a taxi at last! Hi.

M   Hello. Where to, ma'am?

W   To the National Museum of Art, please.

M   Sure. No problem.

W   How much do you think the fare will be?

M   Around 20 dollars... not including a tip, of course.

W   That much? It must take a long time to get there.

M   Well, with traffic, it'll take 30 minutes or so.

Q: Which is correct according to the conversation?
(a) The man expects the trip to last 20 minutes.
(b) The woman has to pay a total of 20 dollars.
(c) The woman is going to a history museum.
(d) The museum is at least 30 minutes away.

40

M That book looks like an antique.

W Well, it's old, but not quite that old.

M Where did you get it?

W I came across it in a used bookstore.

M Well, it looks quite old, although the cover is beautiful.

W Yes, it's in good shape for its age.

Q: Which is correct about the book?
(a) It has a pretty cover.
(b) It looks old for its age.
(c) The woman bought it new.
(d) The woman borrowed it from the man.

41

M Hello. I'm calling about the job you advertised.

W Oh, yes. That position is still available.

M Great. Then, I'd like to apply.

W Do you have any experience dealing with customers?

M Yes, I worked at LJ's Department Store for five years.

W Oh, good. Then, why don't you visit our showroom for an interview, say at 2 pm?

M Sure. Thank you. I look forward to it.

Q: Which is correct according to the conversation?
(a) The man has experience with a relevant position.
(b) The job that was advertised is no longer available.
(c) The man currently works at LJ's Department Store.
(d) The woman wants to interview the man over the phone.

42

W May I help you?

M Yes. I need a birthday card and a gift for my wife.

W Certainly, our birthday cards are right here.

M OK, thanks. And where can I buy jewelry?

W Our jewelry is at the counter over there.

M They can do engravings, can't they?

W Oh, yes, but it costs a little extra.

Q: Which is correct according to the conversation?
(a) The store does not carry birthday cards.
(b) The man wants to buy two gifts for his wife.
(c) The man has some jewelry he wants to engrave.
(d) The cost for engraving is not included in purchases.

43

M A safety officer visited my factory today!

W Without prior notice?

M Yes. None whatsoever. And she found a number of violations.

W That must have been embarrassing.

M It was, especially for my boss.

W No doubt he'll make some safety improvements soon, then.

M I'm sure he will.

Q: What kind of event is being discussed?
(a) A surprise safety inspection.
(b) A meeting about factory safety.
(c) A mistake the man's boss made.
(d) A visit by the company president.

44

M It's a bit cold, isn't it?

W Yes, is the heater on?

M I think so. I'll check the control panel.

W What does the panel show?

M The settings seem OK. It's set at 25.

W Let me see... Yeah, the buttons work, but there's no heat.

Q: What can be inferred from the conversation?
(a) The control panel has an error message.
(b) The control panel buttons are not working.
(c) The man put the settings at the wrong level.
(d) The heater is not responding to the controls.

45

M You need to make a right turn just up ahead.

W Oh! The traffic is so heavy... I can't get into the right lane.

M Watch out! There's a car right beside you!

W Hey! He just blocked me off! And I had my blinker on!

M He should've let you in. How rude.

W What'll I do now? Can we take another way?

M Yeah, just make a U-turn at the next light.

W I hate driving in this heavy traffic.

Q: What can be inferred from the conversation?
(a) The woman missed her planned turn.
(b) The woman is not an experienced driver.
(c) The man and woman are arguing in a car.
(d) The man regrets having let the woman drive.

46

Hi, I'm Mike the Travel Guy. On today's "Traveler's Guide" radio program, I'm going to explain how to make your travel vacation less stressful. First of all, organize your schedule so you can take things slowly. Don't rush from tourist spot to tourist spot trying to see everything there is in one day. Also, try to stay a minimum of three nights in each city you visit. That way, you can get some rest from all the traveling.

Q: What is the speaker's main point about traveling?
(a) Avoid stress by taking your time.
(b) Plan every detail of your vacation.
(c) Try not to go on any package tours.
(d) Just spend time at the best tourist spots.

47

So far in this German language and culture class, we've talked about Berlin's history. Now let's look at what modern Berliners think of their city. In a recent survey, it was found that 55 percent of Berliners do not enjoy living there—that's over half the city population! Why are so many residents of Berlin unhappy there? Well, climate may be part of the reason. In Berlin, it is bitterly cold in the winter and terribly hot in the summer.

Q: What is the main idea of the lecture on Berlin?
(a) It has cold winters and hot summers.
(b) It has had a long and troubled history.
(c) Most residents are proud of their city.
(d) Many of its residents do not like living there.

48

Arab Adventures is now offering a nine-day trip to Egypt at an unbelievably low price. Travelers will explore exotic bazaars, ancient monasteries and desert oases—all for only $520! How did we make it so cheap? It's simple: we arrange for you to travel with the locals on public transportation such as trains, taxis and even donkey carts, and you'll have meals and lodgings in family-run guest houses. So, if you've always wanted to see the real Egypt but thought it was too expensive, contact Arab Adventures today!

Q: What is mainly being advertised?
(a) A trip to Egypt by train.
(b) A low-budget tour to Egypt.
(c) A tour of Egypt's main historical sites.
(d) A new travel company specializing in Egypt.

49

Distinguished coworkers, guests and supporters, thank you for inviting me to speak on our organization's current program in Africa. Our Africa program intends to bring down poverty levels among village farmers in Uganda by widening the availability of animal health services. We are now educating poor farmers to be community-based animal health workers or so-called "barefoot veterinarians" who can provide fundamental animal health services to the local villages. We hope this project will become self-sustaining in the next couple of years.

Q: What is the mission of the project in Uganda?
(a) To fight poverty through better animal care.
(b) To teach farmers new ways of raising animals.
(c) To raise awareness of poverty on farms in Africa.
(d) To help farmers set up animal breeding programs.

50

In health news today, lawmakers have introduced a new bill aimed at stemming childhood obesity. The bill would effectively ban the sale of soft drinks in public schools. It would also limit the sale of snack foods. Not everyone is happy with the bill, however. The food and beverage companies that supply school vending machines with sodas and snacks say jobs will be lost if the bill is passed. Also, school boards worry about profit losses from not being able to sell popular food and drink brands.

Q: What is the main topic of the report?
(a) Reactions to a proposed obesity bill.
(b) The difficulty of passing an obesity bill.
(c) How the obesity bill will change the food industry.
(d) Whether a bill on childhood obesity will be effective.

51

In today's class, we will talk about the Serengeti Plain in Tanzania, Africa. The Serengeti is most renowned for its yearly cycle of animal migrations. More than a million gnus and zebras move southward during the months of October and November. Then, after the rainy season passes in June, they return to the north. Their primeval instinct to migrate is so powerful that no drought or crocodile-infested river can stop them.

Q: What is the main topic of the lecture?
(a) Some life forms in the Serengeti Plain
(b) Ancient instincts among African animals
(c) The cycle of rain and drought in Tanzania
(d) The annual migrations of Serengeti animals

52

As economics students, you shouldn't be surprised that China's ongoing structural changes make its economy more sensitive to interest rates. For one, state companies now often have to repay their loans, and so they have become more concerned about rising interest rates. Moreover, private companies are increasingly accessing credit, making them more sensitive to interest rates as well. And finally, consumers are becoming more sensitive to rate changes because they are borrowing more from banks.

Q: What is the main topic of the lecture?
(a) China's economic problems as a result of rising interest rates.
(b) Chinese companies' increasing tendency to access credit.
(c) The importance of interest rates in the Chinese economy.
(d) The financial danger Chinese state companies are facing.

53

In entertainment news, 17,000 rock fans have already booked tickets for Patty O'Malley's concert scheduled for June 15th at the Delta Center. If it is anything resembling the Patty O'Malley shows held earlier this month in Paris, the fans can expect an exhilarating show. The Irish rocker played two highly successful gigs at a gigantic soccer stadium in northern Paris. Although the concerts during the US tour will be scaled down for indoor venues, the show itself and its emotional intensity should be practically the same.

Q: Which is correct about Patty O'Malley according to the report?
(a) He will perform at open-air venues on his US tour.
(b) Tickets for his Delta Center concert are sold out.
(c) His US performances will be similar to those in Paris.
(d) His concert at the Delta Center will be his largest ever.

54

As we have learned in US History class, the US has five military branches. The smallest of these is the Coast Guard, which has existed since 1790. It originally began as a loose network of fast sailing boats that protected the coastline from smugglers and pirates in the late 1800s. Since then, it has evolved into a large force that serves numerous other purposes as well.

Q: Which is correct about the Coast Guard?
(a) It first began in 1800.
(b) It can be divided into five branches.
(c) It was created to stop illegal immigrants.
(d) It now fulfills a large number of purposes.

55

Thank you everyone for coming to today's lecture. Before you leave, I'd like to remind you that next week's lecture for this class will be delivered by guest speaker Dr. Barbara Stein, who is professor of English Literature at the University of Rhodesia. Her lecture is titled "Beyond Multiculturalism: The Making of a New American Identity through Fiction." Please make sure that you attend. Dr. Stein will also be participating in an informal discussion afterwards, from 12:15 to 1:30, in the Women's Building Lounge.

Q: Which is correct about Dr. Stein's lecture?
(a) It is for University of Rhodesia students.
(b) It will be held during the next class time.
(c) It will be held in the Women's Building Lounge.
(d) It is based on a book about English Multiculturalism.

56

As art history students, you should know that the Baroque period is not clearly distinguished from that of the late Renaissance. Nonetheless, the term "Baroque Art" is generally acknowledged to mean the art of the period roughly from 1600 to 1750. It began when the Catholic Reformation movement was in its final phase. The emergence of Baroque art, in fact, was directly influenced by the Catholic Reformation.

Q: Which is correct according to the lecture?
(a) The Catholic Reformation took place in 1750.
(b) The early Renaissance followed the Baroque period.
(c) Art in the Baroque period influenced Renaissance art.
(d) Baroque art was an outcome of the Catholic Reformation.

57

Before we begin class today, I have a brief announcement: from July 3rd to the 6th, the East Asia Institute at our university will be holding the first annual Asian Relations Conference. The purpose of this conference is to promote research on international relations in East Asia, and this year's focus will be on Japan. Leading scholars on Japanese affairs will be delivering the addresses. If you are interested in attending, please take one of these information brochures on your way out.

Q: Which is correct about the conference?
(a) Prominent academics will be speaking.
(b) It promotes research on Japan annually.
(c) Students must fill out an application to attend.
(d) It marks the start of a new direction in East Asian studies.

58

I am dismayed that many of our Asian economies still don't have adequate social welfare systems. Asia's leaders keep on saying that such systems are not needed in Asia because of "Asian values," meaning that community values are such that people will automatically take care of each other in a crisis. Well, the fact is, they don't. And, since people don't take care of each other as leaders claim they do, there is a need for a social welfare system that will provide that care.

Q: What will the speaker most likely talk about next?
(a) The benefits of "Asian values."
(b) The need for economic improvements in Asia.
(c) The kind of welfare system that is needed in Asia.
(d) The reasons why Asian leaders do not provide welfare.

59

In today's class, I'll introduce you to how geological maps are made. First, geologists travel to a region to gather geological data, such as information on faults, folds and other physical features. In the field, this data is recorded onto aerial photographs, or, occasionally, directly onto a topographic base map. Then, back at the office, all of the information is combined and digitized to produce a final geological map.

Q: What can be inferred from the lecture?
(a) There are many different kinds of geological maps.
(b) Geological fieldwork is indispensable for creating maps.
(c) Information on the final maps is based on years of research.
(d) Geological maps are of better quality when they are handmade.

60

In reference to Mr. Kyle's comments in the press on the veracity of the evidence during the Stanley murder trial, I would like to contend on behalf of my client that as a journalist he is not qualified to pass judgment. Mr. Kyle has spent time neither studying nor working in forensic pathology. For him to pontificate on which evidence is admissible and which is inadmissible in the case is farcical. I fully espouse the rights of the press, but proper dissemination of information to the public is also important.

Q: What can be inferred about the speaker?
(a) He is an attorney involved in a homicide case.
(b) He regards Mr. Kyle's comments as personal slander.
(c) He objects to Mr. Kyle's curtailing the freedom of the press.
(d) He is worried about negligence in the course of a murder trial.

Answer Keys

Listening Comprehension

1 (a)	**2** (a)	**3** (b)	**4** (b)	**5** (d)	**6** (c)	**7** (d)	**8** (a)	**9** (d)	**10** (c)
11 (d)	**12** (d)	**13** (d)	**14** (b)	**15** (a)	**16** (d)	**17** (a)	**18** (a)	**19** (d)	**20** (b)
21 (c)	**22** (b)	**23** (a)	**24** (b)	**25** (c)	**26** (d)	**27** (b)	**28** (d)	**29** (c)	**30** (b)
31 (a)	**32** (b)	**33** (c)	**34** (c)	**35** (a)	**36** (b)	**37** (d)	**38** (c)	**39** (b)	**40** (c)
41 (c)	**42** (d)	**43** (a)	**44** (d)	**45** (b)	**46** (d)	**47** (a)	**48** (c)	**49** (a)	**50** (c)
51 (b)	**52** (c)	**53** (c)	**54** (a)	**55** (a)	**56** (d)	**57** (d)	**58** (b)	**59** (b)	**60** (c)

Grammar

1 (b)	**2** (c)	**3** (c)	**4** (a)	**5** (c)	**6** (d)	**7** (d)	**8** (c)	**9** (d)	**10** (b)
11 (b)	**12** (b)	**13** (c)	**14** (d)	**15** (d)	**16** (b)	**17** (b)	**18** (d)	**19** (b)	**20** (d)
21 (a)	**22** (b)	**23** (a)	**24** (c)	**25** (a)	**26** (d)	**27** (a)	**28** (b)	**29** (a)	**30** (c)
31 (a)	**32** (b)	**33** (c)	**34** (b)	**35** (d)	**36** (d)	**37** (c)	**38** (c)	**39** (d)	**40** (d)
41 (b)	**42** (b)	**43** (d)	**44** (a)	**45** (c)	**46** (d)	**47** (a)	**48** (b)	**49** (c)	**50** (c)

Vocabulary

1 (a)	**2** (c)	**3** (b)	**4** (c)	**5** (a)	**6** (c)	**7** (b)	**8** (a)	**9** (c)	**10** (b)
11 (a)	**12** (b)	**13** (b)	**14** (d)	**15** (c)	**16** (c)	**17** (a)	**18** (c)	**19** (d)	**20** (a)
21 (b)	**22** (a)	**23** (c)	**24** (b)	**25** (b)	**26** (a)	**27** (a)	**28** (d)	**29** (d)	**30** (a)
31 (c)	**32** (c)	**33** (a)	**34** (c)	**35** (c)	**36** (b)	**37** (a)	**38** (d)	**39** (b)	**40** (a)
41 (b)	**42** (d)	**43** (c)	**44** (a)	**45** (b)	**46** (a)	**47** (b)	**48** (c)	**49** (d)	**50** (a)

Reading Comprehension

1 (c)	**2** (a)	**3** (d)	**4** (b)	**5** (c)	**6** (c)	**7** (d)	**8** (d)	**9** (c)	**10** (c)
11 (d)	**12** (c)	**13** (d)	**14** (c)	**15** (a)	**16** (d)	**17** (a)	**18** (b)	**19** (a)	**20** (d)
21 (b)	**22** (b)	**23** (d)	**24** (b)	**25** (d)	**26** (c)	**27** (c)	**28** (c)	**29** (b)	**30** (b)
31 (c)	**32** (b)	**33** (c)	**34** (d)	**35** (d)	**36** (a)	**37** (d)	**38** (b)	**39** (c)	**40** (c)

Answer Keys

Listening Comprehension

1	(c)	**2**	(d)	**3**	(d)	**4**	(a)	**5**	(b)	**6**	(c)	**7**	(d)	**8**	(c)	**9**	(c)	**10**	(b)
11	(c)	**12**	(d)	**13**	(c)	**14**	(a)	**15**	(d)	**16**	(c)	**17**	(a)	**18**	(a)	**19**	(d)	**20**	(a)
21	(a)	**22**	(a)	**23**	(c)	**24**	(d)	**25**	(a)	**26**	(d)	**27**	(c)	**28**	(c)	**29**	(b)	**30**	(b)
31	(a)	**32**	(c)	**33**	(d)	**34**	(b)	**35**	(c)	**36**	(b)	**37**	(b)	**38**	(a)	**39**	(b)	**40**	(d)
41	(b)	**42**	(b)	**43**	(d)	**44**	(c)	**45**	(c)	**46**	(b)	**47**	(c)	**48**	(d)	**49**	(d)	**50**	(b)
51	(a)	**52**	(b)	**53**	(c)	**54**	(b)	**55**	(a)	**56**	(b)	**57**	(a)	**58**	(b)	**59**	(d)	**60**	(d)

Grammar

1	(d)	**2**	(b)	**3**	(d)	**4**	(a)	**5**	(a)	**6**	(d)	**7**	(c)	**8**	(b)	**9**	(d)	**10**	(a)
11	(c)	**12**	(a)	**13**	(d)	**14**	(a)	**15**	(c)	**16**	(d)	**17**	(a)	**18**	(a)	**19**	(c)	**20**	(c)
21	(c)	**22**	(d)	**23**	(b)	**24**	(a)	**25**	(c)	**26**	(a)	**27**	(b)	**28**	(d)	**29**	(a)	**30**	(c)
31	(b)	**32**	(a)	**33**	(b)	**34**	(d)	**35**	(d)	**36**	(c)	**37**	(b)	**38**	(c)	**39**	(d)	**40**	(c)
41	(a)	**42**	(b)	**43**	(d)	**44**	(c)	**45**	(d)	**46**	(d)	**47**	(b)	**48**	(c)	**49**	(b)	**50**	(c)

Vocabulary

1	(c)	**2**	(d)	**3**	(b)	**4**	(a)	**5**	(d)	**6**	(a)	**7**	(b)	**8**	(c)	**9**	(a)	**10**	(b)
11	(d)	**12**	(b)	**13**	(a)	**14**	(b)	**15**	(c)	**16**	(c)	**17**	(c)	**18**	(d)	**19**	(c)	**20**	(b)
21	(c)	**22**	(d)	**23**	(a)	**24**	(d)	**25**	(d)	**26**	(b)	**27**	(d)	**28**	(c)	**29**	(d)	**30**	(d)
31	(a)	**32**	(d)	**33**	(a)	**34**	(a)	**35**	(b)	**36**	(a)	**37**	(c)	**38**	(a)	**39**	(c)	**40**	(a)
41	(c)	**42**	(d)	**43**	(a)	**44**	(b)	**45**	(d)	**46**	(b)	**47**	(d)	**48**	(b)	**49**	(a)	**50**	(c)

Reading Comprehension

1	(b)	**2**	(d)	**3**	(a)	**4**	(c)	**5**	(b)	**6**	(b)	**7**	(c)	**8**	(c)	**9**	(a)	**10**	(c)
11	(b)	**12**	(d)	**13**	(d)	**14**	(b)	**15**	(a)	**16**	(d)	**17**	(c)	**18**	(c)	**19**	(c)	**20**	(a)
21	(b)	**22**	(d)	**23**	(a)	**24**	(d)	**25**	(d)	**26**	(c)	**27**	(c)	**28**	(c)	**29**	(d)	**30**	(b)
31	(d)	**32**	(c)	**33**	(d)	**34**	(b)	**35**	(c)	**36**	(c)	**37**	(b)	**38**	(b)	**39**	(c)	**40**	(b)

Answer Keys

Listening Comprehension

1 (b)	2 (d)	3 (c)	4 (a)	5 (a)	6 (c)	7 (d)	8 (b)	9 (b)	10 (d)
11 (b)	12 (b)	13 (b)	14 (d)	15 (d)	16 (d)	17 (d)	18 (c)	19 (c)	20 (d)
21 (a)	22 (d)	23 (a)	24 (c)	25 (b)	26 (b)	27 (b)	28 (d)	29 (a)	30 (a)
31 (a)	32 (d)	33 (d)	34 (d)	35 (a)	36 (c)	37 (a)	38 (c)	39 (d)	40 (c)
41 (b)	42 (c)	43 (c)	44 (d)	45 (a)	46 (b)	47 (c)	48 (b)	49 (a)	50 (a)
51 (c)	52 (d)	53 (a)	54 (a)	55 (c)	56 (b)	57 (c)	58 (d)	59 (b)	60 (b)

Grammar

1 (a)	2 (c)	3 (a)	4 (b)	5 (a)	6 (a)	7 (d)	8 (d)	9 (a)	10 (d)
11 (b)	12 (d)	13 (c)	14 (b)	15 (d)	16 (b)	17 (d)	18 (c)	19 (c)	20 (b)
21 (b)	22 (b)	23 (c)	24 (d)	25 (c)	26 (d)	27 (d)	28 (d)	29 (a)	30 (b)
31 (c)	32 (b)	33 (d)	34 (c)	35 (b)	36 (c)	37 (c)	38 (c)	39 (c)	40 (c)
41 (d)	42 (d)	43 (c)	44 (a)	45 (d)	46 (b)	47 (a)	48 (c)	49 (c)	50 (d)

Vocabulary

1 (b)	2 (c)	3 (a)	4 (d)	5 (c)	6 (b)	7 (c)	8 (b)	9 (a)	10 (b)
11 (b)	12 (a)	13 (a)	14 (c)	15 (d)	16 (a)	17 (c)	18 (b)	19 (b)	20 (b)
21 (c)	22 (b)	23 (a)	24 (c)	25 (b)	26 (b)	27 (b)	28 (a)	29 (c)	30 (c)
31 (d)	32 (c)	33 (a)	34 (a)	35 (b)	36 (b)	37 (b)	38 (c)	39 (a)	40 (b)
41 (d)	42 (b)	43 (c)	44 (b)	45 (d)	46 (c)	47 (a)	48 (a)	49 (d)	50 (a)

Reading Comprehension

1 (d)	2 (a)	3 (b)	4 (d)	5 (d)	6 (b)	7 (d)	8 (a)	9 (d)	10 (d)
11 (a)	12 (d)	13 (d)	14 (c)	15 (c)	16 (a)	17 (d)	18 (a)	19 (d)	20 (c)
21 (b)	22 (c)	23 (a)	24 (a)	25 (c)	26 (b)	27 (a)	28 (c)	29 (a)	30 (a)
31 (a)	32 (c)	33 (d)	34 (c)	35 (c)	36 (d)	37 (c)	38 (b)	39 (b)	40 (a)

Answer Keys

Listening Comprehension

1 (c)	**2** (c)	**3** (a)	**4** (c)	**5** (b)	**6** (b)	**7** (b)	**8** (b)	**9** (a)	**10** (c)
11 (a)	**12** (c)	**13** (b)	**14** (c)	**15** (b)	**16** (c)	**17** (a)	**18** (a)	**19** (d)	**20** (b)
21 (c)	**22** (b)	**23** (b)	**24** (a)	**25** (d)	**26** (c)	**27** (c)	**28** (d)	**29** (b)	**30** (a)
31 (a)	**32** (a)	**33** (c)	**34** (d)	**35** (a)	**36** (c)	**37** (d)	**38** (b)	**39** (a)	**40** (d)
41 (d)	**42** (b)	**43** (b)	**44** (d)	**45** (d)	**46** (b)	**47** (c)	**48** (d)	**49** (c)	**50** (a)
51 (c)	**52** (d)	**53** (d)	**54** (c)	**55** (d)	**56** (d)	**57** (d)	**58** (a)	**59** (d)	**60** (d)

Grammar

1 (b)	**2** (a)	**3** (a)	**4** (b)	**5** (a)	**6** (b)	**7** (b)	**8** (c)	**9** (c)	**10** (b)
11 (b)	**12** (c)	**13** (d)	**14** (d)	**15** (b)	**16** (b)	**17** (a)	**18** (c)	**19** (a)	**20** (d)
21 (c)	**22** (a)	**23** (a)	**24** (a)	**25** (a)	**26** (d)	**27** (d)	**28** (c)	**29** (d)	**30** (a)
31 (c)	**32** (a)	**33** (b)	**34** (d)	**35** (a)	**36** (c)	**37** (a)	**38** (c)	**39** (a)	**40** (d)
41 (c)	**42** (d)	**43** (c)	**44** (b)	**45** (b)	**46** (b)	**47** (c)	**48** (d)	**49** (c)	**50** (d)

Vocabulary

1 (c)	**2** (c)	**3** (a)	**4** (c)	**5** (b)	**6** (c)	**7** (a)	**8** (b)	**9** (a)	**10** (a)
11 (c)	**12** (d)	**13** (d)	**14** (b)	**15** (b)	**16** (d)	**17** (d)	**18** (d)	**19** (d)	**20** (c)
21 (d)	**22** (b)	**23** (c)	**24** (a)	**25** (a)	**26** (c)	**27** (d)	**28** (c)	**29** (d)	**30** (d)
31 (c)	**32** (b)	**33** (c)	**34** (a)	**35** (b)	**36** (d)	**37** (b)	**38** (b)	**39** (c)	**40** (b)
41 (d)	**42** (c)	**43** (d)	**44** (d)	**45** (a)	**46** (c)	**47** (c)	**48** (d)	**49** (b)	**50** (b)

Reading Comprehension

1 (d)	**2** (d)	**3** (a)	**4** (b)	**5** (b)	**6** (d)	**7** (b)	**8** (c)	**9** (d)	**10** (c)
11 (a)	**12** (a)	**13** (b)	**14** (c)	**15** (a)	**16** (a)	**17** (b)	**18** (c)	**19** (a)	**20** (b)
21 (a)	**22** (d)	**23** (c)	**24** (b)	**25** (b)	**26** (c)	**27** (c)	**28** (c)	**29** (c)	**30** (c)
31 (c)	**32** (d)	**33** (c)	**34** (c)	**35** (a)	**36** (d)	**37** (c)	**38** (b)	**39** (d)	**40** (c)

Listening Comprehension

1 (c)	2 (c)	3 (a)	4 (a)	5 (a)	6 (a)	7 (b)	8 (b)	9 (d)	10 (b)
11 (d)	12 (d)	13 (b)	14 (b)	15 (d)	16 (c)	17 (b)	18 (d)	19 (c)	20 (a)
21 (a)	22 (d)	23 (c)	24 (c)	25 (d)	26 (c)	27 (c)	28 (b)	29 (a)	30 (a)
31 (a)	32 (a)	33 (d)	34 (a)	35 (d)	36 (a)	37 (c)	38 (a)	39 (d)	40 (c)
41 (d)	42 (d)	43 (a)	44 (b)	45 (d)	46 (b)	47 (d)	48 (a)	49 (d)	50 (c)
51 (d)	52 (a)	53 (c)	54 (b)	55 (c)	56 (b)	57 (c)	58 (d)	59 (d)	60 (b)

Grammar

1 (b)	2 (a)	3 (b)	4 (a)	5 (c)	6 (b)	7 (a)	8 (b)	9 (c)	10 (d)
11 (c)	12 (c)	13 (c)	14 (d)	15 (c)	16 (c)	17 (d)	18 (b)	19 (c)	20 (c)
21 (d)	22 (a)	23 (a)	24 (c)	25 (b)	26 (a)	27 (b)	28 (d)	29 (b)	30 (a)
31 (c)	32 (a)	33 (c)	34 (c)	35 (a)	36 (c)	37 (c)	38 (b)	39 (a)	40 (c)
41 (b)	42 (c)	43 (d)	44 (d)	45 (a)	46 (b)	47 (a)	48 (b)	49 (a)	50 (d)

Vocabulary

1 (d)	2 (b)	3 (a)	4 (b)	5 (d)	6 (d)	7 (a)	8 (d)	9 (b)	10 (d)
11 (a)	12 (a)	13 (a)	14 (c)	15 (b)	16 (c)	17 (d)	18 (a)	19 (a)	20 (c)
21 (d)	22 (d)	23 (c)	24 (a)	25 (a)	26 (c)	27 (b)	28 (b)	29 (a)	30 (c)
31 (c)	32 (d)	33 (a)	34 (d)	35 (b)	36 (a)	37 (d)	38 (d)	39 (d)	40 (a)
41 (a)	42 (b)	43 (b)	44 (d)	45 (a)	46 (d)	47 (d)	48 (b)	49 (b)	50 (d)

Reading Comprehension

1 (d)	2 (b)	3 (a)	4 (a)	5 (d)	6 (a)	7 (b)	8 (d)	9 (c)	10 (b)
11 (d)	12 (d)	13 (c)	14 (b)	15 (a)	16 (b)	17 (d)	18 (d)	19 (d)	20 (b)
21 (b)	22 (a)	23 (b)	24 (c)	25 (c)	26 (b)	27 (c)	28 (d)	29 (d)	30 (d)
31 (b)	32 (b)	33 (d)	34 (c)	35 (b)	36 (c)	37 (c)	38 (b)	39 (b)	40 (c)

Answer Keys

Listening Comprehension

1 (d)	2 (d)	3 (b)	4 (b)	5 (a)	6 (c)	7 (c)	8 (d)	9 (c)	10 (a)
11 (c)	12 (d)	13 (b)	14 (b)	15 (c)	16 (d)	17 (a)	18 (a)	19 (d)	20 (b)
21 (b)	22 (d)	23 (b)	24 (a)	25 (c)	26 (a)	27 (c)	28 (c)	29 (c)	30 (b)
31 (b)	32 (c)	33 (b)	34 (b)	35 (a)	36 (a)	37 (d)	38 (a)	39 (d)	40 (a)
41 (a)	42 (d)	43 (a)	44 (d)	45 (a)	46 (a)	47 (d)	48 (b)	49 (a)	50 (a)
51 (d)	52 (c)	53 (c)	54 (d)	55 (b)	56 (d)	57 (a)	58 (c)	59 (b)	60 (a)

Grammar

1 (b)	2 (d)	3 (c)	4 (b)	5 (a)	6 (c)	7 (d)	8 (b)	9 (c)	10 (c)
11 (c)	12 (a)	13 (c)	14 (c)	15 (d)	16 (b)	17 (d)	18 (c)	19 (d)	20 (b)
21 (b)	22 (a)	23 (c)	24 (c)	25 (b)	26 (a)	27 (a)	28 (c)	29 (a)	30 (d)
31 (a)	32 (d)	33 (b)	34 (a)	35 (b)	36 (a)	37 (b)	38 (a)	39 (d)	40 (d)
41 (a)	42 (c)	43 (a)	44 (b)	45 (a)	46 (b)	47 (d)	48 (a)	49 (a)	50 (c)

Vocabulary

1 (c)	2 (d)	3 (b)	4 (b)	5 (a)	6 (c)	7 (d)	8 (d)	9 (b)	10 (d)
11 (c)	12 (a)	13 (a)	14 (b)	15 (c)	16 (a)	17 (b)	18 (a)	19 (b)	20 (b)
21 (b)	22 (b)	23 (c)	24 (c)	25 (d)	26 (d)	27 (c)	28 (a)	29 (b)	30 (c)
31 (c)	32 (d)	33 (c)	34 (b)	35 (c)	36 (d)	37 (a)	38 (b)	39 (d)	40 (d)
41 (c)	42 (c)	43 (b)	44 (c)	45 (a)	46 (d)	47 (b)	48 (a)	49 (d)	50 (a)

Reading Comprehension

1 (c)	2 (b)	3 (c)	4 (a)	5 (b)	6 (c)	7 (d)	8 (c)	9 (a)	10 (d)
11 (d)	12 (a)	13 (a)	14 (c)	15 (c)	16 (a)	17 (b)	18 (c)	19 (a)	20 (a)
21 (b)	22 (c)	23 (a)	24 (a)	25 (a)	26 (a)	27 (b)	28 (b)	29 (b)	30 (c)
31 (a)	32 (b)	33 (b)	34 (d)	35 (c)	36 (d)	37 (c)	38 (c)	39 (d)	40 (a)

i-TEPS Review

국내 최초 통합 영어능력 평가
integrated-TEPS

⇨ 의사소통에 필요한 듣기, 말하기, 읽기, 쓰기 능력을 통합하여 평가한다.

듣기, 말하기, 읽기, 쓰기 능력은 서로 밀접한 관계를 가진 요소로 듣기, 읽기 능력 혹은 말하기, 쓰기 능력만을 단순히 측정해서는 정확한 영어능력을 평가하기 어렵다. *i*-TEPS는 유기적인 연관성을 지닌 이 네 가지 의사소통 능력을 통합적으로 측정하여 수험자의 영어능력을 정확하게 평가한다.

⇨ 변별력과 신뢰도가 있는 시험이다.

i-TEPS는 국내 최고 권위의 영어능력 평가로 듣기, 읽기 분야에서 탁월한 변별력을 인정받은 TEPS와 국내 최초 CBT 방식의 영어 말하기 · 쓰기 시험인 TEPS-Speaking & Writing의 성공 노하우를 바탕으로 개발되었다. 실전 영어능력을 보다 정밀하게 측정할 수 있도록 세분화된 채점 요소를 적용하고 있으며, 출제자와 채점자를 어학 분야의 최고 전문가들로 선정하여 높은 신뢰도와 탁월한 변별력을 지니고 있다.

⇨ 실전 영어능력을 측정한다.

간단한 대화를 할 수 있는 능력부터 도표를 보고 발표하는 분석력과 구성력까지, 접하는 상황에 따라 필요한 영어능력도 다양하다. *i*-TEPS는 유학이나 비즈니스 등 특정한 분야에서의 영어 활용 능력을 집중적으로 평가하는 타 시험과는 달리, 비즈니스 상황을 포함한 다양한 영어 사용 환경을 재현하여 실질적으로 활용 가능한 영어능력을 평가한다.

⇨ 경제성과 효율성을 갖춘 시험이다.

i-TEPS는 타 통합 영어능력 평가시험에 비해 응시료가 저렴하다. 한 번의 시험으로 듣기, 말하기, 읽기, 쓰기 능력을 종합적으로 평가하여 각각의 영역을 별도로 평가해야 하는 타 시험과 비교해도 응시료 부담이 적다. *i*-TEPS는 최소의 시간과 비용으로 수험자의 영어능력을 정확히 측정하는 높은 효율성을 갖춘 시험이다.

i-TEPS 영역별 유형 및 설명

i-TEPS는 기존의 TEPS와 TEPS-Speaking & Writing 시험을 토대로 듣기, 말하기, 읽기, 쓰기 능력을 종합적으로 측정하는 통합형 시험으로 개발되었다. Listening, Grammar & Vocabulary, Reading, Speaking, Writing의 5개 영역에 걸쳐 약 3시간 동안 진행되며, 총 143문항, 400점 만점으로 구성되어 있다.

영역		문제유형	문항수	시간		총점
Listening	Part 1	짧은 대화를 듣고 이어질 대화로 가장 적절한 답 고르기	15	35분		80점
	Part 2	긴 대화를 듣고 질문에 가장 적절한 답 고르기	15			
	Part 3	담화를 듣고 질문에 가장 적절한 답 고르기	10			
Grammar & Vocabulary	Part 1	대화문의 빈칸에 가장 적절한 답 고르기	15	20분		20점
	Part 2	단문의 빈칸에 가장 적절한 답 고르기	15			
	Part 3	대화문의 빈칸에 가장 적절한 어휘 고르기	15			20점
	Part 4	단문의 빈칸에 가장 적절한 어휘 고르기	15			
Reading	Part 1	지문을 읽고 빈칸에 가장 적절한 답 고르기	10	40분		80점
	Part 2	지문을 읽고 질문에 가장 적절한 답 고르기 (1지문 1문항)	19			
	Part 3	지문을 읽고 질문에 가장 적절한 답 고르기 (1지문 2문항)	6			
Speaking	Part 1	간단한 질문에 대답하기	1(3)		답변 10초	100점
	Part 2	소리내어 읽기	1	준비 30초	답변 45초	
	Part 3	일상 대화 상황에서 질문에 답하기	1(5)	준비 15초	답변 10초	
	Part 4	그림 보고 연결하여 이야기하기	1	준비 60초	답변 60초	
	Part 5	도표 보고 발표하기	1	준비 120초	답변 90초	
Writing	Part 1	받아쓰기	1	10분		100점
	Part 2	이메일 쓰기	1	15분		
	Part 3	의견 쓰기	1	30분		
계						400점

TEPS 등급표

등급	점수	영역	능력검정기준(Description)
1⁺급 Level 1⁺	901~990	전반	**외국인으로서 최상급 수준의 의사소통 능력** 교양 있는 원어민에 버금가는 정도로 의사소통이 가능하고 전문분야 업무에 대처할 수 있음. (Native Level of Communicative Competence)
1급 Level 1	801~900	전반	**외국인으로서 거의 최상급 수준의 의사소통 능력** 단기간 집중 교육을 받으면 대부분의 의사소통이 가능하고 전문분야 업무에 별 무리 없이 대처할 수 있음. (Near-Native Level of Communicative Competence)
2⁺급 Level 2⁺	701~800	전반	**외국인으로서 상급 수준의 의사소통 능력** 단기간 집중 교육을 받으면 일반분야 업무를 큰 어려움 없이 수행할 수 있음. (Advanced Level of Communicative Competence)
2급 Level 2	601~700	전반	**외국인으로서 중상급 수준의 의사소통 능력** 중장기간 집중 교육을 받으면 일반분야 업무를 큰 어려움 없이 수행할 수 있음. (High Intermediate Level of Communicative Competence)
3⁺급 Level 3⁺	501~600	전반	**외국인으로서 중급 수준의 의사소통 능력** 중장기간 집중 교육을 받으면 한정된 분야의 업무를 큰 어려움 없이 수행할 수 있음. (Mid Intermediate Level of Communicative Competence)
3급 Level 3	401~500	전반	**외국인으로서 중하급 수준의 의사소통 능력** 중장기간 집중 교육을 받으면 한정된 분야의 업무를 다소 미흡하지만 큰 지장 없이 수행할 수 있음. (Low Intermediate Level of Communicative Competence)
4⁺급 Level 4	201~400	전반	**외국인으로서 하급 수준의 의사소통 능력** 장기간의 집중 교육을 받으면 한정된 분야의 업무를 대체로 어렵게 수행할 수 있음. (Novice Level of Communicative Competence)
5⁺급 Level 5	10~200	전반	**외국인으로서 최하급 수준의 의사소통 능력** 단편적인 지식만을 갖추고 있어 의사소통이 거의 불가능함. (Near-Zero Level of Communicative Competence)

Memo

TEPS

Test of English Proficiency
developed by
Seoul National University

TEPS

Test of English Proficiency
developed by
Seoul National University

수험번호
Registration No.

성명 한글
Name 한자

문제지번호
Test Booklet No.

감독관확인란

청 해 Listening Comprehension	문 법 Grammar	어 휘 Vocabulary	독 해 Reading Comprehension

주민등록번호
National ID No.

고사실란
Room No.

수험번호
Registration No.

비밀번호
Password

좌석번호
Seat No.

서 약 — 본인은 필기구 및 기재오류와 답안지 훼손으로 인한 책임을 지고, 부정행위 처리규정을 준수할 것을 서약합니다.

답안작성시 유의사항

1. 답안 작성은 반드시 **컴퓨터용 싸인펜**을 사용해야 합니다.
2. 답안을 정정할 경우 수정테이프(수정액 불가)를 사용해야 합니다.
3. 본 답안지는 컴퓨터로 처리되므로 훼손해서는 안되며, 답안지 하단의 타이밍마크(|||)를 찢거나, 낙서 등으로 인한 훼손시 불이익이 발생할 수 있습니다.

4. 답안은 문항당 정답을 1개만 골라 ● 와 같이 정확히 기재해야 하며, 필기구 오류나 본인의 부주의로 잘못 표기한 경우에는 당 관리위원회의 OMR판독기의 판독결과에 따르며, 그 결과는 본인이 책임집니다.
   Good ●   Bad ◖ ◉ ◑ ✕ ✓
5. 감독관의 확인이 없는 답안지는 무효처리됩니다.

TEPS

Test of English Proficiency
developed by
Seoul National University

성 영문

명 서명

응시일자 : 20   년   월   일

성   명 (성·이름순으로 기재)

EX HONG GIL DONG

| | A | B | C | D | E | F | G | H | I | J | K | L | M | N | O | P | Q | R | S | T | U | V | W | X | Y | Z |

〈부정행위 및 규정위반 처리규정〉

1. 모든 부정행위 및 규정위반 적발 및 이에 대한 조치는 TEPS관리위원회의 처리규정에 따라 이루어집니다.

2. 부정행위 및 규정위반 행위는 현장 적발 뿐만 아니라 사후에도 적발될 수 있으며 모두 동일한 조치가 취해집니다.

3. 부정행위 적발 시 당해 성적은 무효화되며 사안에 따라 최대 5년까지 TEPS관리위원회에서 주관하는 모든 시험의 응시자격이 제한됩니다.

4. 문제지 이외에 메모를 하는 행위와 시험 문제의 일부 또는 전부를 유출하거나 공개하는 경우 부정행위로 처리됩니다.

5. 각 파트별 시간을 준수하지 않거나, 시험 종료 후 답안 작성을 계속할 경우 규정위반으로 처리됩니다.

단체구분

학생	일반
○	○

질 문 란

1. 귀하의 TEPS 응시목적은?
   - ⓐ 입사지원 ⓑ 인사정책
   - ⓒ 개인실력측정 ⓓ 입시
   - ⓔ 국가고시 지원 ⓕ 기타

2. 귀하의 영어권 체류 경험은?
   - ⓐ 없다 ⓑ 6개월 미만
   - ⓒ 6개월 이상 1년 미만 ⓓ 1년 이상 3년 미만
   - ⓔ 3년 이상 5년 미만 ⓕ 5년 이상

3. 귀하께서 응시하고 계신 고사장에 대한 만족도는?
   - ⓐ 0점 ⓑ 1점
   - ⓒ 2점 ⓓ 3점
   - ⓔ 4점 ⓕ 5점

4. 최근 2년내 TEPS 응시횟수는?
   - ⓐ 없다 ⓑ 1회
   - ⓒ 2회 ⓓ 3회
   - ⓔ 4회 ⓕ 5회 이상

학 력

학력	재학	졸업
초등학교	○	○
중 학 교	○	○
고등학교	○	○
전문대학	○	○
대 학 교	○	○
대 학 원	○	○

전 공

- 인 문 학 ○
- 사회과학·법학 ○
- 경제학·경영학 ○
- 자 연 과 학 ○
- 의학·약학·간호학 ○
- 공 학 ○
- 교 육 학 ○
- 음악·미술·체육 ○
- 기 타 ○

직 업

- 공 무 원 ○
- 고시준비 ○
- 교 사 ○
- 군 인 ○
- 의 료 인 ○
- 자 영 업 ○
- 학 생 ○
- 회 사 원 ○
- 무 직 ○
- 기 타 ○

직 종

- 고 위 임 직 원 ○
- 전문직(과학.공학) ○
- 전 문 직 (교육) ○
- 전문직(법률.회계.금융) ○
- 기 술 직 ○
- 영 업 ○
- 홍 보 ○
- 총 무 ○
- 인 사 ○
- 경 리 ○
- 기 획 ○
- 구 매 ○

- 무 역 ○
- 외 환 ○
- 자 금 ○
- 공 무 ○
- 업 무 ○
- 품 질 관 리 ○
- 전 산 ○
- 행 정 직 ○
- 생 산 관 리 ○
- 서 비 스 ○
- 기 타 ○

직 책

- 임 원 ○
- 부 장 ○
- 차 장 ○
- 과 장 ○
- 대 리 ○
- 계 장 ○
- 사 원 ○
- 인 턴 ○
- 기 타 ○

앞면(Side1)

TEPS

Test of English Proficiency
developed by
Seoul National University

수험번호
Registration No.

성명
Name
한글
한자

문제지번호
Test Booklet No.

감독관확인란

청 해 Listening Comprehension	문 법 Grammar	어 휘 Vocabulary	독 해 Reading Comprehension

주 민 등 록 번 호
National ID No.

고사실란
Room No.

수 험 번 호
Registration No.

비밀번호
Password

좌석번호
Seat No.

서 약

본인은 필기구 및 기재오류와 답안지 훼손으로 인한 책임을 지고, 부정행위 처리규정을 준수할 것을 서약합니다.

답안작성시
유 의 사 항

1. 답안 작성은 반드시 **컴퓨터용 싸인펜**을 사용해야 합니다.

2. 답안을 정정할 경우 수정테이프(수정액 불가)를 사용해야 합니다.

3. 본 답안지는 컴퓨터로 처리되므로 훼손해서는 안되며, 답안지 하단의
   타이밍마크(|||)를 찢거나, 낙서 등으로 인한 훼손시 불이익이 발생할 수 있습니다.

4. 답안은 문항당 정답을 1개만 골라 ● 와 같이 정확히 기재해야 하며, 필기구 오류나 본인의 부주의로
   잘못 표기한 경우에는 당 관리위원회의 OMR판독기의 판독결과에 따르며, 그 결과는 본인이 책임집니다.
   Good ●   Bad ◖ ◔ ◑ ✗ ◉

5. 감독관의 확인이 없는 답안지는 무효처리됩니다.

뒷면(Side2)

TEPS

Test of English Proficiency
developed by
Seoul National University

성명	
영문	
서명	

응시일자 : 20 년 월 일

<부정행위 및 규정위반 처리규정>

1. 모든 부정행위 및 규정위반 적발 및 이에 대한 조치는 TEPS관리위원회의 처리규정에 따라 이루어집니다.
2. 부정행위 및 규정위반 행위는 현장 적발 뿐만 아니라 사후에도 적발될 수 있으며 모두 동일한 조치가 취해집니다.
3. 부정행위 적발 시 당해 성적은 무효화되며 사안에 따라 최대 5년까지 TEPS관리위원회에서 주관하는 모든 시험의 응시자격이 제한됩니다.
4. 문제지 이외에 메모를 하는 행위와 시험 문제의 일부 또는 전부를 유출하거나 공개하는 경우 부정행위로 처리됩니다.
5. 각 파트별 시간을 준수하지 않거나, 시험 종료 후 답안 작성을 계속할 경우 규정위반으로 처리됩니다.

성 명 (성 · 이름순으로 기재)

EX	H	O	N	G		G	I	L		D	O	N	G							
A	A	A	A	A	A	A	A	A	A	A	A	A	A	A	A	A	A	A	A	A
B	B	B	B	B	B	B	B	B	B	B	B	B	B	B	B	B	B	B	B	B
C	C	C	C	C	C	C	C	C	C	C	C	C	C	C	C	C	C	C	C	C
D	D	D	D	D	D	D	D	D	D	D	D	D	D	D	D	D	D	D	D	D
E	E	E	E	E	E	E	E	E	E	E	E	E	E	E	E	E	E	E	E	E
F	F	F	F	F	F	F	F	F	F	F	F	F	F	F	F	F	F	F	F	F
G	G	G	G	G	G	G	G	G	G	G	G	G	G	G	G	G	G	G	G	G
H	H	H	H	H	H	H	H	H	H	H	H	H	H	H	H	H	H	H	H	H
I	I	I	I	I	I	I	I	I	I	I	I	I	I	I	I	I	I	I	I	I
J	J	J	J	J	J	J	J	J	J	J	J	J	J	J	J	J	J	J	J	J
K	K	K	K	K	K	K	K	K	K	K	K	K	K	K	K	K	K	K	K	K
L	L	L	L	L	L	L	L	L	L	L	L	L	L	L	L	L	L	L	L	L
M	M	M	M	M	M	M	M	M	M	M	M	M	M	M	M	M	M	M	M	M
N	N	N	N	N	N	N	N	N	N	N	N	N	N	N	N	N	N	N	N	N
O	O	O	O	O	O	O	O	O	O	O	O	O	O	O	O	O	O	O	O	O
P	P	P	P	P	P	P	P	P	P	P	P	P	P	P	P	P	P	P	P	P
Q	Q	Q	Q	Q	Q	Q	Q	Q	Q	Q	Q	Q	Q	Q	Q	Q	Q	Q	Q	Q
R	R	R	R	R	R	R	R	R	R	R	R	R	R	R	R	R	R	R	R	R
S	S	S	S	S	S	S	S	S	S	S	S	S	S	S	S	S	S	S	S	S
T	T	T	T	T	T	T	T	T	T	T	T	T	T	T	T	T	T	T	T	T
U	U	U	U	U	U	U	U	U	U	U	U	U	U	U	U	U	U	U	U	U
V	V	V	V	V	V	V	V	V	V	V	V	V	V	V	V	V	V	V	V	V
W	W	W	W	W	W	W	W	W	W	W	W	W	W	W	W	W	W	W	W	W
X	X	X	X	X	X	X	X	X	X	X	X	X	X	X	X	X	X	X	X	X
Y	Y	Y	Y	Y	Y	Y	Y	Y	Y	Y	Y	Y	Y	Y	Y	Y	Y	Y	Y	Y
Z	Z	Z	Z	Z	Z	Z	Z	Z	Z	Z	Z	Z	Z	Z	Z	Z	Z	Z	Z	Z

단체구분

학생	일반
▢	▢

질 문 란

1. 귀하의 TEPS 응시목적은?
   - a 입사지원
   - b 인사정책
   - c 개인실력측정
   - d 입시
   - e 국가고시 지원
   - f 기타

2. 귀하의 영어권 체류 경험은?
   - a 없다
   - b 6개월 미만
   - c 6개월 이상 1년 미만
   - d 1년 이상 3년 미만
   - e 3년 이상 5년 미만
   - f 5년 이상

3. 귀하께서 응시하고 계신 고사장에 대한 만족도는?
   - a 0점
   - b 1점
   - c 2점
   - d 3점
   - e 4점
   - f 5점

4. 최근 2년내 TEPS 응시횟수는?
   - a 없다
   - b 1회
   - c 2회
   - d 3회
   - e 4회
   - f 5회 이상

학력	재학	졸업	전공	직업
초등학교	▢	▢	인문학 ▢	공무원 ▢
중학교	▢	▢	사회과학 · 법학 ▢	고시준비 ▢
고등학교	▢	▢	경제학 · 경영학 ▢	교사 ▢
전문대학	▢	▢	자연과학 ▢	군인 ▢
대학교	▢	▢	의학 · 약학 · 간호학 ▢	의료인 ▢
대학원	▢	▢	공학 ▢	자영업 ▢
			교육학 ▢	학생 ▢
			음악 · 미술 · 체육 ▢	회사원 ▢
			기타 ▢	무직 ▢
				기타 ▢

직종		직책
고위임직원 ▢	무역 ▢	임원 ▢
전문직(과학.공학) ▢	외환 ▢	부장 ▢
전문직(교육) ▢	자금 ▢	차장 ▢
전문직(법률.회계.금융) ▢	공무 ▢	과장 ▢
기술직 ▢	업무 ▢	대리 ▢
영업 ▢	품질관리 ▢	계장 ▢
홍보 ▢	전산 ▢	사원 ▢
총무 ▢	행정직 ▢	인턴 ▢
인사 ▢	생산관리 ▢	기타 ▢
경리 ▢	서비스 ▢	
기획 ▢	기타 ▢	
구매 ▢		

앞면(Side1)

TEPS

Test of English Proficiency
developed by
Seoul National University

| 수험번호 Registration No. | | 문 제 지 번 호 Test Booklet No. | 감독관확인란 |
| 성 명 Name | 한글 / 한자 | | |

| 청　해 Listening Comprehension | 문　법 Grammar | 어　휘 Vocabulary | 독　해 Reading Comprehension | 주 민 등 록 번 호 National ID No. | 고사실란 Room No. |

| 수 험 번 호 Registration No. | 비밀번호 Password | 좌석번호 Seat No. |

서　약　본인은 필기구 및 기재오류와 답안지 훼손으로 인한 책임을 지고, 부정행위 처리규정을 준수할 것을 서약합니다.

답안작성시 유의사항

1. 답안 작성은 반드시 **컴퓨터용 싸인펜**을 사용해야 합니다.

2. 답안을 정정할 경우 수정테이프(수정액 불가)를 사용해야 합니다.

3. 본 답안지는 컴퓨터로 처리되므로 훼손해서는 안되며, 답안지 하단의 타이밍마크(ㅣㅣㅣ)를 찢거나, 낙서 등으로 인한 훼손시 불이익이 발생할 수 있습니다.

4. 답안은 문항당 정답을 1개만 골라 ● 와 같이 정확히 기재해야 하며, 필기구 오류나 본인의 부주의로 잘못 표기한 경우에는 당 관리위원회의 OMR판독기의 판독결과에 따르며, 그 결과는 본인이 책임집니다.
   Good ●　Bad ◖ ◐ ◑ ✕ ✓

5. 감독관의 확인이 없는 답안지는 무효처리됩니다.

TEPS

Test of English Proficiency
developed by
Seoul National University

성	영문	
명	서명	

응시일자 : 20   년   월   일

〈부정행위 및 규정위반 처리규정〉

1. 모든 부정행위 및 규정위반 적발 및 이에 대한 조치는 TEPS관리위원회의 처리규정에 따라 이루어집니다.

2. 부정행위 및 규정위반 행위는 현장 적발 뿐만 아니라 사후에도 적발될 수 있으며 모두 동일한 조치가 취해집니다.

3. 부정행위 적발 시 당해 성적은 무효화되며 사안에 따라 최대 5년까지 TEPS관리위원회에서 주관하는 모든 시험의 응시자격이 제한됩니다.

4. 문제지 이외에 메모를 하는 행위와 시험 문제의 일부 또는 전부를 유출하거나 공개하는 경우 부정행위로 처리됩니다.

5. 각 파트별 시간을 준수하지 않거나, 시험 종료 후 답안 작성을 계속할 경우 규정위반으로 처리됩니다.

성   명 (성·이름순으로 기재)

EX HONG GIL DONG

(A B C D E F G H I J K L M N O P Q R S T U V W X Y Z 마킹란)

단 체 구 분

학생	일반
◯	◯

질 문 란

1. 귀하의 TEPS 응시목적은?
   ⓐ 입사지원   ⓑ 인사정책
   ⓒ 개인실력측정   ⓓ 입시
   ⓔ 국가고시 지원   ⓕ 기타

2. 귀하의 영어권 체류 경험은?
   ⓐ 없다   ⓑ 6개월 미만
   ⓒ 6개월 이상 1년 미만   ⓓ 1년 이상 3년 미만
   ⓔ 3년 이상 5년 미만   ⓕ 5년 이상

3. 귀하께서 응시하고 계신 고사장에 대한 만족도는?
   ⓐ 0점   ⓑ 1점
   ⓒ 2점   ⓓ 3점
   ⓔ 4점   ⓕ 5점

4. 최근 2년내 TEPS 응시횟수는?
   ⓐ 없다   ⓑ 1회
   ⓒ 2회   ⓓ 3회
   ⓔ 4회   ⓕ 5회 이상

학 력 / 전 공 / 직 업

학력	재학	졸업	전공		직업	
초등학교	◯	◯	인 문 학	◯	공 무 원	◯
중 학 교	◯	◯	사회과학·법학	◯	고시준비	◯
고등학교	◯	◯	경제학·경영학	◯	교 사	◯
전문대학	◯	◯	자 연 과 학	◯	군 인	◯
대 학 교	◯	◯	의학·약학·간호학	◯	의 료 인	◯
대 학 원	◯	◯	공 학	◯	자 영 업	◯
			교 육 학	◯	학 생	◯
			음악·미술·체육	◯	회 사 원	◯
			기 타	◯	무 직	◯
					기 타	◯

직 종 / 직 책

직종		직책	
고 위 임 직 원	◯	무 역	◯	임 원	◯
전문직(과학.공학)	◯	외 환	◯	부 장	◯
전 문 직 (교육)	◯	자 금	◯	차 장	◯
전문직(법률.회계.금융)	◯	공 무	◯	과 장	◯
기 술 직	◯	업 무	◯	대 리	◯
영 업	◯	품 질 관 리	◯	계 장	◯
홍 보	◯	전 산	◯	사 원	◯
총 무	◯	행 정 직	◯	인 턴	◯
인 사	◯	생 산 관 리	◯	기 타	◯
경 리	◯	서 비 스	◯		
기 획	◯	기 타	◯		
구 매	◯				

앞면(Side1)

TEPS

Test of English Proficiency
developed by
Seoul National University

| 수험번호 Registration No. | | 문제지번호 Test Booklet No. | 감독관확인란 |
| 성명 Name | 한글 / 한자 | | |

| 청 해 Listening Comprehension | 문 법 Grammar | 어 휘 Vocabulary | 독 해 Reading Comprehension |

주 민 등 록 번 호 National ID No.

고사실란 Room No.

수 험 번 호 Registration No.

비밀번호 Password

좌석번호 Seat No.

서 약   본인은 필기구 및 기재오류와 답안지 훼손으로 인한 책임을 지고, 부정행위 처리규정을 준수할 것을 서약합니다.

답안작성시 유의사항

1. 답안 작성은 반드시 **컴퓨터용 싸인펜**을 사용해야 합니다.

2. 답안을 정정할 경우 수정테이프(수정액 불가)를 사용해야 합니다.

3. 본 답안지는 컴퓨터로 처리되므로 훼손해서는 안되며, 답안지 하단의 타이밍마크(‖‖)를 찢거나, 낙서 등으로 인한 훼손시 불이익이 발생할 수 있습니다.

4. 답안은 문항당 정답을 1개만 골라 ● 와 같이 정확히 기재해야 하며, 필기구 오류나 본인의 부주의로 잘못 표기한 경우에는 당 관리위원회의 OMR판독기의 판독결과에 따르며, 그 결과는 본인이 책임집니다.

    Good ●   Bad ◖ ◒ ◗ ✕ ⦸

5. 감독관의 확인이 없는 답안지는 무효처리됩니다.

TEPS

Test of English Proficiency
developed by
Seoul National University

성	영문	
명	서명	

응시일자 : 20　　년　　월　　일

<부정행위 및 규정위반 처리규정>

1. 모든 부정행위 및 규정위반 적발 및 이에 대한 조치는 TEPS관리위원회의 처리규정에 따라 이루어집니다.

2. 부정행위 및 규정위반 행위는 현장 적발 뿐만 아니라 사후에도 적발될 수 있으며 모두 동일한 조치가 취해집니다.

3. 부정행위 적발 시 당해 성적은 무효화되며 사안에 따라 최대 5년까지 TEPS관리위원회에서 주관하는 모든 시험의 응시자격이 제한됩니다.

4. 문제지 이외에 메모를 하는 행위와 시험 문제의 일부 또는 전부를 유출하거나 공개하는 경우 부정행위로 처리됩니다.

5. 각 파트별 시간을 준수하지 않거나, 시험 종료 후 답안 작성을 계속할 경우 규정위반으로 처리됩니다.

성　명 (성·이름순으로 기재)

EX HONG GIL DONG

A B C D E F G H I J K L M N O P Q R S T U V W X Y Z

단 체 구 분

학생	일반
◯	◯

질 문 란

1. 귀하의 TEPS 응시목적은?
   - a 입사지원　　b 인사정책
   - c 개인실력측정　　d 입시
   - e 국가고시 지원　　f 기타

2. 귀하의 영어권 체류 경험은?
   - a 없다　　b 6개월 미만
   - c 6개월 이상 1년 미만　　d 1년 이상 3년 미만
   - e 3년 이상 5년 미만　　f 5년 이상

3. 귀하께서 응시하고 계신 고사장에 대한 만족도는?
   - a 0점　　b 1점
   - c 2점　　d 3점
   - e 4점　　f 5점

4. 최근 2년내 TEPS 응시횟수는?
   - a 없다　　b 1회
   - c 2회　　d 3회
   - e 4회　　f 5회 이상

학 력 / 전 공 / 직 업

학력	재학	졸업	전공		직업	
초등학교	◯		인 문 학	◯	공 무 원	◯
중 학 교	◯		사회과학·법학	◯	고시준비	◯
고등학교	◯		경제학·경영학	◯	교 사	◯
전문대학	◯		자 연 과 학	◯	군 인	◯
대 학 교	◯		의학·약학·간호학	◯	의 료 인	◯
대 학 원	◯		공 학	◯	자 영 업	◯
			교 육 학	◯	학 생	◯
			음악·미술·체육	◯	회 사 원	◯
			기 타	◯	무 직	◯
					기 타	◯

직 종 / 직 책

직종		직책	
고 위 임 직 원	◯	임 원	◯
전문직(과학.공학)	◯	부 장	◯
전 문 직 (교육)	◯	차 장	◯
전문직(법률.회계.금융)	◯	과 장	◯
기 술 직	◯	대 리	◯
영 업	◯	계 장	◯
홍 보	◯	사 원	◯
총 무	◯	인 턴	◯
인 사	◯	기 타	◯
경 리	◯		
기 획	◯		
구 매	◯		

직종(우)	
무 역	◯
외 환	◯
자 금	◯
공 무	◯
업 무	◯
품 질 관 리	◯
전 산	◯
행 정 직	◯
생 산 관 리	◯
서 비 스	◯
기 타	◯

앞면(Side 1)

TEPS

Test of English Proficiency
developed by
Seoul National University

| 수험번호 Registration No. | | 문 제 지 번 호 Test Booklet No. | 감독관확인란 |
| 성 명 Name | 한글 / 한자 | | |

청 해 — Listening Comprehension

문 법 — Grammar

어 휘 — Vocabulary

독 해 — Reading Comprehension

주 민 등 록 번 호 — National ID No.

고사실란 — Room No.

수 험 번 호 — Registration No.

비밀번호 — Password

좌석번호 — Seat No.

서 약   본인은 필기구 및 기재오류와 답안지 훼손으로 인한 책임을 지고, 부정행위 처리규정을 준수할 것을 서약합니다.

답안작성시 유의사항

1. 답안 작성은 반드시 **컴퓨터용 싸인펜**을 사용해야 합니다.

2. 답안을 정정할 경우 수정테이프(수정액 불가)를 사용해야 합니다.

3. 본 답안지는 컴퓨터로 처리되므로 훼손해서는 안되며, 답안지 하단의 타이밍마크(|||)를 찢거나, 낙서 등으로 인한 훼손시 불이익이 발생할 수 있습니다.

4. 답안은 문항당 정답을 1개만 골라 ● 와 같이 정확히 기재해야 하며, 필기구 오류나 본인의 부주의로 잘못 표기한 경우에는 당 관리위원회의 OMR판독기의 판독결과에 따르며, 그 결과는 본인이 책임집니다.

   Good ● Bad ◖ ◔ ◐ ⊗ ◓

5. 감독관의 확인이 없는 답안지는 무효처리됩니다.

TEPS

Test of English Proficiency
developed by
Seoul National University

성 영문

명 서명

응시일자 : 20 년 월 일

<부정행위 및 규정위반 처리규정>

1. 모든 부정행위 및 규정위반 적발 및 이에 대한 조치는 TEPS관리위원회의 처리규정에 따라 이루어집니다.

2. 부정행위 및 규정위반 행위는 현장 적발 뿐만 아니라 사후에도 적발될 수 있으며 모두 동일한 조치가 취해집니다.

3. 부정행위 적발 시 당해 성적은 무효화되며 사안에 따라 최대 5년까지 TEPS관리위원회에서 주관하는 모든 시험의 응시자격이 제한됩니다.

4. 문제지 이외에 메모를 하는 행위와 시험 문제의 일부 또는 전부를 유출하거나 공개하는 경우 부정행위로 처리됩니다.

5. 각 파트별 시간을 준수하지 않거나, 시험 종료 후 답안 작성을 계속할 경우 규정위반으로 처리됩니다.

성 명 (성 · 이름순으로 기재)

EX HONG GIL DONG

(마킹란: A B C D E F G H I J K L M N O P Q R S T U V W X Y Z)

단체구분

학생	일반
○	○

질문란

1. 귀하의 TEPS 응시목적은?
   - ⓐ 입사지원
   - ⓑ 인사정책
   - ⓒ 개인실력측정
   - ⓓ 입시
   - ⓔ 국가고시 지원
   - ⓕ 기타

2. 귀하의 영어권 체류 경험은?
   - ⓐ 없다
   - ⓑ 6개월 미만
   - ⓒ 6개월 이상 1년 미만
   - ⓓ 1년 이상 3년 미만
   - ⓔ 3년 이상 5년 미만
   - ⓕ 5년 이상

3. 귀하께서 응시하고 계신 고사장에 대한 만족도는?
   - ⓐ 0점
   - ⓑ 1점
   - ⓒ 2점
   - ⓓ 3점
   - ⓔ 4점
   - ⓕ 5점

4. 최근 2년내 TEPS 응시횟수는?
   - ⓐ 없다
   - ⓑ 1회
   - ⓒ 2회
   - ⓓ 3회
   - ⓔ 4회
   - ⓕ 5회 이상

학력 / 전공 / 직업

학력	재학	졸업	전공		직업	
초등학교			인 문 학	○	공 무 원	○
중 학 교			사회과학 · 법학	○	고시준비	○
고등학교	○		경제학 · 경영학	○	교 사	○
전문대학			자 연 과 학	○	군 인	○
대 학 교	○		의학 · 약학 · 간호학	○	의 료 인	○
대 학 원			공 학	○	자 영 업	○
			교 육 학	○	학 생	○
			음악 · 미술 · 체육	○	회 사 원	○
			기 타	○	무 직	○
					기 타	○

직종 / 직책

직종				직책	
고 위 임 직 원	○	무 역	○	임 원	○
전문직 (과학.공학)	○	외 환	○	부 장	○
전 문 직 (교육)	○	자 금	○	차 장	○
전문직(법률.회계.금융)	○	공 무	○	과 장	○
기 술 직	○	업 무	○	대 리	○
영 업	○	품 질 관 리	○	계 장	○
홍 보	○	전 산	○	사 원	○
총 무	○	행 정 직	○	인 턴	○
인 사	○	생 산 관 리	○	기 타	○
경 리	○	서 비 스	○		
기 획	○	기 타	○		
구 매	○				

앞면(Side1)

TEPS

Test of English Proficiency
developed by
Seoul National University

수험번호
Registration No.

성명 Name
한글
한자

문제지번호
Test Booklet No.

감독관확인란

청 해
Listening Comprehension

문 법
Grammar

어 휘
Vocabulary

독 해
Reading Comprehension

주 민 등 록 번 호
National ID No.

고사실란
Room No.

수 험 번 호
Registration No.

비밀번호
Password

좌석번호
Seat No.

서 약

본인은 필기구 및 기재오류와 답안지 훼손으로 인한 책임을 지고, 부정행위 처리규정을 준수할 것을 서약합니다.

답안작성시
유 의 사 항

1. 답안 작성은 반드시 **컴퓨터용 싸인펜**을 사용해야 합니다.
2. 답안을 정정할 경우 수정테이프(수정액 불가)를 사용해야 합니다.
3. 본 답안지는 컴퓨터로 처리되므로 훼손해서는 안되며, 답안지 하단의 타이밍마크(|||)를 찢거나, 낙서 등으로 인한 훼손시 불이익이 발생할 수 있습니다.

4. 답안은 문항당 정답을 1개만 골라 ● 와 같이 정확히 기재해야 하며, 필기구 오류나 본인의 부주의로 잘못 표기한 경우에는 당 관리위원회의 OMR판독기의 판독결과에 따르며, 그 결과는 본인이 책임집니다.

Good ● Bad ◐ ◑ ◎ ⊗ ⊘

5. 감독관의 확인이 없는 답안지는 무효처리됩니다.

TEPS
Test of English Proficiency
developed by
Seoul National University

성	영문	
명	서명	

응시일자 : 20   년   월   일

<부정행위 및 규정위반 처리규정>

1. 모든 부정행위 및 규정위반 적발 및 이에 대한 조치는 TEPS관리위원회의 처리규정에 따라 이루어집니다.

2. 부정행위 및 규정위반 행위는 현장 적발 뿐만 아니라 사후에도 적발될 수 있으며 모두 동일한 조치가 취해집니다.

3. 부정행위 적발 시 당해 성적은 무효화되며 사안에 따라 최대 5년까지 TEPS관리위원회에서 주관하는 모든 시험의 응시자격이 제한됩니다.

4. 문제지 이외에 메모를 하는 행위와 시험 문제의 일부 또는 전부를 유출하거나 공개하는 경우 부정행위로 처리됩니다.

5. 각 파트별 시간을 준수하지 않거나, 시험 종료 후 답안 작성을 계속할 경우 규정위반으로 처리됩니다.

성   명 (성·이름순으로 기재)

EX H O N G   G I L   D O N G

A B C D E F G H I J K L M N O P Q R S T U V W X Y Z

단체구분

학생	일반
○	○

질문란

1. 귀하의 TEPS 응시목적은?
   - ⓐ 입사지원
   - ⓑ 인사정책
   - ⓒ 개인실력측정
   - ⓓ 입시
   - ⓔ 국가고시 지원
   - ⓕ 기타

2. 귀하의 영어권 체류 경험은?
   - ⓐ 없다
   - ⓑ 6개월 미만
   - ⓒ 6개월 이상 1년 미만
   - ⓓ 1년 이상 3년 미만
   - ⓔ 3년 이상 5년 미만
   - ⓕ 5년 이상

3. 귀하께서 응시하고 계신 고사장에 대한 만족도는?
   - ⓐ 0점
   - ⓑ 1점
   - ⓒ 2점
   - ⓓ 3점
   - ⓔ 4점
   - ⓕ 5점

4. 최근 2년내 TEPS 응시횟수는?
   - ⓐ 없다
   - ⓑ 1회
   - ⓒ 2회
   - ⓓ 3회
   - ⓔ 4회
   - ⓕ 5회 이상

학력 / 전공 / 직업

학력	재학	졸업	전공		직업	
초등학교			인 문 학	○	공 무 원	○
중 학 교			사회과학·법학	○	고시준비	○
고 등 학 교			경제학·경영학	○	교 사	○
전 문 대 학	○	○	자 연 과 학	○	군 인	○
대 학 교	○	○	의학·약학·간호학	○	의 료 인	○
대 학 원	○	○	공 학	○	자 영 업	○
			교 육 학	○	학 생	○
			음악·미술·체육	○	회 사 원	○
			기 타	○	무 직	○
					기 타	○

직종 / 직책

직 종		직 책	
고 위 임 직 원	○	무 역	임 원 ○
전문직(과학.공학)	○	외 환	부 장 ○
전 문 직 (교육)	○	자 금	차 장 ○
전문직(법률.회계.금융)	○	공 무	과 장 ○
기 술 직	○	업 무	대 리 ○
영 업		품 질 관 리	계 장 ○
홍 보		전 산	사 원 ○
총 무		행 정 직	인 턴 ○
인 사		생 산 관 리	기 타 ○
경 리		서 비 스	
기 획		기 타	
구 매			

TEPS

Test of English Proficiency
developed by
Seoul National University

수험번호 Registration No.		문 제 지 번 호 Test Booklet No.	감독관확인란
성 명 Name	한글		
	한자		

청 해 Listening Comprehension	문 법 Grammar	어 휘 Vocabulary	독 해 Reading Comprehension	주 민 등 록 번 호 National ID No.	고사실란 Room No.

서 약 — 본인은 필기구 및 기재오류와 답안지 훼손으로 인한 책임을 지고, 부정행위 처리규정을 준수할 것을 서약합니다.

수 험 번 호 Registration No.

비밀번호 Password

좌석번호 Seat No.

답안작성시 유 의 사 항

1. 답안 작성은 반드시 **컴퓨터용 싸인펜**을 사용해야 합니다.

2. 답안을 정정할 경우 수정테이프(수정액 불가)를 사용해야 합니다.

3. 본 답안지는 컴퓨터로 처리되므로 훼손해서는 안되며, 답안지 하단의 타이밍마크(ㅣㅣㅣ)를 찢거나, 낙서 등으로 인한 훼손시 불이익이 발생할 수 있습니다.

4. 답안은 문항당 정답을 1개만 골라 ● 와 같이 정확히 기재해야 하며, 필기구 오류나 본인의 부주의로 잘못 표기한 경우에는 당 관리위원회의 OMR판독기의 판독결과에 따르며, 그 결과는 본인이 책임집니다.

Good ● Bad 〇 ◑ ◐ ⊗ ⊙

5. 감독관의 확인이 없는 답안지는 무효처리됩니다.

TEPS

Test of English Proficiency
developed by
Seoul National University

성	영문	
명	서명	

응시일자 : 20   년   월   일

<부정행위 및 규정위반 처리규정>

1. 모든 부정행위 및 규정위반 적발 및 이에 대한 조치는 TEPS관리위원회의 처리규정에 따라 이루어집니다.

2. 부정행위 및 규정위반 행위는 현장 적발 뿐만 아니라 사후에도 적발될 수 있으며 모두 동일한 조치가 취해집니다.

3. 부정행위 적발 시 당해 성적은 무효화되며 사안에 따라 최대 5년까지 TEPS관리위원회에서 주관하는 모든 시험의 응시자격이 제한됩니다.

4. 문제지 이외에 메모를 하는 행위와 시험 문제의 일부 또는 전부를 유출하거나 공개하는 경우 부정행위로 처리됩니다.

5. 각 파트별 시간을 준수하지 않거나, 시험 종료 후 답안 작성을 계속할 경우 규정위반으로 처리됩니다.

성   명 (성·이름순으로 기재)

EX HONG GIL DONG

A B C D E F G H I J K L M N O P Q R S T U V W X Y Z

단체구분

학생	일반
○	○

질 문 란

1. 귀하의 TEPS 응시목적은?

ⓐ 입사지원   ⓑ 인사정책
ⓒ 개인실력측정   ⓓ 입시
ⓔ 국가고시 지원   ⓕ 기타

2. 귀하의 영어권 체류 경험은?

ⓐ 없다   ⓑ 6개월 미만
ⓒ 6개월 이상 1년 미만   ⓓ 1년 이상 3년 미만
ⓔ 3년 이상 5년 미만   ⓕ 5년 이상

3. 귀하께서 응시하고 계신 고사장에 대한 만족도는?

ⓐ 0점   ⓑ 1점
ⓒ 2점   ⓓ 3점
ⓔ 4점   ⓕ 5점

4. 최근 2년내 TEPS 응시횟수는?

ⓐ 없다   ⓑ 1회
ⓒ 2회   ⓓ 3회
ⓔ 4회   ⓕ 5회 이상

학 력

학력	재학	졸업
초등학교	○	○
중학교	○	○
고등학교	○	○
전문대학	○	○
대학교	○	○
대학원	○	○

전 공

인 문 학 ○
사회과학·법학 ○
경제학·경영학 ○
자 연 과 학 ○
의학·약학·간호학 ○
공 학 ○
교 육 학 ○
음악·미술·체육 ○
기 타 ○

직 업

공 무 원 ○
고시준비 ○
교 사 ○
군 인 ○
의 료 인 ○
자 영 업 ○
학 생 ○
회 사 원 ○
무 직 ○
기 타 ○

직 종

고 위 임 직 원 ○
전문직(과학·공학) ○
전 문 직 (교육) ○
전문직(법률·회계·금융) ○
기 술 직 ○
영 업 ○
홍 보 ○
총 무 ○
인 사 ○
경 리 ○
기 획 ○
구 매 ○
무 역 ○
외 환 ○
자 금 ○
공 무 ○
업 무 ○
품 질 관 리 ○
전 산 ○
행 정 직 ○
생 산 관 리 ○
서 비 스 ○
기 타 ○

직 책

임 원 ○
부 장 ○
차 장 ○
과 장 ○
대 리 ○
계 장 ○
사 원 ○
인 턴 ○
기 타 ○

TEPS

Test of English Proficiency
developed by
Seoul National University

수험번호 Registration No.		
성명 Name	한글	
	한자	

문 제 지 번 호 Test Booklet No.	감독관확인란

청 해 — Listening Comprehension

문 법 — Grammar

어 휘 — Vocabulary

독 해 — Reading Comprehension

주 민 등 록 번 호 — National ID No.

고사실란 — Room No.

수 험 번 호 — Registration No.

비밀번호 — Password

좌석번호 — Seat No.

서 약	본인은 필기구 및 기재오류와 답안지 훼손으로 인한 책임을 지고, 부정행위 처리규정을 준수할 것을 서약합니다.

답안작성시 유의사항

1. 답안 작성은 반드시 **컴퓨터용 싸인펜**을 사용해야 합니다.

2. 답안을 정정할 경우 수정테이프(수정액 불가)를 사용해야 합니다.

3. 본 답안지는 컴퓨터로 처리되므로 훼손해서는 안되며, 답안지 하단의 타이밍마크(▮▮▮)를 찢거나, 낙서 등으로 인한 훼손시 불이익이 발생할 수 있습니다.

4. 답안은 문항당 정답을 1개만 골라 ● 와 같이 정확히 기재해야 하며, 필기구 오류나 본인의 부주의로 잘못 표기한 경우에는 당 관리위원회의 OMR판독기의 판독결과에 따르며, 그 결과는 본인이 책임집니다.

Good ● 　 Bad ◖ · ◗ ✕ ⦶

5. 감독관의 확인이 없는 답안지는 무효처리됩니다.

TEPS

Test of English Proficiency
developed by
Seoul National University

성	영문	
명	서명	

응시일자 : 20   년   월   일

〈부정행위 및 규정위반 처리규정〉

1. 모든 부정행위 및 규정위반 적발 및 이에 대한 조치는 TEPS관리위원회의 처리규정에 따라 이루어집니다.

2. 부정행위 및 규정위반 행위는 현장 적발 뿐만 아니라 사후에도 적발될 수 있으며 모두 동일한 조치가 취해집니다.

3. 부정행위 적발 시 당해 성적은 무효화되며 사안에 따라 최대 5년까지 TEPS관리위원회에서 주관하는 모든 시험의 응시자격이 제한됩니다.

4. 문제지 이외에 메모를 하는 행위와 시험 문제의 일부 또는 전부를 유출하거나 공개하는 경우 부정행위로 처리됩니다.

5. 각 파트별 시간을 준수하지 않거나, 시험 종료 후 답안 작성을 계속할 경우 규정위반으로 처리됩니다.

성   명 (성 · 이름순으로 기재)

EX HONG GIL DONG

(답안 표기란: A B C D E F G H I J K L M N O P Q R S T U V W X Y Z)

단 체 구 분

학생	일반
◯	◯

질 문 란

1. 귀하의 TEPS 응시목적은?

   a 입사지원   b 인사정책
   c 개인실력측정   d 입시
   e 국가고시 지원 f 기타

2. 귀하의 영어권 체류 경험은?

   a 없다   b 6개월 미만
   c 6개월 이상 1년 미만   d 1년 이상 3년 미만
   e 3년 이상 5년 미만   f 5년 이상

3. 귀하께서 응시하고 계신 고사장에 대한 만족도는?

   a 0점   b 1점
   c 2점   d 3점
   e 4점   f 5점

4. 최근 2년내 TEPS 응시횟수는?

   a 없다   b 1회
   c 2회   d 3회
   e 4회   f 5회 이상

학 력

학 력	재학	졸업
초등학교	◯	◯
중학교	◯	◯
고등학교	◯	◯
전문대학	◯	◯
대학교	◯	◯
대학원	◯	◯

전 공

인 문 학	◯
사회과학 · 법학	◯
경제학 · 경영학	◯
자 연 과 학	◯
의학 · 약학 · 간호학	◯
공 학	◯
교 육 학	◯
음악 · 미술 · 체육	◯
기 타	◯

직 업

공 무 원	◯
고시준비	◯
교 사	◯
군 인	◯
의 료 인	◯
자 영 업	◯
학 생	◯
회 사 원	◯
무 직	◯
기 타	◯

직 종

고 위 임 직 원	◯
전문직 (과학 · 공학)	◯
전 문 직 (교육)	◯
전문직(법률 · 회계 · 금융)	◯
기 술 직	◯
영 업	◯
홍 보	◯
총 무	◯
인 사	◯
경 리	◯
기 획	◯
구 매	◯

직 책

무 역	◯
외 환	◯
자 금	◯
공 무	◯
업 무	◯
품 질 관 리	◯
전 산	◯
행 정 직	◯
생 산 관 리	◯
서 비 스	◯
기 타	◯

임 원	◯
부 장	◯
차 장	◯
과 장	◯
대 리	◯
계 장	◯
사 원	◯
인 턴	◯
기 타	◯

서울대학교 TEPS관리위원회
대표번호. 02-886-3330 홈페이지. www.teps.or.kr
TEPS
Actually...
He is so friendly
When you do TEPS!
진짜 실력을 만나다, 텝스!
민간자격국가공인 영어능력검정 (제2013-10호. 1+급, 1급, 2+급, 2급에 해당)

넥서스 수준별 TEPS 맞춤 학습 프로그램

서울대 기출문제

기출·독해

서울대 텝스 관리위원회 텝스 최신기출 1200제 2016 문제집 2 | 서울대학교 TEPS관리위원회 문제 제공 | 352쪽 | 19,500원
서울대 텝스 관리위원회 텝스 최신기출 1200제 2016 해설집 2 | 서울대학교 TEPS관리위원회 문제 제공 · 넥서스 TEPS연구소 해설 | 480쪽 | 25,000원
서울대 텝스 관리위원회 텝스 최신기출 1200제 2015-2016 문제집 | 서울대학교 TEPS관리위원회 문제 제공 | 352쪽 | 19,500원
서울대 텝스 관리위원회 텝스 최신기출 1200제 2015-2016 해설집 | 서울대학교 TEPS관리위원회 문제 제공 · 넥서스 TEPS연구소 해설 | 480쪽 | 25,000원
서울대 텝스 관리위원회 공식기출 1000 Listening | 서울대학교 TEPS관리위원회 문제 제공 | 432쪽 | 19,000원
서울대 텝스 관리위원회 공식기출 1000 Grammar | 서울대학교 TEPS관리위원회 문제 제공 | 188쪽 | 12,000원
서울대 텝스 관리위원회 공식기출 1000 Reading | 서울대학교 TEPS관리위원회 문제 제공 | 376쪽 | 16,000원
서울대 텝스 관리위원회 최신기출 1000 | 서울대학교 TEPS관리위원회 문제 제공 · 양준희 해설 | 628쪽 | 28,000원
서울대 텝스 관리위원회 최신기출 1200/SEASON 2~3 문제집 | 서울대학교 TEPS관리위원회 문제 제공 | 352쪽 | 19,500원
서울대 텝스 관리위원회 최신기출 1200/SEASON 2~3 해설집 | 서울대학교 TEPS관리위원회 문제 제공 · 넥서스 TEPS연구소 해설 | 472쪽 | 25,000원

실전 모의고사

실전·어휘

How to TEPS 영역별 끝내기 청해 | 테리 홍 지음 | 424쪽 | 19,800원
How to TEPS 영역별 끝내기 문법 | 장보금 · 써니 박 지음 | 260쪽 | 13,500원
How to TEPS 영역별 끝내기 어휘 | 양준희 지음 | 240쪽 | 13,500원
How to TEPS 영역별 끝내기 독해 | 김무룡 · 넥서스 TEPS연구소 지음 | 504쪽 | 25,000원

텝스 청해 기출 분석 실전 8회 | 넥서스 TEPS연구소 지음 | 296쪽 | 19,500원
텝스 문법 기출 분석 실전 10회 | 장보금 · 써니 박 지음 | 248쪽 | 14,000원
텝스 어휘 기출 분석 실전 10회 | 양준희 지음 | 252쪽 | 14,000원
텝스 독해 기출 분석 실전 12회 | 넥서스 TEPS연구소 지음 | 504쪽 | 25,000원

초급 (400~500점)   중급 (600~700점)

영역별

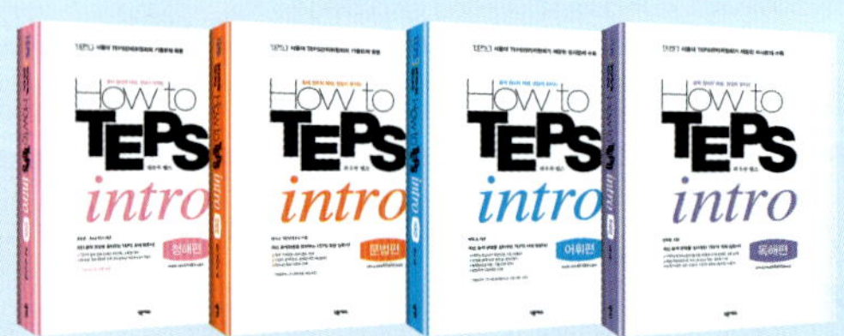 

How to TEPS intro 청해편 | 강소영 · Jane Kim 지음 | 444쪽 | 22,000원
How to TEPS intro 문법편 | 넥서스 TEPS연구소 지음 | 424쪽 | 19,000원
How to TEPS intro 어휘편 | 에릭 김 지음 | 368쪽 | 15,000원
How to TEPS intro 독해편 | 한정림 지음 | 392쪽 | 19,500원

How to TEPS 실전 600 어휘편 · 청해편 · 문법편 · 독해편 | 서울대학교 TEPS 관리위원회 문제 제공(어휘), 이기현(청해), 장보금·써니 박(문법), 황수경·넥서스 TEPS연구소(독해) 지음 | 어휘: 15,000원, 청해: 19,800원, 문법: 17,500원, 독해: 19,000원
How to TEPS 실전 700 청해편 · 문법편 · 독해편 | 강소영 · 넥서스 TEPS연구소(청해), 이신영 · 넥서스 TEPS연구소(문법), 오정우 · 넥서스 TEPS연구소(독해) 지음 | 청해: 16,000원, 문법: 15,000원, 독해: 19,000원

종합서

How to 텝스 뉴스타터 | 넥서스 TEPS연구소 지음 | 584쪽 | 25,900원
How to 텝스 초급용 모의고사 10회 | 넥서스 TEPS연구소 지음 | 296쪽 | 15,000원
How to 텝스 베이직 리스닝 | 고명희 · 넥서스 TEPS연구소 지음 | 320쪽 | 18,500원
How to 텝스 베이직 리딩 | 박미영 · 넥서스 TEPS연구소 지음 | 368쪽 | 19,500원

서울대 텝스 관리위원회 최신기출 Listening | 서울대학교 TEPS관리위원회 문제 제공 · 넥서스 TEPS연구소 해설 | 320쪽 | 19,800원
서울대 텝스 관리위원회 최신기출 Reading | 서울대학교 TEPS관리위원회 문제 제공 · 넥서스 TEPS연구소 해설 | 568쪽 | 24,800원
서울대 텝스 관리위원회 최신기출 스피킹 · 라이팅 | 서울대학교 TEPS관리위원회 문제 제공 · 유경하 해설 | 340쪽 | 28,000원
서울대 텝스 관리위원회 최신기출 i-TEPS | 서울대학교 TEPS관리위원회 문제 제공 · 넥서스 TEPS연구소 해설 | 296쪽 | 19,800원

독해 · 청해 · 문법

How to 텝스 독해 기본편 | 양준희 · 넥서스 TEPS연구소 지음 | 312쪽 | 17,500원
How to 텝스 독해 중급편 | 장우리 지음 | 360쪽 | 17,500원
How to 텝스 독해 고난도편 | 넥서스 TEPS연구소 지음 | 324쪽 | 17,500원
How to 텝스 청해 중급편 | 양준희 지음 | 276쪽 | 18,500원
How to 텝스 문법 고난도편 | 테스 김 · 넥서스 TEPS연구소 지음 | 160쪽 | 12,500원

텝스 기출모의 1200 | 넥서스 TEPS연구소 지음 | 456쪽 | 18,500원
How to TEPS 실전력 500 · 600 · 700 · 800 · 900 | 넥서스 TEPS연구소 지음 | 308쪽 | 실전력 500~800: 16,500원, 실전력 900: 18,000원
서울대 텝스 관리위원회 텝스 실전 연습 5회+1회 | 서울대학교 TEPS관리위원회 문제 제공 | 200쪽 | 9,800원
텝스 기출모의 5회분 | 넥서스 TEPS연구소 지음 | 364쪽 | 14,500원

어휘

서울대 최신기출 TEPS VOCA | 넥서스 TEPS연구소 · 문덕 지음 | 544쪽 | 15,000원
How to TEPS VOCA | 김무룡 · 넥서스 TEPS연구소 지음 | 320쪽 | 12,800원
How to TEPS 넥서스 텝스 보카 | 이기헌 지음 | 536쪽 | 15,000원
How to 텝스 어휘 기본편 | 고명희 · 넥서스 TEPS연구소 지음 | 304쪽 | 15,500원
How to 텝스 어휘 고난도편 | 김무룡 · 넥서스 TEPS연구소 지음 | 296쪽 | 17,000원

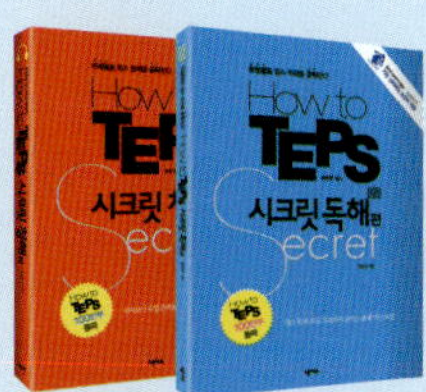

How to TEPS 시크릿 청해편 · 독해편 | 유니스 정(청해), 정성수(독해) 지음 | 청해: 22,500원, 독해: 14,500원
텝스, 어려운 파트만 콕콕 찍어 점수 따기(청해 PART 4 · 문법 PART 3,4) | 이성희 · 진공심 지음 | 170쪽 | 13,000원

고급 (800점 이상)

How to TEPS 실전 800 어휘편 · 청해편 · 문법편 · 독해편 | 넥서스 TEPS연구소 (어휘, 청해, 독해), 테스 김(문법) 지음 | 어휘: 12,800원, 청해: 19,000원, 문법: 16,000원, 독해: 19,000원
How to TEPS 실전 900 청해편 · 문법편 · 독해편 | 김철용(청해), 이용재(문법), 김철용(독해) 지음 | 청해: 17,000원, 문법: 16,500원, 독해: 17,500원

How to TEPS L/C | 이성희 지음 | 400쪽 | 19,800원
How to TEPS R/C | 이정은 · 넥서스 TEPS연구소 지음 | 396쪽 | 19,800원

How to TEPS Expert L | 박영주 지음 | 340쪽 | 21,000원
How to TEPS Expert GVR | 박영주 지음 | 520쪽 | 28,000원
How to TEPS Expert 고난도 실전 모의고사 | 넥서스 TEPS연구소 지음 | 388쪽 | 21,500원

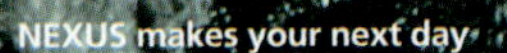

NEXUS makes your next day